IDEAS OF LANDSCAPE

IDEAS OF LANDSCAPE

Matthew Johnson

Blackwell
Publishing

BLACKWELL PUBLISHING
350 Main Street, Malden, MA 02148-5020, USA
9600 Garsington Road, Oxford OX4 2DQ, UK
550 Swanston Street, Carlton, Victoria 3053, Australia

The right of Matthew Johnson to be identified as the Author of this Work has been
asserted in accordance with the UK Copyright, Designs, and Patents Act 1988.

First published 2007 by Blackwell Publishing Ltd

1   2007

Library of Congress Cataloging-in-Publication Data

Johnson, Matthew, 1962–
    Ideas of landscape / Matthew Johnson.
       p. cm.
    Includes bibliographical references and index.
    ISBN-13: 978-1-4051-0159-2 (hardcover : alk. paper)
    ISBN-10: 1-4051-0159-8 (hardcover : alk. paper)
    ISBN-13: 978-1-4051-0160-8 (pbk. : alk. paper)
    ISBN-10: 1-4051-0160-1 (pbk. : alk. paper)   1. Great Britain–Historical geography.
2. Landscape archaeology–Great Britain.   3. Land use–Great Britain–History.   I. Title.

    DA600.J64 2006
    936.2–dc22

                                                                            2005037143

A catalogue record for this title is available from the British Library.

Set in 11/13pt Bembo
by Graphicraft Limited, Hong Kong
Printed and bound in Singapore
by Markono Print Media Pte Ltd

The publisher's policy is to use permanent paper from mills that operate a sustainable
forestry policy, and which has been manufactured from pulp processed using acid-free
and elementary chlorine-free practices. Furthermore, the publisher ensures that the text
paper and cover board used have met acceptable environmental accreditation standards.

For further information on
Blackwell Publishing, visit our website:
www.blackwellpublishing.com

For Rose Amelie Johnson

CONTENTS

LIST OF FIGURES

ACKNOWLEDGEMENTS

The intellectual frame of this book was sketched out in 2002, while I held an Arts and Humanities Research Board (AHRB) Research Leave award; I thank the University of Durham for granting me research leave for one term, and the AHRB for extending it to two. During this time I was a Visiting Scholar at the Department of Archaeology, University of Cambridge, and I thank everyone there for their hospitality and kindness, particularly Catherine Hills as my sponsor. Discussions during that time with Matthew Spriggs, John Robb, Elizabeth Demarrais, Chris Chippindale, and many others directly or indirectly sparked many of the ideas in this book. The book's ideas were further developed in 2004 during two months in Australia, for which I thank Claire Smith and Heather Burke, and at Heidelberg in the spring of 2005, a visit organized by Joseph Maran. Chris Taylor and Andrew Fleming kindly acted as referees, but, more importantly, conversations with both informed the content of this book. John Barrett, David Hinton, Steph Moser, and Jim Wright read the manuscript in detail; Jim alerted me to much pertinent Americanist material. Two anonymous North American reviewers helped sharpen the focus of the book immeasurably. Brian Roberts rightly corrected my thinking about the hachured plan and supplied Figures 4.9 and 5.1. Harold Fox and the University of Leicester kindly supplied the photograph of W. G. Hoskins. I also thank Dave Austin, Simon Coleman, Simon Draper, Tim Earle, Mark Edmonds, Joan Gero, Chris Gerrard, Bob Preucel, Margaret Purser, Wlodzimierz Rackzowski, and Helen Wickstead for pertinent discussions.

Many years ago, in 1982 in the year before I went to university, I spent a field season at Wharram, one of the landscapes discussed in this book; I have not forgotten the kindness shown by those involved in that project to a spotty, inarticulate adolescent. I remember my time there very fondly; Wharram was one of a series of important formative experiences for me.

I thank my wife Becky for her contribution both in the field and in discussion, and for her constant support. The emphasis in this book on the intellectual legacy of Romanticism is due to her influence. I could not have done it without her.

THE ARGUMENT

This book is about the theory and practice of landscape archaeology today. It focuses on the so-called "English landscape tradition" as it has been applied to the historic landscape. It asks why this tradition stands at some distance from North American, from prehistoric, and from other approaches in which "theory" plays a more prominent role. It identifies the ideological underpinnings of this "English" tradition as coming from English Romanticism, in part via the influence of the "father of landscape history," W. G. Hoskins. The strengths and weaknesses of current landscape archaeology of historic periods are shown to mirror the underlying discontents of Romanticism, for example in its politics and in its empiricism. An alternative agenda for historic landscape archaeology is set out. This alternative agenda is argued to map more closely on to the established empirical strengths of archaeology as a discipline, to be more relevant to the thrust of interdisciplinary landscape studies, and also to be more relevant to the social concerns of the present.

PREFACE:
THINKING ABOUT SWALEDALE

I will start not with definitions and theoretical arguments, but by examining a specific landscape, and thinking about how archaeologists, as scholars and as human beings, view that landscape.

Swaledale

Swaledale is in the Yorkshire Dales, in the north of England (Figure P1). Even if the reader has never been there, the appearance of the Dales may well be familiar, either from television adaptations of novels and books set in the Dales or from tourist posters advertising the delights of the English countryside.

The Yorkshire Dales are valleys cut into the Pennines, a belt of limestone uplands forming a north/south "spine" above Midland England. The Pennine hills can be seen in the distance from the train as it speeds north from York on the London–Edinburgh line. Swaledale is the most northerly of the Yorkshire Dales, and one of the harshest in its climate and general appearance. The River Swale runs from west to east, carving the dale from the limestone into a narrow valley.

The character of the dale changes as one drives up from the small market town of Richmond at its mouth. "Lower Swaledale" is less rugged; once one passes the large village of Reeth, however, one enters "Upper Swaledale" and the shape of the dale becomes markedly narrower. Local people habitually refer to Upper and Lower Swaledale in terms that stress their different identities; those of Upper Swaledale have often told me that the dale only "really begins" at Reeth – though it is often unclear whether when they use these terms they

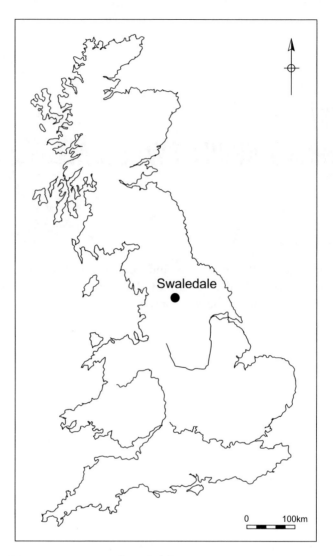

Figure P1 Location map of Swaledale

are referring to the land, or to the human communities that inhabit
the land.

The most obvious landscape feature of Swaledale and of the Dales
generally is the criss-crossing system of dry stone walls (Figure P2).
Viewed from a distance, these walls carve the valley up into pastoral
fields; the fields in the valley bottom all have their own field barn. The
walls appear of uniform design when looked at casually and from afar,
but studied close up they have subtle differences in building method,

Figure P2   View of Swaledale, looking northeast from the road between Grinton and Reeth, showing field walls. Traces of earlier field systems are just visible in the lower fields

and butt-joints indicating where one craftsman or team of labourers stopped and another started (Figure P3).

The archaeologist, coming to the dale for the first time and stopping perhaps on the shoulders of the hills between Grinton and Reeth, becomes aware very quickly that he or she is looking at a complex and multilayered landscape. It is obvious from the start that the archaeology here is so dense, the linear features so complex and criss-crossing, that to mark "archaeological sites" as dots on a map of the dale would be to do its character serious violence. The majority of field walls are of similar construction, suggesting that they were built or rebuilt at largely the same date; however, field and other boundaries in the dale often look very different from one another in their construction, suggesting that they have been built and rebuilt over many different periods, and that some are much more than just a few hundred years old (Figure P4).

There is hardly a single straight line in the dale. Routeways wind from one habitation to the next, along the contours of the valley shoulders. Villages and hamlets are scattered in what is superficially a random pattern.

Figure P3 A "butt-joint" in a field wall, near Grinton, Swaledale

Figure P4 The Ordnance Survey map of the Grinton/Reeth area.
Ancient earthworks are marked in Gothic lettering; two lines of north/
south dykes can be made out, topped by modern field walls. A prehistoric
field system is marked on the moor to the south, and "cultivation terraces"
to the north. The morphology of the village of Reeth, around a central
green, is clearly visible. The place-name element "How" is attributed to
the fifth to eighth centuries A.D., while "Reeth" and other names are of
Scandinavian derivation. The dotted and broken lines indicate tracks and
paths that are public rights of way. *Reproduced by permission of Ordnance
Survey on behalf of HMSO. © Crown copyright 2005. All rights reserved.
Ordnance Survey licence number 100044559*

England is a small and densely occupied country; consequently, for
all its apparent solitude, Swaledale is very close to several centres
of urban population. The universities of Leeds, Bradford, York, and
Durham, and a host of smaller educational institutions, are all within
80 kilometres. As a result, scholars wishing to do field archaeology in

the dale can take off for a day or even just an afternoon; it is possible to undertake significant fieldwork while also undertaking other teaching and administrative duties in the daily and weekly round. Many scholars in England measure buildings and plot earthworks for a day or so or at weekends, often as part of a local amateur group, and then, during the rest of the week while stuck in traffic jams or committee meetings, think inductively about what they have observed. They can then return to the dale to make fresh observations – nothing so formal as "test" their ideas – again and again. The process, then, hardly conforms to a formal scientific model of hypothesis and deduction, but is deeply empirically informed.

Such a pattern of activity is encouraged by the nature of the archaeological and historical record of the dale. The researcher does not have to excavate before he or she can do meaningful archaeology; indeed, there is much that is necessary to do before one can even reach that stage. The dale now is largely under pasture, though this was not always the case in the past. The lack of ploughing means that many archaeological features survive as earthworks. These earthworks are meaningless "humps and bumps" to the untutored eye, but an elementary archaeological training enables the observer to identify and give meaning to them. Most obviously, many of these earthworks are of "ridge and furrow" form, generally taken to be indicative of medieval arable agriculture; others, strip lynchets and other features, are less easily assigned a date. In many cases, one earthwork seems to overlie another, and tentative assignments of relative dates can be attempted.

Many of the features of archaeological interest are still in what Michael Schiffer (1976, 1987) would call "systemic context"; that is, they are still part of a living and functioning cultural system. Thus, for example, Grinton dyke, an ancient ditch and bank running across the dale, is topped with pollarded elm trees (now dying of or killed by Dutch elm disease), while the dyke itself is part of current administrative boundaries, themselves of great antiquity (White 1997:46). The field barns that dot the landscape, built in to the pattern of field walls, are still in use, as most obviously are many of the 17th- and 18th-century farmhouses.

The often subtle nature of these earthworks and remains of buildings, and the complex relationship between them, means that it is best to repeatedly visit the dale in different seasons, times of day, and light conditions; a field that is apparently "empty" for three or four visits can, on the fifth and under particular conditions, turn out to be full of features. The discernment of these features is a craft every bit as complex, and as full of its own field knowledge and lore, as that of excavation (Shanks and McGuire 1996). The steep, V-shaped profile of the dale means that the oblique observations of the landscape from a distance usually only afforded by air photos are here possible from the ground.

Another aid to the researcher is the documentary record. Communities such as Upper and Lower Swaledale have their own parish records, churchwardens' accounts, tax and estate records of various kinds, all kept in various archives and record offices. Many of these records only start around A.D. 1500, but others go back into the medieval period. The transcription and interpretation of these records is a specialized skill and subdiscipline in its own right. The scholar wishing to use them in any detail requires skills of palaeography, and in many cases knowledge of medieval Latin. The existence of these records does mean, however, that we can write a deep and complex history of the dale from material stored in the local record office alone. Indeed the standard history of the dale makes almost no reference whatsoever to its landscape archaeology (Fieldhouse and Jennings 1978).

I know about Swaledale in part because I lived there for some months in the late 1980s, struggling to finish my Ph.D.; its landscape is associated with long walks as I tore my hair out, thinking through some problem with the thesis. I have walked parts of it with Andrew Fleming, the author of the definitive book on the archaeology of the dale (Fleming 1998); while living and working in Durham, I regularly visited Swaledale for Sunday walks, pub lunches, and student field trips. For me, it is a very familiar and much-loved landscape, but however familiar it is, it is one which each visit modifies slightly as I notice some new feature or view a familiar area under slightly different light conditions. As such, the field experience of visiting and thinking about Swaledale has influenced the way I think about landscape archaeology every bit as much as, if not more than, a reading of comparative anthropology, or of theorists such as Heidegger (1953), Tilley (1994) or Thomas (1996). And my suspicion is that many English and European archaeologists would say the same of "their" local and familiar landscapes.

When I teach archaeological theory, I am often pressed to demonstrate the relationship between theory, archaeological practice, and social context. To meet this challenge, I often compare the intellectual and everyday world of Swaledale with that of other writing on landscape archaeology: comparative, heavily theoretical, often taking a world perspective, interested in general questions. The two worlds often seem oblivious to each other. On the one hand, to take an apposite example, Wendy Ashmore and Bernard Knapp's edited volume (1999) has no reference to any of the "giants" (often resonantly termed "founding fathers": see Chapter 6) of English landscape history and archaeology – W. G. Hoskins, Maurice Beresford, Christopher Taylor, O. G. S. Crawford. And conversely, the writings of Hoskins, Beresford, Taylor, and the others contain no reference to North American or other generalizing traditions. For example, one will search in vain for the influence of any kind of general anthropological theory in the two edited volumes of Hooke (2000) and Thirsk (2000).

The two ways of looking at landscape are also conditioned by a very different history of archaeology from that usually familiar to the student. The starting points for most discussions of the history of archaeology are the prehistoric and classical worlds. For example, Trigger (1989), Daniel (1975), and Daniel and Renfrew (1988) all place the "discovery" of human origins, and the study of the classical world, as central to the development of archaeological thought. However, there is a different and complementary story to be told. This might start in the 19th century with the desire to record and restore the great medieval buildings of Europe, itself dependent on a social context of industrialization and perceived loss of medieval values of community; Linda Ebbatson (1994) and Chris Gerrard (2003) have pointed to Victorian explorations of the stratigraphy of medieval buildings. Early journals such as the *Archaeological Journal* included discussions of folk customs and medieval and post-medieval artefacts alongside discussions of prehistory; such topics occupied centre stage in the 19th-century view of "archaeology" (Ebbatson 1994).

One of the things that struck me, as an archaeologist raised in the English landscape tradition, was how objective and disengaged, to my eyes, much generalizing writing on landscape seems to be. It is true that Fleming, Hoskins, and other scholars working within the English landscape tradition all write "objectively," but their prose unfolds in a manner which is often narrative rather than analytical, a narrative which is often personal moreover (see Fleming 1988 for example), and in a way which implies an emotional engagement with the landscape even if this engagement is not explicit. When Lekson writes of the archaeology of the American Southwest in the mode of personal narrative, the story of personal discovery is exciting, but reads as a voyage of scientific discovery rather than a Swaledale-style engagement with a local landscape (Lekson 1999).

To which those archaeologists, on visiting Swaledale, might justifiably reply: Where is your objectivity? Where is your system? How can you responsibly and reliably make anthropological generalizations from this one place? Why should anybody else in any other part of the world be interested in your little patch – why is it anything more than a few humps and bumps? How are you going to use Swaledale to find out not just about a few field boundaries, but about humankind as a whole? And how are you going to test any propositions you come up with? Don't you just end up with some hopelessly particularist, unverifiable just-so story?

Now of course a lot of the apparent divergence between these two traditions is not "real," but framed through background and perception. One can begin to sketch out what a theoretically inspired view of Swaledale might look like: one might start with Fleming's observation of protohistoric linear boundaries marking out different parts of the dale, and then go on to think about Swaledale boundaries as territorial markers that tell us in turn about levels of social development and their relationship to territoriality and varying population levels. Or we might use observations of agricultural earthworks to talk about the dale as a whole as a "marginal environment," occupied and used for arable agriculture during favourable climatic conditions, and abandoned or at least less intensively farmed at other times. It is also easy to forget, with Swaledale, that the area has gone through quite sudden changes and is linked in to the rise and fall of world systems. The foremost example of the intersection of the dale with wider processes is seen in the extensive archaeological record of lead mining in the dale – the sides and tops of the slopes are littered with spoil heaps, buildings, and debris from this industrial phase of the dale's history. In its later forms, lead mining was financed from London; the sudden abandonment of the lead mines in the face of cheaper imported lead was, then, tied in to global flows of goods and capital (White 1997).

However, the archaeological record is much more than simply a passive sounding-board for the prejudices of scholars. The "data set," or more accurately the field experience that Swaledale offers, does affect archaeologists' interpretations and does limit what archaeologists can or cannot say about it. The postmodern turn has meant that we have become very practised at charting how our cultural perceptions shape our view of landscape or indeed any other aspect of the archaeological record. There is nothing wrong with this; indeed, I would argue that it is part of the "loss of innocence" that any responsible science such as archaeology has to undergo. However, I think that archaeologists have been less good at turning this equation on its head: at examining precisely how the land shapes academic perceptions, and hence how the "data," however defined (and as I write I feel English landscape historians shuddering at the use of such a dry, scientific term), help to shape academic conceptions of what landscape is.

For example, the density of archaeology in Swaledale means that a linear approach with complex horizontal stratigraphy is possible. An archaeologist seeing a lynchet running across an earlier enclosure, itself apparently on top of some earlier feature, is led very quickly into thinking about time over a long scale – several centuries, if not millennia. Stress, then, on a view of continuing use of a landscape – whether agricultural, social or "ritual" – spanning several periods, and with it an emphasis on ideas such as place, memory, tradition, and the long term, is not just an intellectual fashion; it is something strongly suggested by the evidence itself.

We are all students of the past; archaeologists all claim to have a common goal, the study of human beings. Yet the way in which archaeologists have come to understand landscapes in different areas of the globe is, at least at first sight, utterly different. Surely this cannot be right? Surely we cannot descend into utter relativism – in this case, a kind of sociological relativism between academic communities, embedded in the belief that different localities and intellectual communities have their own, quite different way of doing things, each no better and no worse than the other?

If it is agreed that such a coming together is a noble aim, and one productive of academic insight, then a first step in doing it is to understand something of where the tradition whose surface here we have only scratched actually comes from. In other words, we need to trace something of the intellectual history and ancestry of different views of landscape. That is the initial task of this book.

Chapter One

INTRODUCTION

This book is about how scholars have thought, and are thinking, about landscape. It is about how scholars have interpreted past landscapes; it takes as its primary focus the work of historical archaeologists working within the "English landscape tradition," though we shall find other archaeologists, prehistorians, anthropologists, geologists, geographers, historians, and others – even poets and artists – entering the scene from time to time, and I hope that its conclusions will be of interest to a much wider audience. It is very far from being a complete account of all the ideas of landscape ever proposed; such a volume would be an encyclopaedia, if it were possible at all. Rather, I shall be looking at a few selected strands of thought, a narrow sample of the literature.

This is not a book about theories or ideologies of landscape as such; nor is it a book primarily about techniques of landscape archaeology. Rather, it is a book about *habits of thought*. It asks the question: why do different communities of archaeologists and scholars habitually think about and do landscape archaeology in the way that they do? Such a topic spans both theory and practice, and moves back and forth between wider ideologies on the one hand (environmental determinism; landscape as subjectively constituted) and "mere techniques" (air photographs; field survey; mapping) on the other.

Part of the problem with writing a general book about landscape interpretation has been its double nature. Landscape studies are simultaneously one of the most fashionable and avant-garde areas of scholarly enquiry, and also, paradoxically, one of the most theoretically dormant areas. Two schools of landscape studies seem to currently exist, each hermetically sealed from the other. It is easy to read the studies in Ashmore and Knapp (1999), Bender (1993, 1998), Bradley (1993, 1998), Adam Smith (2003), Ucko and Layton (1999) and geographers such as Denis Cosgrove (1984,

2000), Stephen Daniels (1992), David Harvey (1990), Derek Gregory (1994), and Felix Driver (2001) and come to the conclusion that wide-ranging discussions of the meanings of landscape sit at the forefront of theoretical debate. Conversely, it is easy to peruse the pages of *Landscape History*, *Journal of the Medieval Settlement Research Group*, and *Landscapes* and conclude that landscape archaeology remains firmly in the grip of the most unreflective empiricism in which "theory" is a dirty word and the only reality worth holding on to is that of muddy boots – a direct, unmediated encounter with the "real world." Mick Aston's *Interpreting the Landscape* (1985), for example, one of the best books on the techniques of landscape archaeology, contains almost no reference to theoretical debate of this kind, while approaches drawing on Foucault and literary theory such as those taken by the author (Johnson 1996) have been seen as "wild" and "mystical" by respected figures in what might be termed the empirical school (Williamson 2000:56).

This mutual ignorance can lead to paradoxical views and statements. When Richard Muir (2000:147), for example, writes that the "sense of place is . . . a subjective phenomenon: it cannot be expressed and gauged with precision by the professional archaeologist or historian . . . The objective approach cultivated in the universities is admirable for most purposes, but the exclusion of emotion from intellect and symbol from reason in Western science does not equip us to recognise and relate to sense of place factors which may have motivated our distant forebears . . . The academic study of the relationship between landscape and human behaviour is in its infancy," he seems to be genuinely unaware of any of the writings of university-based phenomenologists from Heidegger (1953), Gadamer (1975), and Benjamin (1999, though he was writing before 1940) onwards. Conversely, when postprocessual writers speak of the need to develop personal, subjective, and hermeneutic approaches to landscape in contradistinction to "processual" approaches, they often seem unaware of a strong and continuing tradition of finding meaning in local landscapes through traditional forms of landscape history and archaeology. The point I am making here is not an adverse criticism of any of these writers; it is rather to draw attention to the depth and breadth of a divide in scholarship that allows this mutual ignorance to exist.

Definitions of Landscape

Here is a range of definitions of landscape, the majority of which were first collated by Rodaway (1994:127):

Landscape is a kind of backcloth to the whole stage of human activity. (Appleton 1975:2)

"Landscape", as the term has been used since the 17th century, is a construct of the mind as well as a physical and measurable entity. (Tuan 1979:6)

A landscape is a cultural image, a pictorial way of representing, structuring or symbolising surroundings . . . Landscape is a social and cultural product, a way of seeing projected onto the land and having its own techniques and compositional forms; a restrictive way of seeing that diminishes alternative modes of experiencing our relations with nature. (Cosgrove 1984:1 and 269)

When we consider landscape, we are almost always concerned with a visual construct. (Porteous 1990:4)

Landscape is not merely an aesthetic background to life, rather it is a setting that both expresses and conditions cultural attitudes and activities, and significant modifications to landscapes are not possible without major changes in social attitudes . . . Landscapes are therefore always imbued with meanings that come from how and why we know them. (Relph 1976:122)

A working country is hardly ever a landscape. The very idea of landscape implies separation and observation. (Williams 1973:120)

When collective labour and the struggle with nature had ceased to be the only arena for man's encounter with nature and the world – then nature itself ceased to be a living participant in the events of life. Then nature became, by and large, a "setting for action", its backdrop; it was turned into landscape, it was fragmented into metaphors and comparisons serving to sublimate the individual and private affairs and adventures not connected in any real or intrinsic way to nature itself. (Bakhtin 1986:217)

Landscape came to mean a prospect seen from a specific standpoint. (Tuan 1974:133)

I shall return to these themes again and again in the rest of the text; what I want to note in these initial comments is that any study of the way archaeologists view "landscape," at least within Western traditions of thought, will perforce involve at least two elements:

1   The "land" itself, however defined: the humanly created features that exist "objectively" across space, and their natural context. Landscape archaeology in this sense is a very simple term to define: it is about what lies beyond the site, or the edge of the excavation.

2   How "the land" is viewed – how we, and people in the past, came to apprehend and understand the landscape, and what those systems of apprehension and understanding are, the cognitive systems and processes of perception.

"Landscape" is, in this second sense, a *way of seeing*, a way of thinking about the physical world. This particular way of thinking and seeing is, in many conceptions of the subject including the quotes given above, what transforms the "land" and its study into "land-scape."

In the preface we have already seen these two ideas come into play. A simple description of the physical realities of Swaledale, interesting though it was, was not enough on its own to explain its "land-scape" – in this case, how scholars and popular audiences have viewed it, the meanings that have become attached to it, and the ways of thinking about it that have become habitual and taken for granted. To begin to understand the landscape, we had to make reference not just to its physical features, whether natural or humanly made, but also to the scholarly traditions that had been brought to bear on both, and behind scholarly tradition make reference to popular perceptions and culture.

Part of the enduring problem with landscape archaeology has been that scholars of all theoretical stripes have not always been very careful to distinguish these two ideas of landscape. We talk about "prehistoric land-scape use," "landscapes of the mind," "historic landscape characteriza-tion," and so on. Clearly both elements rattle around our heads as we use these phrases. Some would say that these two elements should be separated; some would accord one element dominance over the other. Some would argue that the first simply does not exist apart from the second (for example, in the view that objective description of space is an impossibility; or in the view that the creation of a monument or field system was simultaneously a physical action and also part of a changing system of understanding the landscape). Some would add a third concept: landscape as engagement with the world – a process or way of doing things rather than a thing or an idea (cf. David and Wilson 2002:6).

Traditions of thought outside the West, such as those of many "indigenous" cultures, often deny any opposition between land and land-scape, or simply reject the Cartesian system of thought that set the opposition up in the first place. For the indigenous peoples of Australia, for example, the notion of a distinction between a process of living in the world and one's spiritual or emotional preconceptions about it is a quite alien concept (see Ucko and Layton 1999 for this and other examples).

The Origins of Landscape Studies

Humans have tried to observe, monitor, and understand the land around them for many thousands of years. It has been argued that Palaeolithic cave art is in part an attempt to control the environment through sympathetic magic. Certainly the siting of the rock art of many gatherer-hunter communities, for example of Australia, both makes reference to the land around and is very carefully sited within it with respect to visibility, or lack of visibility; and "natural" features such as rocks and hills acquire significance and meaning, meaning often encoded in the action of story-telling (David and Wilson 2002).

More directly physical means of carving up the landscape can be seen in early agricultural societies, for example large-scale woodland clearance and the laying out of field systems (Fleming 1988). Such activities were rarely purely utilitarian in nature; they clearly had a cognitive component and were in part about understanding and symbolically appropriating the land around them. It has been convincingly argued, for example, that new agricultural systems went hand in hand with new ways of thinking about human relations with the environment and with each other (Hodder 1990; Thomas 1991). It has been a recurrent, and highly controversial, theme of studies of early state societies that their origins are bound up with large-scale modification of the landscape through irrigation agriculture (Wittfogel 1957). While the "irrigation hypothesis" has been debated back and forth through the decades, the dimensions of early state landscapes other than those related to subsistence – the religious, symbolic, and political landscape – have been seen as increasingly important by recent scholars (Smith 2003). Much activity within the Roman empire can also be seen in this light: vast schemes of "centuriation" or the creation of grid-like patterns of fields were as much statements of imperial power over the land as they were utilitarian (Schubert 1996).

The classical world also made a contribution to the *ideology* of landscape that can hardly be overestimated. Classical texts, for example the poets Virgil and Ovid and their works in the "pastoral" genre, created a series of images that were reworked by later writers and which indirectly structure much of the way we think about landscape today. Many of these ideas are so much part of our habit of thought that we do not even recognize their classical origin. Discourses with a classical origin include, for example, ideas of productive husbandry (Thirsk 1992), the pastoral, the rural idyll, of Arcadia, and of *genius loci* (the presiding spirit of a locality). More broadly, a conception of "Nature" was forged by classical authors and kept alive through subsequent centuries of classical learning. Of course, all these ideas actually said more about the realities of living amongst the bustle and squalor of republican and imperial Rome than they did about rural realities; since this date, as we shall see, the city and the country have been intertwined (Williams 1973). Classical writers also established a gendering of Nature and of fertility as feminine, for example through the cult of the corn goddess Demeter. This was a gendering that was continued into Christian thought through the association of the Virgin Mary with fertility (Warner 1976:273–84).

In the Middle Ages, we can see the emergence of a theme that continues to dominate ideas of landscape: that the carving up of the land, whether mental or material, has a close relationship to the carving up of society: that the spatial grid maps on to the social grid, if you will. Kathleen Biddick writes suggestively:

> Before the enclosure and partitioning of time and space in the 12th century of England, personhood and status did not operate as compartmentalised juridical categories . . . [12th-century] enclosure and partitioning . . . partitioned status out as an enclosed space or property, an object . . . Lords, the state, the courts thus conjoined disciplinary practices to grid the English landscape and create places where individuals supposedly could be produced. The fiscal, the juridical, the spatial, and the textual superimposed and overlapped in a palimpsest of disciplinary practices. (Biddick 1993:15–16)

This enclosure and partitioning was carried out through the division of land, the fossil record of which can still be seen in the English and European landscape (Figure 1.1), and also through the deployment of new administrative techniques that have left their trace in medieval estate and court records. Large feudal estates were owned by individual lords, the Crown, or religious institutions. Bureaucratic records of the administration of these estates often survive, to the extent that they overflow the record offices and archives of Europe. They have been used by historians, armed with a knowledge of medieval Latin and palaeography, to reconstruct the workings of the medieval economy (for example Dyer 1980, or the citations in Hatcher and Bailey 2001). The immediate concern of these records was administrative; however, they were also resources of power. The basic administrative unit became the manor, and manorial records recorded customary practices such as who had what rights over which piece of land (Seebohm 1884).

Peasants knew the power of these written records. A recurring feature of late medieval peasant revolts was the burning of such documents,

Figure 1.1 Appleton-le-Moors, North Yorkshire, a village on the edge of the North York Moors. The modern land divisions fossilize a medieval partitioning of land including "tenements," church, manor house, back lane, and fields beyond. *Copyright reserved Cambridge University Collection of Air Photographs*

in order to destroy the basis of evidence used to keep peasants in unfree status or to legitimate the extraction of rents and services (Hilton 1977). It has been argued that medieval peasants had their own different tradition, which might be seen as complementary to that of the landlord or set up in resistance to it, of common land and of rights over the land enshrined not in documents but in everyday action and social memory (Shoard 1999:164).

If the everyday landscape of the medieval world was conceived of in a complex and contested way, the same was also true of the representation of the world through medieval geographical thinking. Medieval knowledge of the world was, of course, mediated through the Church, but was not as unsystematic or as divorced from a modern Cartesian appreciation as non-medievalists might think. For example, the practice of creating *mappae mundi* (maps of the world) was widespread across medieval Europe. Jerusalem was always at their centre, but they were not simply primitive distortions of geographical "reality" (Harvey 1996). Much of this cartographic knowledge was bound up with religious experience, the world being God's creation; thus the three continents of Europe, Asia, and Africa were often placed in geometrical harmony and symmetry around the Holy Land.

Renaissance Landscapes

Historical geographers, most notably Denis Cosgrove (1984), have argued cogently that the rise of "modern" views of landscape is bound up with the ideas and attitudes that were part and parcel of the Renaissance, however that historical period is defined. In particular, they argue for a connection between the idea of land-scape, in the second sense defined earlier, with that of the gaze from a single, often elevated, viewpoint and of perspective in art. Several different ideas are bound up in this general proposition.

First, the very term Renaissance implies "rediscovery," for example of the classical authors described above, and with that rediscovery a new encounter with the ideas of landscape first framed by those authors. It is not the case that classical ideas of landscape were forgotten in the Middle Ages; the choice of sites for medieval monasteries, for example, was influenced by classical texts in their manipulation of the landscape, as well as by the hermetic tradition of St Augustine. Many monasteries were sited in locations that might be described as rural retreats, and some even evicted the residents of medieval villages in order to create these (Greene 1992). However, it is certainly true that European gentlemen, taught to spend time reading Latin and Greek and to model themselves on the great Hellenic and Roman heroes, became more aware of some of the classical ideas and models described above.

One such classical theme was taken from Livy's history of the rise of Rome: that of Horatius at his farm (Luce 1998). The Roman warrior Horatius, after doing his duty to Rome and becoming a hero on the battlefield, left the public life and retired to his country retreat; he is presented by Livy as making an active decision to forsake the worldly bustle and political ambition of the metropolis for a simpler country life. Texts such as Livy's became more and more widely known in 16th- and 17th-century Europe. The 17th-century English poet John Milton rewrote the story of Horatio at his farm; Virgil's poems about bee-keeping were given an increased circulation. Joan Thirsk has shown elegantly how, in the later 16th century, the increased circulation of such ideas marked a shift away from the cultivated lack of interest of the medieval knight. English gentlemen became more aware of such poetry and sought to live after models such as that of Horatius. The result of this awareness was increased gentlemanly interest in the every-day practicalities of farm management, an interest which fed directly in to the pace of agricultural innovation and agrarian change in the early modern period (Thirsk 1992).

However, the reading of classical texts was not simply an intellectual process: it was tied up with secularization and changes in culture in the gentry classes. As these classical texts were produced in printed editions for the first time, they became less and less the exclusive preserve of the manuscript libraries of the Church. Further, they were often translated into the vernacular, so that a knowledge of Latin and Greek was no longer a prerequisite. The printing press meant books were more freely and cheaply available, and rising levels of literacy in the 16th and 17th centuries meant that those of the gentry and middling social classes were better able to read them. Advice books and agricultural manuals contained information on sowing crops, household management, and care of the agricultural landscape. For example, Thomas Tusser's *Five Hundred Points of Good Husbandry*, published in 1586, contained advice (expressed in execrable verse) on household management and culti-vation of the fields. This genre continued through the 17th and 18th centuries (Johnson 1996:84–6). And perhaps most significantly, the Bible could now be read in socially middling homes across much of Europe (16th-century authorities attempted to legislate against its printing and dissemination, with little success). Ordinary people could now read of landscapes, particularly in the Old Testament, that were bound up with powerful and religious and political meanings – the Garden of Eden, the Promised Land, the wilderness (Hill 1993).

In all such texts, the linking of land and social order was espe-cially apparent. However, such thinking about landscape could be double-edged: it could carry both authoritarian and subversive mean-ings. Richard Helgerson (1992) has shown how, in the Middle Ages, ideas of the monarch and of the kingdom were coterminous. As a result, he suggests, it was intellectually inconceivable to lead a revolt

Figure 1.2 The "Ditchley Portrait" of Elizabeth I. Elizabeth stands on a map of England and Wales, with one foot resting on Ditchley in Oxfordshire; the south coast and Isle of Wight are visible in the foreground. The composition is obviously symbolic and allegorical, with the pairing of light and dark and the flat rendering of Elizabeth's body. © *National Portrait Gallery, London*

against monarchy, on the one hand, and in the name of the kingdom or commonwealth on the other. He shows how a conceptual divide between monarch and the idea of the nation arose in the 16th and 17th centuries, in part due to the production and dissemination of the map. Maps of the kingdom showed how the nation-state had a geographical existence in its own right, independent of that of the monarch. This potentially subversive divide between the idea of monarch and nation is expressed in the famous "Ditchley Portrait" of Elizabeth I, in which the queen stands on a map of England, one of her feet directly upon Ditchley (Figure 1.2): the point being that the divide between nation and monarch is subtly reinforced in a stylized and allegorical propaganda portrait of Elizabeth's sovereignty. By the 1640s, argues Helgerson, this intellectual divide had become so great as to allow the English Parliament to put on trial and proceed to execute King Charles for treachery, in the name of the "nation." The parliamentary leaders could make an argument that would have been alien to the Middle Ages: that loyalty to the nation was quite separate to loyalty to the monarch.

Enclosure

At a national level, then, appreciation of the physical landscape was bound up with that of the social and moral – and changes in that appreciation were driven in part by the production of maps. The same was true at the local level, and was especially true in England with the early development in that country of rural capitalism. From the 15th century onwards, the customary, medieval landscape of England was under attack from material and social forces both within and without. A generation of landlords, famously seen by the historian Richard Tawney and others as the first harbingers of the new capitalist order, carved up the medieval landscape and gave much of it over to sheep-runs. In the process, great numbers of medieval villages were deserted (Figure 1.3), a phenomenon that caused anger, condemnation and ineffectual legislation from the authorities (Tawney 1912; Dyer 1994 summarizes the historical reassessment of this process and takes the position that the phenomenon of aggressive "depopulation" by landlords has been exaggerated, a position that is now largely undisputed).

More generally, the population and other changes of the later Middle Ages were tied up with the transformation of large parts of the

Figure 1.3 A deserted village: Hamilton in Leicestershire. Parts of Hamilton were excavated by W. G. Hoskins and his students in 1948. *Copyright reserved Cambridge University Collection of Air Photographs*

landscape. Landlords and wealthier peasants enclosed fields, switched from arable to pasture, and built up wealth in the countryside. They were assisted in this process by the techniques of the survey and in particular the local map. The surveyor was seen in popular discourse as the land-lord's friend and the enemy of the peasant farmer; popular sentiment correctly identified the drawing up of an apparently objective survey as the first step towards enclosure and dispossession. Norden's famous treatise on surveying consists of a dialogue between a surveyor and a farmer, in which the former tries to persuade the latter of the validity of his pursuit and elaborates on how the survey is done (Richeson 1966:93).

In the early modern period, early scholarly understandings were bound up with the politics of rights and access. Opponents of enclosure

Figure 1.4 Enclosure "by agreement," later fields running along the lines of earlier ridge-and-furrow at Brassington, Derbyshire, showing how medieval land divisions can be preserved in the process of small-scale enclosure. *Copyright reserved Cambridge University Collection of Air Photographs*

and defenders of common land, standing in local courtrooms attempting to defend their rights, routinely cited "custom since time out of mind," or in other words a particular conception of traditional usage of the land justified with reference to the past. Drawing on traditions going back to the Middle Ages, ordinary people engaged in resistance to enclosure through modifications to the landscape – specifically, throwing over and destroying, often in a small-scale and symbolic way, the hedges and ditches of enclosed land (Thompson 1991). The Levellers, the radical and proto-socialist group thrown up by the upheavals of the English Revolution, took their name not from an egalitarian desire as such, but rather from the action of levelling these ditches and fences (Hill 1993:133). Similar views were attributed to other rebellious groups: "Shall they, as have brought hedges about common pastures, enclose with their intolerable lusts also all the commodities and pleasures of this life, which Nature, the parent of us all, would have common? . . . Now that it comes to extremity, we will also prove extremity: rend down hedges, fill up ditches, make way for every man into the common pasture" (cited in Patterson 1989:42–3). By the 17th century if not before, the landscape had become an established metaphor for the state of the political realm. Denham's poem "Coopers Hill" referenced the landscape against protagonists in the English Revolution: the narrator of the poem, standing on Coopers Hill, lifts his gaze upwards to the prospect of the noble seats of royalist families and lowers it again to the sites of parliamentarian iniquity: "the mist of aerial perspective corresponds to the malignant fog of Puritan business, and the romantic horror of the ruin-piece to political thuggery" (Turner 1979:55).

At the same time, the everyday actions of surveyors and map-makers were closely tied in both to an emerging sensibility to landscape and to the antiquities contained therein and to the politics of the state. The great 16th-century topographers Leland and Camden wrote their descriptions of England in a context dominated by the rise of the Tudor state; the increased frequency of the production of national and regional maps (Helgerson 1992:105–46). Norden published *The Surveiors Dialogue* in 1618, in which the surveyor explicates the methods of surveying in justification to a farmer whose view is that the former is a stooge of the landlord whose aim in drawing up a survey is simply to find an excuse to extract more rent (Richeson 1966:93; Johnson 1996:70–96). Norden's anxieties were a symptom of a deeper sense in which topography presented itself as neutral, but was actually ideological:

Topography claims to be a "science", that is, a discourse of technical, objective, rational Enlightenment knowledge. Such knowledge is often claimed to be universal in its scope and free of cultural or political interests. But topography (like cartography) also is a "practice", knowledge put to use, knowledge in the service of power that is deeply intertwined in the cultural, social and political webs of a society. Such knowledge is intended to describe the way in which a social formation is made visible on the face of the earth. It is a practice which describes boundaries, including property relations, and thereby objectifies them, rationalises them and makes them seem like objects of nature through the legitimising tropes of the discourse of science . . . Topography is also therefore a science of domination – confirming boundaries, securing norms and treating questionable social conventions as unquestioned social facts. (Duncan and Ley 1993:1)

If topography was complicit with a nascent science of domination and dispossession, much of 17th- and 18th-century English literature was a culture of protest against that process. Many of the classic evocations of landscape in the history of English literature were written in the context of direct opposition to landscape change. The Anglo-Irish writer Oliver Goldsmith's classic poem "The Deserted Village," written in 1770, is a moral condemnation of enclosing landlords and the social and economic forces behind them.

Landscapes of Colonialism

As Europe reorganized itself internally, so it redefined its physical, moral, and political landscapes with reference to the lands and peoples outside its boundaries. European explorers and colonists had to accommodate to the shock of the "discovery" of new continents, upsetting the medieval symmetry of the world discussed above. They then had to come to terms with what they saw on those continents. For many, most famously the Puritan settlers of New England, this accommodation was a struggle for mastery. Just as the Puritan was engaged in constant struggle to discipline his own wills and desires, and just as the Puritan head of household struggled to discipline his family and servants, so Puritans perceived themselves as engaged in a struggle to master a wild, untamed landscape, a savage howling wilderness (Johnson 1993a:170–6). The conceptual challenge these landscapes presented, in the view of many historians, set off a ferment of theorizing among the intellectual circles of early modern Europe (Greenblatt 1991).

Of course, the "wilderness" encountered by European settlers was not a real one in any sense, but a constructed idea. From Ireland to Virginia to New England, the land had been settled and occupied by human societies for millennia. But the indigenous inhabitants appeared to the narrow-eyed English settlers to have failed in the God-given duty to cultivate the landscape. Cultivation in this view meant not simply use of the land, but arable agriculture, with fields bounded and divided by hedges and fences. These indigenous people had no bounded landscapes, no fences, no idea of property, no cultivation; a failing indissolubly linked with their lack of true religion (the Irish, being Catholic, were barely better, in the Protestant view, than the pagan

Americans). Their lack of imprint on the landscape, in the view of English Protestants, was testament to their savagery and ample moral justification for their dispossession (Vaughan 1979).

The Birth of Landscape Archaeology

I have dwelt on the social and cultural changes of the Renaissance, and their implications for the study of landscape, at some length because the intellectual frame of this period helps us understand a series of practices and disciplinary techniques that were central to the development of the modern academic and popular understanding of landscape, and of modern archaeology.

Perhaps the most central element to all these practices was the map. We have seen how the production of local and national maps by surveyors was tied in with the history of enclosure, and must be seen in the context of developing ideas of the nation-state. Most early maps were bounded with ideological representations that referred back to a past of ancestry and genealogy – coats of arms, dedications to the wealthy and landed families of the areas portrayed. Bound up with the production of maps, then, was the emerging discipline of topography. The task of the "topographer," usually a gentleman or a man of socially middling origins, was to translate the natural and humanly made landscape of a locality into words. The *Oxford English Dictionary* defines topography as "the science or practice of describing a particular place" (1603); its definition occurs around the same time as the term "mapping" (1586). The closely related practice of "chorography," defined as "the art of describing, or of delineating on a map, particular regions or districts," is also later 16th-century in date. The role of the early topographers and chorographers in studies of the landscape and the elements in it, and the way these studies fed into the development of what would later be termed archaeology, is well known (Daniel and Renfrew 1988; Trigger 1989:47–52). Arguably the first of these, John Leland, gained a commission from the great Tudor centralizer, Henry VIII; it is no coincidence that Henry and his ministers also went on to oversee and implement an explosion of bureaucratic record and control in the service of the creation of an early modern nation-state. Leland travelled the length and breadth of the country, writing down what he saw.

The development of the language and habits of thought of topography and chorography shows an intimate connection with the class struggles of the early modern period. By the 17th century, the "descriptions" written by topographers were privileging "vision," or the direct evidence of one's own eyes, above what they saw as "hearsay" or the traditions upheld by local, rural communities. These latter traditions of "hearsay," relying on ideas of customary practice "since time out of mind," may have incurred the disfavour of learned antiquarians, but they were the cornerstone of the assertion of rights by such local communities against the forces of enclosure discussed earlier. By the 18th century, the roles and definitions of the topographer and chorographer had coalesced into that of the antiquarian; again, this evolution has been well charted by historians of archaeology. The famous figure of William Stukeley, recorder of Stonehenge and Avebury, stands not just at the origins of modern archaeology, but at the end of a long line of topographical tradition going back to the Renaissance.

However, I am going to argue that the later 18th century also saw a break, and the establishment of a new horizon of ideas about the landscape. This set of ideas is associated with a new intellectual movement, that of Romanticism. In the next chapter I will begin to look at the values, strengths, and discontents of Romanticism, and begin to sketch out the argument that English Romanticism forms the backdrop to a large part of archaeological thinking about landscape today.

Chapter Two

LONELY AS A CLOUD

I wandered lonely as a Cloud
That floats on high o'er Vales and Hills,
When all at once I saw a crowd
A host, of golden Daffodils
. . . .
I gazed – and gazed – but little thought
What wealth the shew to me had brought:

For oft when on my couch I lie
In vacant or in pensive mood,
They flash upon that inward eye
Which is the bliss of solitude . . .

(William Wordsworth, Daffodils)

poets make the best topographers

(Hoskins 1955:17)

An old English teacher of mine once stated that you could know someone's literary tastes (and thus, he implied, know everything valuable about that person), by enquiring who they felt was the Third Greatest Poet in the English language. For my teacher, the first two names were self-evident to any civilized human being and a matter of canonical truth: William Shakespeare and Geoffrey Chaucer. The third name, he charitably granted, was a matter of personal choice, but he clung to his preferred candidate with vehement passion: William Wordsworth. (Others have named the 17th-century revolutionary poet John Milton as number two but retain Wordsworth in the third spot: Bragg 1996:58; see also Easthope 1999.) Wordsworth (1770–1850) was

Figure 2.1 Benjamin Robert Haydon, Wordsworth on the summit of the Lakeland peak Helvellyn, painted in 1842 when Wordsworth was 72. © *National Portrait Gallery, London*

the central figure in the English version of the cultural and intellectual movement known to us as Romanticism (Figure 2.1).

Wordsworth loved the landscape: central to Wordsworthian Romanticism was a set of firmly held ideas and convictions about landscape appreciation, both aesthetic and scholarly. He spent much of his life in the mountains and hills of the Lake District in northwest England, with his sister Dorothy to keep house. While Dorothy cooked and cleaned, kept a diary, and occasionally accompanied him on his walks with notebook in hand, ready to record her brother's great thoughts, William concentrated on higher and more aesthetic pursuits. Above all, he loved walking – his friend and associate Thomas De Quincey asserts that he walked over 175,000 miles during his lifetime (Shoard 1999:64). Wordsworth loved being on his own, or at least a few paces ahead of Dorothy, and he loved looking at views across the Cumbrian countryside.

But most of all William Wordsworth loved the exercise of turning the landscape he saw laid out before him into words:

> The act of turning what he saw into words was, for Wordsworth, an act that combined rationality with emotion. Merely describing what he saw was not enough: "It became with him an instinct to judge of a natural scene in the light of an artistic composition, in which all irrelevant detail sinks into its proper insignificance, and the main features of the landscape stand out in bold relief against the sky. Let him but gather it into "a heart that watches and receives", and express it through the medium of intense imaginative feeling, and it is a poem that spoke of the landscape in "the figured language of vitalising love." (de Selincourt 1906:xxi–xxii, citing Wordsworth himself)

However, the translation of turning the landscape into words need not be simply a poem. Other textual forms, factual and documentary as well as poetic, might be subjected to this process of transformation through intense feeling. Wordsworth wrote one of the first ever guidebooks in the English language for visitors to the countryside, the famous *Guide through the District of the Lakes*. This guide was a topographical description of and meditation on his beloved Lake District. It was addressed to "the Tourist," or more specifically "Persons of taste, who might be inclined to explore the District of the Lakes with that degree of attention to which its beauty may fairly lay claim" (de Selincourt 1906:1).

Central to the *Guide* is the primacy of the gaze or view. Sometimes this view will be from below, gazing up at a sublime prospect such as a waterfall or great crag; but more frequently, the view was downwards. In particular, Wordsworth's descriptions of the Lakes are animated by the idea of a panoramic view from above, looking over the landscape from a great height and taking in all detail, from the most colossal mountain to the tiniest human figure, under one single, imperious gaze (Figure 2.2). In this concentration on a view from above, seen also in the citation from "Daffodils" at the start of this chapter, Wordsworth was influenced by his travels on the Continent. While visiting Lucerne in Switzerland he had observed a model

Figure 2.2 View of the Lakes, from near Wordsworth's home in Grasmere. *Photo by Tony Richards*

of the Alpine country . . . The Spectator ascends a little platform, and sees mountains, lakes, glaciers, rivers, woods, waterfalls, and valleys, with their cottages, and every other object contained in them, lying at his feet . . . It may easily be conceived that this exhibition affords an exquisite delight to the imagination, tempting it to wander at will from valley to valley, from mountain to mountain, through the deepest recesses of the Alps. But it supplies also a more substantial pleasure: for the sublime and beautiful region, with all its hidden treasures, and their bearings and relations to each other, is thereby comprehended and understood at once. (de Selincourt 1906:21)

For Wordsworth, this aerial, superhuman, even God-like view that comprehended all the region "at once," in one imperious sweep of the gaze, and which accorded such power and intellectual primacy to "the imagination," included human settlement and social relations as well as the natural landscape. Viewed from the vantage point of one of the Lake District's peaks, houses, fields, and the tiny figures moving around them became objects of aesthetic appreciation, as necessary to the aesthetic composition of the scene as cloud formations or craggy peaks. Indeed, the distinction in Wordsworth's mind, and that of the Romantic mind in general, between aesthetic criticism and appreciation of the natural world, and criticism and appreciation of the human world, was not always clear.

This dovetailing of the natural and human, and the control of both by the all-encompassing gaze, was certainly evident in Romantic art. Contemporary painting, following the tradition of the picturesque, routinely included in the foreground of any landscape composition some small human figures, arranged in a suitably bucolic or pastoral manner, alluding back to the classical motifs discussed in the last chapter: perhaps some dairy maids and cattle, or shepherds tending their sheep. The picturesque artist John Gilpin, for example, was quite explicit about the compositional qualities of such figures (Bermingham 2000). In colonial contexts, such as the early years of the Australian penal colonies, these dairy maids and sheep were often replaced by dimly lit and indistinct small groups of indigenous peoples (Radford and Hylton 1995:15, 23).

Human relations were aestheticized by this process. That is, they became part of the artistic or literary composition, bounded in to the same (aesthetic) rules. They became part of a wider landscape that was to be judged in compositional and aesthetic terms. The social and political realities of those human relations were consequently, it has been argued by critics of Romanticism, pushed into the background (McGann 1984; Brookner 2000).

We can take this observation further. The panoramic view from above tended to lead directly and seamlessly from observation to interpretation. That is, it connected a visual comprehension and understanding to a direct moral and political injunction linking landscape, human activity and the aesthetic in terms of preservation of natural beauty. For Wordsworth, the Lakes were a naturally beautiful place, but had been deformed in recent years by the works of humans. Wordsworth railed against over-grand building, follies, and white roughcast, and the use of conifers and exotics. All such excrescences were unfaithful to what he called the *genius loci* of the area. In referring to *genius loci* in this way, Wordsworth drew from one of the classical traditions and images of the landscape outlined in the last chapter, that of a presiding spirit of a locality or place:

> *Singula de nobis anni praedantur euntes.* This is in the course of things; but why should the genius that directed the ancient architecture of the vales have deserted them? For the bridges, churches, mansions, cottages, and their richly fringed and flat-roofed outhouses, venerable as the grange of some old abbey, have been substituted structures, in which baldness

only seems to have been studied, or plans of the most vulgar utility. (de Selincourt 1906:65)

Such a sentiment can be seen as part of the origins of the ethics of architectural and environmental conservation today; this railing against the vulgar utility of the moderns led directly to an ethic of preservation. One of the great achievements of the Romantics, aside from the poetry and prose that they wrote, was the development of an environmental sensibility. Wordsworth has been seen by literary critics and historians as the first "nature poet," and, more arguably, as the first conservationist (Bate 1991). It is certainly true that Romanticism marked a decisive turn in European and North American attitudes to the landscape. Before Romanticism, "wild" landscapes, craggy peaks such as those of Cumbria just as much as the savage howling wildernesses so detested by the Puritans in New England, were seen as hostile, terrifying, physically ugly. Who could be ignorant, after all, of the fact that such hideous, craggy mountains and deformed hillsides were thrown up after the fall of Adam, as a sign of God's displeasure with man? The English traveller and writer Daniel Defoe, author of the seminal colonialist text *Robinson Crusoe*, explicitly linked the inhospitable, uncultivated nature of the Scottish landscape with what he saw as the unreformed nature of Scottish society and culture (Rogers 1989:198).

The stress on conservation was also implicitly nationalist. Wordsworth wanted to encourage Britons to view and appreciate the landscape around them, and this landscape was seen in national terms. Wordsworth was writing at a particular historical moment. Earlier generations of wealthy aristocrats had completed their education with the Grand Tour, a trip around Europe, often accompanied by a tutor, in which the cultural highlights of the Continent would be experienced. Wordsworth was no aristocrat, but his earlier work was itself informed by an engagement with Continental Romanticism and in particular the Swiss Alps. However, after the French Revolution of 1789 and the ensuing intermittent wars with France, culminating in the conflict with Napoleon not resolved until 1815, the Grand Tour was difficult if not impossible to undertake. Wordsworth was inviting his countrymen, then, to turn inwards and engage with the local scenery of the British Isles at a particularly propitious moment. He wrote: "my object is to reconcile a Briton to the scenery of his own country, though not at the expense of truth." For Wordsworth, in a phrase that would come to reverberate down the centuries, the Cumbrian Lakes were "a sort of national property, in which every man has a right and interest who has an eye to perceive and a heart to enjoy" (de Selincourt 1906:106, 92, 145).

However, for Wordsworth, not everyone had an eye to perceive and a heart to enjoy. The gentle classes, those at or near the apex of society, had such eyes and hearts, but not necessarily anyone else. The ability to appreciate a landscape could be taught to an extent, but was nevertheless not easily acquired by ordinary folk. Wordsworth disliked railways, and not simply because he felt they were physically ugly; they also led in his view to "railway inundations" of common folk, spoiling his solitude and appreciation of the countryside. The Lake District was indeed a national treasure, but it was so difficult to acquire the training needed to appreciate it: "the perception of what has acquired the name of picturesque and romantic scenery is so far from being intuitive, that it can be produced only by a slow and gradual process of culture . . . as a consequence, that the humbler ranks of society are not, and cannot be, in a state to gain material benefit from a more speedy access" (de Selincourt 1906:160, 157). In this view, Wordsworth contrasted the landscape with urban and metropolitan institutions such as the British Museum and National Gallery, into which ordinary folk could walk at any time and so imbibe some culture without straying too far from their proper social and physical place. Some decades later, the National Gallery's weekly afternoon when admission was free was satirized by contemporary cartoons in the humorous magazine *Punch*.

It is worth noting in passing that what, precisely, the necessary training or education was to "correctly" understand the landscape is not entirely explicit. "A slow and gradual process of culture" is not a satisfactory definition; indeed, it is so vague as to lead the reader to suspect that there is no real definition, outside the general sense of having mastered a particular set of jargon, and of appearing through one's manner, speech, and appearance to have the correct social and intellectual background.

Wordsworth's view of landscape was also explicitly backward-looking. He wrote that a rising awareness of the past meant that "we are setting out to travel backwards" (de Selincourt 1906:140). By this he meant that the care and management of the landscape in feudal times were to be commended, in that feudal power expressed itself in the vastness of the open countryside. However, Romanticism as a project was closely tied up also with the presence of antiquity in the landscape. If picturesque artists placed figures in the foreground of their paintings, ruins were often placed in the background. Many of Wordsworth's poems meditate deeply on the links between present and past in contemplation of the landscape (Wallace 2004:37–52).

To summarize: for Wordsworth, then, understanding the landscape was:

- a solitary experience
- rooted in the gaze from above
- an act of aesthetic appreciation
- an act of translation from landscape to text
- embedded in the particular (*genius loci*) and the national
- setting out to travel backwards
- rooted in bodily activity – walking miles
- somehow ineffable and intuitive, yet
- the product of rigorous training, and therefore
- socially restricted.

Romantic philosophy is notoriously difficult to define (Brookner 2000). Its political content is double-edged. On the one hand, Romanticism has been part of an explicitly socialist and libertarian programme, from the Continental influence of Rousseau, embracing figures such as the early Wordsworth, the mystic and freethinker William Blake, and the radical and revolutionary Thomas Paine. In the 19th century figures such as William Hazlitt, George Crabbe, and William Cobbett formed a distinct radical and populist tradition; from there, it can be traced through the formation of the socialist Labour Party to figures such as George Orwell, and politicians such as Michael Foot and Tony Benn. As such, Romanticism has often been conceived of as a primary formative influence on a distinctively English tradition of left-wing politics.

This whole tradition had strongly emotive, egalitarian, and populist overtones. Romantic poetry had a distinctively democratic and populist edge. In his preface to the *Lyrical Ballads*, Wordsworth asserted that the poet should employ "simple speech, the language really spoken by men" (cited in Montefiore 1994:9). In his youth Wordsworth was a political radical, though as he aged he became steadily more reactionary. In subsequent generations, the Romantic vision has proved a fertile source for a vibrant egalitarian vision in English art, culture, and politics. This vision owes much more to Romanticism than it does to Marx (Woodcock 2000; see also Chapter 6 below). This is not to deny the contribution of Romanticism to Marxism. The young Marx saw himself as a Romantic, and many of the philosophical underpinnings of "early Marx" owe much to German Romantic philosophy (Kiernan 1989:96).

It has also informed the thinking of the famous post-war generation of British Marxist historians, including Christopher Hill and Eric Hobsbawm, radicalized by the war and turning to Marxism and the Communist Party on their return. Many of these figures subsequently distanced themselves from the Stalinist Soviet Union, in particular after its invasion of Hungary. The most famous example of such a tradition is the work of E. P. Thompson, whose classic book *The Making of the English Working Class* (1963) stressed the traditions and sentiments of the emergent working classes of industrial England. It took as its theme the thoughts and actions of artisans and workers caught up in the Industrial Revolution, with the aim of saving them from the "enormous condescension of history." In this respect, it complemented the more analytical strands of thought within Marxism, stressing that men and women make themselves, and are not simply made by the forces and relations of production. Thompson took the implicit critique further in his *The Poverty of Theory* (1978), an impassioned and sustained attack on what he saw as the formality and sterility of French structural Marxism; not far below the surface here was an English Romantic's impatience with a perceived Gallic obsession with formal structures at the expense of real human beings. Again, the point of attack was structural Marxism's alleged inability to comprehend or engage seriously with human agency.

For better or worse, then, the impact of Romanticism on English and British culture and politics cannot be overstressed. It represents a political, cultural, social, and aesthetic backdrop that is often unspoken in British intellectual circles. It is because of its unspoken and therefore unexamined nature that Romanticism remains an enduring habit of thinking (Easthope 1999).

The Discontents of Romanticism

The central problem with Wordsworth, and with Romanticism generally, for the landscape archaeologist is the epistemology being proposed: in other words, how we know what we know about the landscape and past human life. At a very basic level, it proposes that understanding a landscape is about opening one's heart and mind and simply seeing (or sensing). Literary critics have subjected the writings of the Romantics to textual exegesis of infinite complexity. However, in a vulgar view, the message of Romanticism to the scholar seeking to understand the landscape is: walk for a long enough distance, position yourself in front of the most sublime views, and as long as you open your mind out in the proper manner and have the proper education, you will somehow, by a process that is at least partly ineffable and beyond analysis, grasp what is in front of you.

As thus expressed, a Romantic view of landscape involves an unrestrained empiricism. Empiricism is the belief that the data will speak for themselves, with no need for any intervening theory. This may seem a strange comment to make, because Romanticism is often associated in both philosophy and popular thought with idealism and a celebration of subjective experience. In particular, Romantic philosophy owes much to the influence of the idealism of Kant, which proposes that the world of thought and ideas takes priority over that of empirical experience. Indeed, Wordsworth's friend and fellow poet Coleridge critiqued the idea of the mind as a passive absorber of information (Kitson 1991).

However, when unexamined and implicit, empiricist and idealist views actually fit together like lock and key: the one presupposes the existence of the other. In archaeology, Shanks and Tilley famously rejected the series of dualisms established in Western thought between subjective and objective (1987:24 and *passim*). They argue that each actually implies its obverse. For example, the split between culture and nature also tends to reinforce a dualism between culture and nature, between the viewer and the viewed. The Romantics may have rejected a model in which culture was required to take precedence over nature; a scene of cultivated fields was no longer to be preferred over craggy mountains; unrestrained nature was now sublime rather than hideous. However, in so doing, they reinforced this dualism and elevated the significance of nature. As a result, the underlying split between culture and nature was not itself questioned, and nature remained passive. However, far from being a simple, passive, easily defined object, nature is actually "the most complex word in the [English] language" (Williams 1976:184). The feminist Val Plumwood has called the overturning and reinscription of this nature/culture dualism the "Cavern of Reversal," and observed how in this view nature remains both passive and gendered as feminine, albeit in a complex way (Plumwood 1993:41–69).

There is a second dualism here that Romanticism reinforces: between landscape and poem, or more broadly between material culture and text, or for that matter archaeology and documents. Wordsworth translates landscape into words, and emphasizes how difficult and exacting such an effort is – the peculiar intractability of the translation and the cultural training needed to effect it. In so emphasizing the intellectual and affective difficulty of the translation, he reinforces the separateness of the two domains.

It is here that epistemological issues lead us to the other side of double-edged Romantic politics. An unrestrained empiricism leads naturally into a political quietism, in which all one can do is observe the world rather than act upon it; or it can even go further, into a reactionary politics. This process can best be seen in Wordsworth's own career. He famously started as a leading supporter of the French Revolution, but disillusionment set in, and in his later life he became a political reactionary. Romanticism – wandering lonely as a cloud, retreating into a solitary existence and aesthetic appreciation of the natural world, away from the human mêlée of the metropolis – can be seen as a personal response to political defeat and disillusionment. Kiernan explores how Wordsworth's early activism slid slowly into quietism and retreat from action. By the time of his poem "The Lonely Cottage," poverty is a moving spectacle, not a spring for political protest (Kiernan 1989:102).

Conceptions of the picturesque, which in many ways was the artistic representation of literary Romanticism, went through a subtle parallel transition in which early radicalism gave way to political conservatism and reaction. Anne Bermingham (2000) has argued that the picturesque formulas of artists like Gilpin, reducing artistic appreciation of the landscape to a series of formulaic rules, went alongside formulaic proposals for government, such as the radical Thomas Paine's *Rights of Man* and the Jacobin party of the French Revolution – or indeed the American Constitution. As England retreated into nationalism and reactionary politics in response to the Jacobin ascendancy in France and the ensuing French wars, culminating in the struggle against Napoleon, so the counter-assertion that the principles and practice of government should be based on memory, complexity, history, and antecedent, rather than on abstract formula, gained intellectual ascendancy. Such a conservative view stressed the cultural and political landscape as both ineffable (its essence cannot be analysed and consequently critiqued according to abstract principles) and one of continuity. This position was expressed politically through Edmund Burke's *Reflections on the Revolution in France*. Bermingham argues that reflections on picturesque art went through a parallel change. Gilpin's formulas fell from favour; instead, Wordsworth and others saw the landscape as complex, ineffable, and increasingly full of history.

Wordsworth was certainly acutely aware of social distinctions, and was not slow in making those around him conscious of them too. In conversation, he quickly distinguished between those worth talking to and the great mass of others. This led him to alienate and estrange many of his greatest friends and admirers, most notably Thomas De Quincey, whom he never forgave for marrying into the vulgar sort. According to De Quincey, those Wordsworth considered outside "the sacred and privileged pale" of thinking like himself "he did not even appear to listen [to]; but as if what they said on such a theme might be childish prattle, turned away with an air of perfect indifference" (Wright 1970:326).

Such criticisms of Wordsworth and the Romantic tradition generally are not new. De Quincey rolled up many of them into a pithy and satirical critique of the Wordsworth poem "The Lonely Cottage," in which the solitary figure of Wordsworth contemplates the sad and picturesque ruin of a cottage; he is told the story of its hapless inmates by a passing traveller, who recalls talking to the woman who lived there. Racked by poverty, her husband left to join the army, but never returned, leaving her to bring up the children alone and in hardship. Wordsworth tells this story in order to excite the appropriate feelings of pity in the heart of the reader, and there is more than a hint in his writing that the excitement of these emotional sensibilities, the *feeling* of feeling emotional, is an end in itself; De Quincey hints that this is more than a little narcissistic (Wright 1970). He drily points out that instead of standing back and passively viewing the melancholy scene in purely aesthetic terms, the traveller might have been better employed in advising the woman to apply to the army administration for information on her husband's whereabouts, which would have been readily obtainable, and thereafter exercise her right under British army regulations to half his pay.

De Quincey's humour may be laboured to our eyes (the comment loses much in the paraphrasing, and I urge the reader to consult the more witty original); however, there is a serious point here. For Wordsworth, it is implied, aesthetic appreciation of the scene is far more worthy of poetic celebration than practical action to deal with the social problems contained therein. A divide is thus reinforced between the aesthetic and the social. This divide does not merely lead to political quietism: it impoverishes the scholar's appreciation of the way "the aesthetic" is not an isolated category at all. Raymond Williams comments that the idea of the aesthetic "is a key formation in a group of meanings which . . . is an element in the divided modern consciousness between art and society." Williams comments that "the isolation can be damaging, for there is something irresistibly displaced and marginal about the now common and limiting phrase 'aesthetic considerations', especially when contrasted with practical or utilitarian consideration, which are elements of the same basic division" (1976:28). Two centuries earlier, this attitude was satirized by William Blake, who pointed out that: "Pity would be no more | If we did not make somebody poor." Wordsworth's poem "The Old Cumberland Beggar" epitomizes this debate; in characteristic fashion the reactionary critic Harold Bloom

(1961:173–8) simply denies that politics are relevant to an understanding of this poem.

McGann and Liu have both argued that "Wordsworth developed a creed of the all-powerful, redeeming Imagination . . . as a kind of compensation for his political disillusionment" (Bate 1991:3). Somewhere, then, in later Romantic writings, the spectacle of the landscape comes to erase the real social relations contained therein. Romanticism becomes a mask or ideology in which the search for the aesthetic is held somehow to transcend socio-economic reality; political action to eradicate the causes of rural poverty was abandoned in favour of a search for the sublime. This turning away from social reality had racist and colonial as well as nationalist overtones. It has been argued that the development of Wordsworth as a poet, and specifically his "sublime turn," was a move away from a confrontation with the horrors of slavery and imperialism towards a fictional "imaginative freedom nationed specifically English" (Persyn 2002:1). Such a critique can be applied to other Romantic poets such as Keats, who wrote "To Autumn" at the same time as the Peterloo riots were taking place.

As a result, Romanticism becomes in many of its guises an ideology of liberal individualism, with all the strengths and discontents that go with such a position:

> concepts like the "concrete", the "natural", the "sublime", and the "organic" became popular slogans sustaining autonomous individualism . . . The creation of the "individual" as a simultaneously fundamental, immediate, transcendental, and textualized presence is compressed in Wordsworth's famous three questions about the function of the poet: "What is meant by the word Poet? What is a Poet? To whom does he address himself?" And in his answer that the poet is "a man speaking to other men." (Privateer 1991:1)

What About Dorothy?

A man speaking to other men . . . Wordsworth, of course, took the theme and much of the imagery of his most famous poem "Daffodils" from his sister Dorothy's journal for 15 April 1802:

> there was a long belt of [daffodils] along the shore . . . I never saw daffodils so beautiful they grew among the mossy stones about and about them, some rested their heads upon these stones as on a pillow for weariness and the rest tossed and reeled and danced and seemed as if

they verily laughed with the wind that blew upon them over the lake, they looked so gay ever glancing ever changing . . . (Wordsworth 1987:123)

The serious and more wide-ranging point here is that the Romantic imagination is, for many feminist writers, masculine. The "Romantic imagination" is "a masculine mode of writing and relationship . . . concerned with self-centered imperialism, with a 'pursuit of the infinitude of the private self' that we, in the 20th century, regard with some embarrassment" (Yaeger 1989). Janet Todd expands on this point:

> Romanticism . . . is, in many of its guises and receptions, a reassertion of masculinity. The cry for manliness, mastery and virility echoes through the manifestos of Schlegel and Goethe. Coleridge demands the penetrating and mastering in art and rails against the effete and the effeminate, while Wordsworth, wanting a language available to all classes, sounds "man" and "men" with cumulative force through his prefaces . . . The Romantic poet's world is infinite, eternal and one, and the one, like the one of matrimony, is male. (Todd 1988:113–14)

Todd goes on to argue that in Romanticism "the female enters not usually as creating subject but as the symbol of otherness and immanence" (1988:114). One might add: the subject viewing the landscape is male/active; the viewed is female/passive. In Romantic writing, the older classical motif of the muse is replaced by the landscape as a source of inspiration (de Man 1984:125); the Muse is explicitly gendered as female, and by this act of substitution the landscape is gendered also. If the landscape in Romanticism becomes a passive object, it also becomes gendered as feminine; when Wordsworth is not writing poems about the landscape, when women are more than tiny, beetling creatures viewed from above, his favourite subject, as we have seen in "The Lonely Cottage," is the poor, suffering, helpless woman.

If the landscape is gendered female, the women who populate it either become passive, another element of the natural landscape, or disappear completely. It has been suggested that such a gendering is a deep-seated and continuing feature of English writing about the landscape. In the late 19th century, the great novelist of regional England Thomas Hardy used this technique: Ralph Pite argues that he employed the roving and controlling eye of the tourist to control his women characters (Pite 2002).

Wandering lonely as a cloud is, in many senses, a characteristically male activity. In responding to the great Romantic texts, women have tended to empathize more with sister Dorothy, trailing behind the imperious strides of her illustrious brother and tending to his every material need. Feminist critics have also tended to see the identity of the poet as "a man speaking to other men" in more complex terms, where to speak is not an unproblematic exercise (Kaplan 1986:83–5, 222) and where women are often excluded. Such a gendered identity tied in to Romanticism's nationalist agenda: for Mary Shelley, the unrestrained foreign travel of the Grand Tour made Englishmen half-men, only half-English (Brewer 1998).

Conclusion

If for some Wordsworth is the Third Greatest Poet, for others he is one of the worst, or at least one might argue in more temperate terms that his influence has been detrimental to the course of writing in English. With the notable and honourable exception of William Blake, the Romantics turned English poetry and literature away from one of its most exciting, vibrant, and politically charged phases – the world of Dean Swift's *Modest Proposal* in which the cruelties of English policy in Ireland were viciously lampooned, the world of Pope and Dr Johnson, the merciless yet morally charged artistic caricature of William Hogarth, the witty, merry, and often crude, brutal, and violent world of 18th-century satire (Rogers 1980).

The landscapes of 18th-century satire are populated with naughtiness, travelling, drinking, whoring, and sharp comment on the social iniquities of the day. Romanticism replaced this vibrant comedy of manners and its attendant trenchant, dangerous social comment with sentimentality, and presaged the advent of a dreary, dreadful Victorian mawkishness. It presaged the absorption in self of the middle-aged male. In Wordsworth's own words: "a thing unprecedented in Literary history that a man should talk so much about himself"; "I had nothing to do but describe what I had felt and thought" and "therefore could not easily be bewildered" (de Selincourt 1967:586–7). In this sense, Wordsworth is the forerunner of Sigmund Freud, and also of a contemporary literary trend in which the inner anxieties of the middle-aged male writer are thought to be a subject of infinite interest to the chattering classes.

But there is more to this debate than a parlour game of debating the moral and aesthetic merits of different literary periods. The politics of Wordsworth's poetry have been gone over again and again; for literary critics it is a tired subject, one moreover with far more complexities and nuances than have been covered here. I have covered this old ground at some length here because, in the remainder of this book, I argue that *Romanticism has provided the intellectual underpinning for the implicit theoretical position of much of landscape history and archaeology*. It is tempting to go further and say that if scholars want to understand contemporary approaches to landscape archaeology, and ask why English scholars in particular approach the landscape in the way that they do, we might be better off setting Heidegger and Husserl to one side for the moment and turning instead to English Romanticism.

The formative influence of Romanticism on landscape archaeology has rarely been overtly acknowledged, and many practitioners are clearly not even aware that it is there. Romanticism is a state of mind, a set of cultural assumptions – one of the most successful discourses ever in terms of its infiltration into the cultural being and habits of thought of modern intellectual life, in that its assumptions have become so normal and natural as to be unspoken. Its success in dominating the disciplinary techniques of landscape archaeology comes in part from the fact that its influence was not direct, and is not therefore so easily pinned down. Rather, it comes to us second-hand. Romanticism was refracted, in part, through the work of the self-styled landscape historian William George Hoskins. Hoskins worked within an intellectual horizon set out by Wordsworth, and we shall see how, although prehistory took a different turn, the landscape archaeology of historic periods in Britain works within an intellectual horizon that was set out by Hoskins and his contemporaries. And so it is to William George Hoskins that we must now turn.

Chapter Three

A GOOD PAIR OF BOOTS

The real work [in the study of landscape] is accomplished by the men and women with the muddy boots and aching joints who do most of the work, even if the credit flies off in a different direction.

(*Muir 2000:xiii*)

[The author's] hobby is exploring England on foot, a pursuit of inexhaustible interest in which he reckons to make at least one major "discovery" each week.

(*Hoskins 1954b:back flyleaf*)

If I had to name one person who has made English landscape archaeology the discipline it is today, it would not be the latest phenomenologist or even a great excavator: indeed, it would not be a trained archaeologist at all; it would be an economic and landscape historian who saw the need to get his boots muddy, William George Hoskins (1908–82; see Figure 3.1).

Much of this influence is indirect. Hoskins was a contemporary and great influence on a number of landscape historians and archaeologists such as Maurice Beresford, John Hurst, and others, who went on to dominate the emergent field of historic landscape archaeology in the 1950s and 1960s. At the same time, his books, most notably *The Making of the English Landscape*, and subsequent radio and television contributions, had a tremendous impact on the public consciousness of the historic landscape. As a result, Hoskins's approach and theme have become implicit within much of the current sweep of landscape studies even if his name is not explicitly mentioned.

Hoskins begins his most famous book, *The Making of the English Landscape*, with a direct appeal to Wordsworth's *Guide through the District of the Lakes*: he calls it "one of the best guide-books ever written,

Figure 3.1 W. G. Hoskins towards the end of his career, filming for the television series *English Landscapes* (University of Leicester)

for poets make the best topographers" (1955:17), and both here and elsewhere in his work quotes extensively from it (1955:203–4; 1983:177–8). He describes the structure of Wordsworth's guide, a structure Hoskins had already broadly followed in his 1954 guide to Devon, and then cites Wordsworth's comments and imagery on the "primeval freshness" of the landscape before the arrival of humans. Hoskins comments in terms that could have been lifted directly from Wordsworth's own prose:

How often has one tried to form these images in various parts of England, seated beside a wide, flooding estuary as the light thickens on a winter evening, dissolving all the irrelevant human details of the scene, leaving nothing but the shining water, the sky, and the darkening hills, and the immemorial sounds of curlews whistling over the mud and fading river-beaches. This, we feel, is exactly as the first men saw it . . . for a moment or two we succeed in entering into the minds of the dead . . . (Hoskins 1955:17)

I am going to argue, then, in this chapter that the intellectual project of Hoskins, and to a great extent many of his contemporaries in this formative period of landscape history and archaeology, was the Romantic project of Wordsworth and his age, translated into academic practice. It follows therefore that the intellectual project, and the field programmes and fieldwork habits that it engendered, which came to be shaped by the thinking and research of Hoskins and many of his contemporaries, shares many of the intellectual qualities – and flaws – of Romanticism.

Hoskins's Life and Career

The facts about Hoskins's life and career are well worth recounting, for they help us to understand the social context of his writings and of landscape history and archaeology, and they contain clues to its subsequent development.

Hoskins was born in 1908. He was the son of an Exeter baker; in later life he referred repeatedly to his socially middling origins, and to his "forefathers" as Devon yeomen; the latter became the subject of at least one academic paper (Hoskins and Finberg 1952). He spent much of his early years exploring the Devon landscape; he records that he started making notes at the age of 15 (1954b:xvii). Hoskins's retrospective account of these early researches is revealing of his method as subsequently developed, and also contains more than a distant echo of the style and tone of Wordsworth's long autobiographical poem *The Prelude*. He recounts how he puzzled over the features he observed on his summer holidays in the Devon countryside – a prehistoric hill fort, a Norman font in an otherwise 15th-century church, the scattering of farms rather than nucleation in a village. "I used to come home from these holidays and get histories of Devon out of the library, but they never answered my questions . . . I pored over the one-inch [Ordnance Survey] map for hours, trying to read it like a document written in a foreign language, but I got nowhere with it . . . Similarly

I kept on tackling the translated text of Domesday Book for Devon, hoping that some light would flash on that cryptic shorthand text if I went back to it often enough." Some "tantalising remarks" of the great medieval historian Maitland written at the end of the 19th century added to Hoskins's conviction, however, that "the ordnance map was the most rewarding single document we could have for the study of English topography, and that *fields, walls and hedges were all saying something about the past if only one could decipher the language*" (1967:16–17; italics mine).

Hoskins was brought up in an early 20th-century England riven by class divides, elitism, and inequality, an experience that clearly affected him as someone from socially middling origins. He was later to assert, in his inaugural lecture as Professor of Local History at Leicester,

> A hundred years ago rickets was known as "the English disease". Today I am inclined to think it is a secret preoccupation – not with sex which is now openly discussed in all its aspects – but with social class. However hidden this preoccupation may be, it remains as powerful and crippling as ever in some academic fields. It is a sort of mental rickets, keeping people intellectually deformed, mentally bandy. Historians are very prone to it. I believe, as Flaubert once said, that class distinctions belong to the realm of archaeology. (Hoskins 1966b:9)

However, the British class system traditionally and famously offered some opportunity for those of humble social origins who were exceptionally talented to move up the social scale through the educational system (Jackson and Marsden 1962). Thanks to this, Hoskins's ability and efforts won him scholarships, first to grammar school, then to University College Exeter. Hoskins was trained as an economic historian, and in the 1930s was appointed as a lecturer at Leicester University College.

During the 1930s Hoskins taught evening classes at Vaughan Working Men's College and, in conjunction with his students, who took his classes in the evenings and at weekends, made excursions to explore the landscape around Leicester. The documentary research he and his students undertook during this period was later published as *The Midland Peasant* in 1957 (though it was ready for publication in the 1940s). He later described this period as the happiest of his life. Hoskins also became a leading light in the local Leicestershire Archaeology and History Society.

Hoskins spent the war years working in London. He hated the metropolis, but it was an experience that prompted further reflection on what he wanted to say about the landscape. During his "five years' imprisonment in London," "the only way to keep sane among the rootless millions of 'countrymen on the road to sterility', as E. M. Forster has so truly described them, was to reflect on [his time in the Midlands countryside]. I often reflected on how one could best convey the essential quality of the peaceful, quiet English midlands to anyone who did not know them" (Hoskins 1949:v; the reference to E. M. Forster, a novelist often seen as quintessentially English, is revealing here). After the war he returned to Leicester, and made field visits around the Leicestershire countryside. He was accompanied on these trips by the principal of the college, F. L. Attenborough, who acted as photographer and chauffeur (Hoskins reportedly never learnt to drive). Attenborough appointed him Reader in English Local History at Leicester in 1947/8. However, in 1951 Hoskins was appointed Reader in Economic History at Oxford University.

Hoskins was not happy at Oxford. Traditionally, Oxford lecturers were offered a college fellowship, but the university never got around to doing so to Hoskins; it has been reported that he was about to be offered one when he left twenty years later. There is some hint in his obituaries (Millward 1992; Scarfe 1992; Thirsk 1992) that, as a "grammar-school boy" of relatively humble lower-middle-class origins, Hoskins did not "fit in" to the rather stuffier Oxford environment with its "reek of privilege" (Anonymous 1992:145). The fact that his interests in local history and landscape were not easily classified within the established academic structures of Oxford compounded his discontent. He continued to live and work outside Oxford during this time, and returned to Leicester when appointed professor there in 1965. However, he soon became alienated by what he saw as the excessive demands of university politics and administration, and took early retirement in 1968. Subsequently, Hoskins worked for the BBC in presenting two television series on the landscape, series which at the time were highly innovative and were published as the popular books *English Landscapes* (1973) and *One Man's England* (1978).

Hoskins enjoyed great status as an "orthodox" economic historian, and in addition to his work on landscape and the countryside wrote extensively on topics such as urban history (see for example Hoskins 1957 and 1960). His ideas on and approaches to landscape had much of their impact on popular consciousness through his television work. However, two books, both published in the mid-1950s, stand out as of central significance in the subsequent development of landscape history and archaeology.

The first of these was *Devon* (1954b). This large volume of over six hundred pages was in the format of a county guide, with roughly half the book in the form of thematic and chronological chapters and the other half an alphabetical series of gazetteer entries. It is still a wonderful book to tour the county with, like taking a knowledgeable and charming yet often intemperate friend around as one potters from village to village, and it is the object of enduring admiration (the religious historian Eamon Duffy calls it "the best book ever written about Devon": Duffy 2001:xiv) and is still in print. *Devon* was not written on the spot: it was composed in Leicester, but, as one of his obituaries commented, "Wordsworth found his poetry as recollected in tranquillity" (Millward 1992:66, though this is not entirely true; as we have seen, he relied on his sister Dorothy's diaries and notebooks).

A year later Hoskins published his second great book: *The Making of the English Landscape*. Two themes animate this book, though in keeping with the style and tone of such a passionate and humanistic work they are implicit within the text rather than stated overtly in a formal theoretical excursus; Hoskins's development of these ideas is more apparent in the introduction he wrote for later editions (1977:11–16).

The first of these ideas is the great age of the landscape – "everything is older than we think" is spelt out in italics in the later introduction (1977:12) – and in particular that the landscape can be decoded or deciphered through careful observation and analysis of its physical characteristics – the shape and form of the woods and fields, the location and fabric of the farmsteads. Drawing both on his own experiences and on O. G. S. Crawford's 1953 book *Archaeology in the Field*, Hoskins proposed that these traces, many recorded on his beloved Ordnance Survey maps, could be "decoded" and assembled into a sequential account of the historical development of the landscape or region.

The second idea, or theme, as Charles Phythian-Adams has noted (1992), is a use of the story thus assembled to bemoan the effects of industrialization and the modern world. It is encapsulated in perhaps the most famous passage from Hoskins's entire oeuvre – a moral condemnation of modernity and its effects on the English landscape:

> What else has happened in the immemorial landscape of the English countryside? Airfields have flayed it bare . . . Poor devastated Lincolnshire and Suffolk! And those long gentle lines of the dip-slope of the Cotswolds, those misty uplands of the sheep-grey oolite, how they have lent themselves to the villainous requirements of the new age! Over them drones, day after day, the obscene shape of the atom-bomber, laying a trail like a filthy slug upon Constable's and Gainsborough's sky. England of the Nissen-hut, the "pre-fab", and the electric fence, of the high barbed wire around some unmentionable devilment; England of the arterial by-pass, treeless and stinking of diesel oil, murderous with lorries;

England of the bombing-range wherever there was once silence . . .
Barbaric England of the scientists, the military men, and the politicians;
let us turn away and contemplate the past before all is lost to the
vandals. (Hoskins 1955:231–2)

Hoskins goes on to record that these lines are written from his then
home in Oxfordshire, where his contemplation of the delimited, rural,
local view, "an epitome of the gentle unravished English landscape"
which he could see from his window, was regularly interrupted by the
hated atom-bombers from the local American airbase flying over
(Hoskins 1955:233; Millward 1992:66).

Hoskins and Wordsworth

As thus described, the intellectual parameters of Hoskins's project are,
I suggest, directly derived from, and constitute a species of, English
Romanticism. The comments in Chapter 2 on Wordsworth have an
all-too-familiar ring to the field archaeologist raised in the English landscape tradition. Go out, walk across the landscape, feel the cold air on
your face, get your boots muddy, and somehow this experience will
lead you to a greater sensibility of the past, a sensibility moreover that
is privileged, that is connected to a particular location and defies comparative analysis in its rootedness to a specific place. It is a sentiment
that is at once completely Romantic but also completely empiricist: the
experience speaks for itself, without the need for any intervening theory.

Let us recall the key features of Wordsworth's approach to the
experience of landscape.

A solitary experience

For the Romantic, understanding landscape was a solitary experience,
and one moreover conditioned by the physical activity of walking. We
have seen Hoskins's autobiographical description of how, as a youth,
he wandered alone over the Devon countryside. Elsewhere he expresses a preference for "the scholar and the library" over "some shiny
new academic palace" (Hoskins 1966b:21). More fundamentally, Hoskins
follows the Romantic tradition of individual response to a landscape,
for example in his choice of title for his books – *One Man's England*
(1978) being the most obvious example. It should be acknowledged
that walking was a recurring theme of the inter-war years, for example

in the work of the 1930s anti-modernist writer H. J. Massingham, whose 1936 and 1939 books *The English Downland* and *The English Countryside* prefigured this emphasis (Matless 1998:73–9).

The individual is manifested in other ways: for example, in the rhetorical use of an autobiographical narrative to set out the processes of doing fieldwork in local history (Hoskins 1967:15–19), or in a preference for seeing history as actively made rather than the result of massive impersonal forces. In this sense, Hoskins and E. P. Thompson are cousins with a common ancestor: *The Making of the English Landscape* and *The Making of the English Working Class* share not only the appeal in their titles to the active making of human history, but also the Romantic insistence that "we must strive to hear the men and women talking and working, and creating what has come down to us" (Hoskins 1967:184).

The critic Paul de Man insists that all writing is autobiographical, and Romantic writing especially so:

> Autobiography, then, is not a genre or a mode, but a figure of reading or of understanding that occurs, to some extent, in all texts. The autobiographical moment happens as an alignment between the two subjects involved in the process of reading in which they determine each other by mutual reflexive substitution . . . This specular structure is interiorised in a text in which the author declares himself the subject of his own understanding, but this merely makes explicit the wide claim to authorship that takes place whenever a text is stated to be by someone . . . Which amounts to saying that any book with a readable title page is, to some extent, autobiographical. (de Man 1984:70)

And this goes for reading the landscape as well: Hoskins constitutes himself through the English landscape as much as the landscape is constituted or "reconstructed" by him, as much in his descriptive passages as in his more flowery autobiographical moments.

Rooted in the gaze from above

Key to these early experiences was the act of examining and "reading" or understanding the Ordnance Survey map and relating it to the patterns of landscape on the ground. The classic mode of explanation by example in *The Making of the English Landscape* is an excerpt from the Ordnance Survey map or photograph, accompanied by an extended caption explaining to the reader what he or she is looking at (see for example Figure 3.2). Hoskins frequently places the view photographed

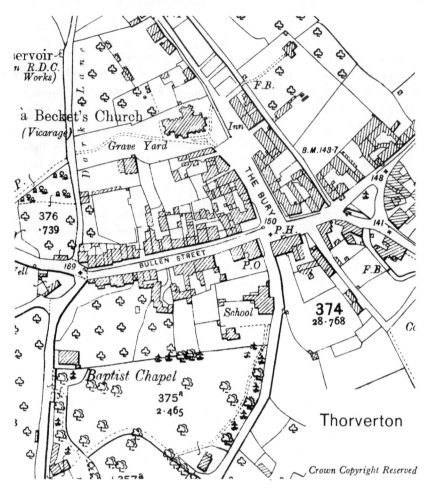

Figure 3.2 One of the maps from *The Making of the English Landscape*. The caption reads: "PLAN OF THORVERTON IN EAST DEVON. Thorverton is a village of Saxon foundation, first settled in all probability in the seventh century. The original nucleus was the large rectangular open space beside the stream, with the significant name of the Bury (from the Saxon word *burh*, meaning 'a fortified place'). The reference must be to the Saxon earthwork or other fortification which formed the original nucleus, as there is not the slightest trace of any Roman or pre-Roman fort here. This significant name is also found on a similar site in the neighbouring village of Silverton, founded at the same date. The parish church lies at one end of the *burh*, again a very characteristic position. The original large space has been halved in area by the encroachment of domestic building on its eastern side, probably in medieval or sub-medieval times." (Hoskins 1955:51)

from above at the centre of his text; this can be said of no less than eight of the first thirteen plates in *The Making of the English Landscape*, though the relative number decreases in the rest of the book. He also reluctantly admits that the one good thing one can say about railways is that they offer excellent viewing platforms for the landscape: "true that the railway did not invent much of this beauty, but it gave us new vistas of it" (1955:206). Hoskins also drew on O. G. S. Crawford's explorations of the emerging field of air photography (see below).

An act of aesthetic appreciation

Many times Hoskins expresses the need to understand the landscape in aesthetic terms. For example, he writes in terms that echo E. M. Forster's opening to the "classic English novel" *Howards End*:

> One may liken the English landscape . . . to a symphony, which it is possible to enjoy as an architectural mass of sound, without being able to analyse it in detail or to see the logical development of the structure. The enjoyment may be real, but it is limited in scope and in the last resort vaguely diffused in emotion. But if instead of hearing merely a symphonic mass of sound, we are able to isolate the themes as they enter, to see how one by one they are intricately woven together and by what magic new harmonies are produced, perceive the manifold subtle variations on a single theme, however disguised it might be, then the total effect is immeasurably enhanced. So it is with the landscapes of historic depth and physical variety that England shows almost every-where. Only when we know all the themes and harmonies can we begin to appreciate its full beauty, or to discover in it new subtleties every time we visit it. Nor is it only a programme of symphonies that the English landscape provides . . . There is as much pleasure to be had in the chamber music of Bedfordshire or Rutland; perhaps, one might say, a more sophisticated pleasure in discovering the essence of these simpler and smaller landscapes. (Hoskins 1955:19)

A key point here is that Hoskins is taking a stand against what he sees as the unsystematic, untrained nature of much writing on the English countryside – against what he sees as the unrestrained and slushy nos-talgia of writers like H. J. Massingham (1936 and 1939) and H. V. Morton (1927), for example. Only by critically analysing and under-standing its form and structure, he insists, can we properly understand what we are looking at. In the work of Hoskins, Crawford, and their contemporaries, "Modern expertise is countered by experienced and knowledgeable observation, enabling the writer to spot the bumps in fields that others never notice, the fonts overlooked by run-of-the-mill guides" (Matless 1998:274–7).

Yet there is a hint that the converse is also true; that is, that the historical analysis of landscape is itself a means to an end – the end being an appreciation of beauty and/or a heightened sense of place, of *genius loci*. Such an end is one that is deeply Romantic, and, many would continue to argue, completely valid as an intellectual project. However, it stands at some distance from what a processual archaeologist might see as the object of analysis, namely a systematic and comparative description and explanation of past human lifeways or social systems.

We see here a similar tension to that raised by Wordsworth's "The Lonely Cottage": we are invited to contemplate the melancholy and beauty of a scene, but there is more than a hint that the aesthetic appreciation of that scene is its own end rather than a critical analysis, appreciation, or indeed moral condemnation of the social relations embedded therein. When Hoskins stresses the importance of hearing past human beings talking and working, he continues: "creating what has come down to us, after so long a time, *for our present enjoyment*" (1967:184; italics mine; see also Hoskins 1960:132).

An act of translation from landscape to text

To state the obvious, for all his insistence on muddy boots and direct observation of the landscape, Hoskins communicates his vision to us via his books. For Hoskins as for Wordsworth, the act of translation is the moment of genius. His beloved Devon in this respect falls short of Wordsworth's Lakes, in part because of its allegedly feminine quality:

> The billowy, feminine beauty of so much of Devon does not lend itself to great poetry. It lacks austerity and the elements of nobility and sadness. Even Dartmoor has produced no literature or poetry of the highest order. No Hardy or Brontë has ever felt its power and translated it into immortal words. (Hoskins 1954b:284)

Further, the governing metaphor for this movement from the observation of the landscape to the printed page is one of reading. The Ordnance Survey map is a document in a foreign language, which at least in the early stages of his life Hoskins did not feel he knew how to translate; the landscape needs to be "read" or decoded. The metaphor of reading has come to be a dominant one in landscape studies (for example Richard Muir's title *Reading the Landscape*, 2000). We will look in more detail at the metaphor of the palimpsest later (see below). In the trials of physical infirmity in later life, for both Wordsworth and Hoskins, the text came to take over completely from the landscape. Wordsworth's *Excursion* describes a man who compensates for his deafness by substituting the reading of books for the sounds of nature; in his final years Hoskins compensated for his lack of mobility by reading, specifically poetry and novels (Thirsk 1992).

Embedded in the particular (genius loci) and the national

It was the details and the particularities of a scene that gave reward and pleasure to Hoskins. It is very rare that mention is made of any study outside England and Wales; it is telling that a brief mention of Burma (Hoskins 1967:144) is a personal communication from "Colonel C. P. H. Wilson" rather than a reference to the literature (though the cross-cultural observations of Lewis Mumford were in his notebooks and on his reading-lists for students: Phythian-Adams 1992:150). While the approach and philosophy of the radical poet William Blake cannot easily be assimilated to those of Wordsworth, it is nevertheless revealing that he is quoted with approval as the epigraph to *Provincial England*:

> To generalise is to be an Idiot;
> To particularise is the Alone Distinction of Genius.
> (Hoskins 1965)

Hoskins's hatred of what he perceived as the rootless, transient millions of London was distinctive of a certain kind of anti-metropolitan Englishness; indeed it is a sentiment whose intellectual and emotional ancestry goes back to the classical trope mentioned in the introduction, of Horatio's retreat from Rome to his farm. Elsewhere Hoskins chooses as an epigraph the classical poet Horace: *Ille terrarium mihi praeter omnes | Angulus ridet*, which he translates as: "It is that corner of the world, above all others | Which has a smile for me" (Hoskins 1983:xvi).

Yet at the same time this stress on locality is interdependent with a strong sense of nationalism and of national identity. The final words of *The Making of the English Landscape* are a direct quotation from an unnamed antiquarian which makes this interdependence explicit: "Know most of the rooms of thy native country before thou goest over the threshold thereof. Especially seeing England presents thee with so many observables." Hoskins's particular places are assembled within a national narrative – it is the *English landscape* that is being made, not a multitude of local places – just as Wordsworth's appreciation of particular localities was framed within a national consciousness, and just as Romanticism was complicit with nationalism across early 19th-century Europe. The titles of Hoskins's books bear testament to this – *English Landscapes, One Man's England, The Making of the English Landscape, Local History in England* . . . The Midlands are the most ignored and "the most English of all the various provinces" (1949:v). In this view, some parts of England get more attention than others: thus London is either condemned or left out entirely, while Northumberland is rarely mentioned, and then only in terms of its nature as a border county with Scotland (Hoskins 1978). There are also very few mentions of Kent and the Home Counties around London.

When, in his more reflective pieces, Hoskins tackles the issue of generalization, he equates it with the making of valid statements about England, not about the world (1966b). And when Hoskins chooses to place at the centre of his work a celebration of that most stereotypically "English" of social classes, the solid, socially middling yeoman, he is following the lead of Wordsworth (Malachuk 2002).

It must be stressed that Hoskins's own explicit political orientation was anything but unthinkingly nationalist or xenophobic. His writing contains little of the unsavoury bunker mentality of G. K. Chesterton, for example (Wright 2005). Hoskins often remarks on his distaste for class distinctions and social snobbery. He was a councillor for the Liberal Party in Exeter; after its collapse as a major political party in the years after 1918, the Liberals continued to benefit from a strong regional tradition in southwest England. Hoskins was motivated by a desire to conserve Exeter from post-war redevelopment. However, he came unstuck in Exeter after making too many potentially slanderous remarks about other politicians. In his written work, he remarks bitterly on the "savage" nature of local politics (1966a:xiii; 1976:103).

In *The Age of Plunder* (1976), his study of Tudor England, the choice of title resonates with Hoskins's view of an affluent and materialist present: Hoskins notes that "the most effective weapon for diminishing the gap between rich and poor is a swingeing taxation policy" (1976:210); the subtle switch to the present tense is striking here. Elsewhere he describes Henry VIII as the "Stalin of Tudor England" and his ministers as "the most unprincipled gang of political adventurers and predators that England had seen for many centuries," and he writes with apparent bitterness: "membership of the governing body brought what opponents thought were flagrant abuses of power, but which might charitably be regarded as the rewards for spending so much time and money on public affairs. English local government, in the boroughs at least, still works on this principle (or lack of principle)"

(1976:232–3, 103). In Margaret Irwin's novel *Young Bess*, published in 1944, the same group of 16th-century politicians is portrayed as well-meaning but misconceived ideologically driven Labourite social reformers who come to an inevitable sticky end.

Hoskins took care to distance himself from any kind of vulgar or jingoistic nationalism – for example, he manages to turn the German bombing of his beloved Exeter during the Second World War into an internationalist condemnation of "barbarians" of whatever nationality:

> [The 1945 burning of Würzburg was] a completely unnecessary and wanton act of destruction . . . There could not be a more powerful illustration of the utter folly of war, of the fact that as any war goes on the barbarians always get the upper hand and the voice of reason and magnanimity is gradually shouted down by those warped beings who have the lust to destroy . . . Savage though the burning of Exeter was, it was little compared with the blind havoc wreaked upon some of the most beautiful cities of Europe later in the war, notably the utter wrecking of Würzburg and Dresden. For this there was no possible shadow of an excuse. But by this time the savages on both sides, and we had our savages as well as the Germans, had got the upper hand. (Hoskins 1960:131)

Setting out to travel backwards

Wordsworth railed against the vulgar utility of the moderns, and stated that a growing awareness of the past meant that "we are setting out to travel backwards" in our understanding and appreciation of landscape (de Selincourt 1906:140). Hoskins opened *Midland England* (1949) with a famous quotation from the 17th-century poet Henry Vaughan, whose meditations on nature were one influence on Wordsworth: "Some men a forward motion love | But I by backward steps will move." *The Making of the English Landscape* cites Wordsworth's views on railways at length and with approval, commenting: "the conservatives, however right they were – and we have lost nearly all our privacy and our silence since they wrote – lost all along the line" (1955:262).

Less explicitly, Hoskins's turning away from the modern world after his time in London during the Second World War echoes the turning inwards of Wordsworth and the Romantics during the Napoleonic Wars. It also echoes other contemporary English writing, most obviously the familiar strain of J. R. R. Tolkien's fantasy *The Lord of the Rings*, also written in the middle of the 20th century. Tolkien's explicit purpose here and in *The Hobbit* was to write an origin myth for the English to parallel the rich mythology of the Welsh, Scots, and Irish

(White 2001). His heroic hobbits return from the wars in foreign lands to find their beloved Shire turned from a homely green into an industrial dystopia. Tolkien had in mind the experience of soldiers returning from the First World War to a changed England, but the master narrative of betrayal and loss of traditional rural England, and its environmental and conservationist overtones, is the same (Curry 1998).

Somehow ineffable and intuitive

"I felt in my bones that the landscape itself was speaking to me," Hoskins said of his younger self (1978:10). For Wordsworth, writing was mimetic; that is, it claimed to be a reflection of reality or what Wordsworth would call nature. Neither man's writings contain any hint of the Marxist critic Raymond Williams's point that nature is "perhaps the most complex word in the language" and has gone through a cultural evolution of its own (1976:184). Elsewhere, Hoskins writes: "the historian who walks along [a town's streets], rather than reads about them in a rate-book, will absorb unconsciously a feeling for his chosen place, even in its dimmer parts, that will eventually reveal itself in the warmth of his writing" (1983:129).

There is complete silence in Hoskins over how we might see the landscape, beyond Wordsworthian quotations such as an "an eye to perceive and a heart to enjoy." This silence, which carries the strong implication that looking and seeing are a matter of common sense and not in need of further reflection, is not simply a product of the time in which he was writing. The question of how to view the natural world, by what rules and conventions it can be represented, had been a long-debated theme in art and art history. For example, it could be said to have driven the modernist movement in art, and was certainly a pressing theme in English landscape art of Hoskins's time (Woodcock 2000). As a result, Hoskins's view of the landscape, relying as it does on simply standing and seeing, is deeply empiricist in the narrow sense of that term. That is, the landscape simply speaks for itself without need for intervening theory, even if the language in which it does so needs to be decoded.

The product of rigorous training, and therefore socially restricted

At the same time, there is no question for both Hoskins and Wordsworth that only a certain kind of eye and mind can perceive and enjoy. It was certainly a mind that was familiar with different elements of modern scholarship. Hoskins wrote in *The Making of the English Landscape* that

"One needs to be a botanist, a physical geographer, and a naturalist, as well as an historian, to be able to feel certain that one has all the facts right before allowing the imagination to play over the small details of a scene" (1955:18); it is striking that this insistence on knowledge and rigour is combined with a Romantic methodology – the imagination being allowed to play – for reconstruction of the past. As with the appreciation of a symphony discussed above, formless appreciation is "not enough; they may entrance for the moment but they make no abiding impression on the mind. One needs the fourth dimension of time to give depth to the scene" (1949:v). Without rigorous training, the result is the "sentimental and formless slush which afflicts so many books concerned only with superficial appearances" (1955:13). That phrase disappears from the 1977 introduction, but the sentiment remains. For example he later wrote scathingly that "there have been innumerable books on the English village, many of them just picture-books strung together with second-hand text" before praising the book under review for its author's dual training as a historian and an archae-ologist (1979:157).

Both Wordsworth and Hoskins are characterized by a tension between, on the one hand, their own relatively humble social origins, and a desire to write simply and accessibly for the "common man," and, on the other, a distaste for the vulgar masses. In Wordsworth's case, this was an outright snobbishness. With Hoskins the sentiment is more complex, but it is clear that behind his dislike of the phenomena of mass culture lies a preference for silence and for being alone. It is striking that Hoskins does not appear to mention working-class engage-ments with landscape; one searches in vain in his work for mention of the 1932 Kinder mass trespass, in which over 400 working-class ramblers organized a deliberate trespass over the grouse moors of the local landowner. The ensuing conflict and court proceedings are a celebrated event in socialist and rambling history (Rothman 1982), yet receive, as far as I am aware, no mention in Hoskins's work. There is also no qualification to his bemoaning of the railways that these did open up experience of the countryside to the urban masses; when he writes of railways destroying "our privacy and silence," the Words-worthian sentiment is clear (1955:204). Hoskins's hated time in London was actually spent in part working on a commission with L. Dudley Stamp to investigate the social and environmental issue of the common fields, subsequently published (Hoskins and Stamp 1963). This was a classic piece of post-war social reform: "as a member of the Royal Commission on Common Land, 1955–8, which recom-mended that the remaining 1/5 million acres of common land should be preserved for public access and regarded in the same light as national parks" (Anonymous 1992:145–6).

There is also a particular sharpness in the condemnation of Alfred Watkins's *The Old Straight Track*, about which Hoskins comments that "The number of intelligent people (and others) who have been seduced by the arguments in this book is legion . . . It is better never to have read *The Old Straight Track*, but if you have read it, try to forget it" (1983:238). Watkins had argued that if one took the Ordnance Survey map and drew straight lines through churches, burial mounds, and other archaeological sites in the English countryside, one "discovered" the existence of "leys" or straight lines linking up these different sites (1925). Watkins interpreted these "leys" as ancient trackways, though later generations of "alternative" writers saw them as lines of mystical power (for example Devereux 2001). Now ley lines clearly do not exist, and Hoskins is quite right to assert that they do not; the point made by both Hoskins and Crawford that "sites" are so densely scattered on the English landscape that it would be impossible to draw a line on the map without "clipping" a great number is quite undisputed by any serious scholar. What is revealing though is the Wordsworthian sharpness with which wrong thinking is dismissed. Tom Williamson and Liz Bellamy later delivered a comprehensive refutation of ley lines, but were careful to discuss sympathetically the widespread belief in their existence within its contemporary social context (Williamson and Bellamy 1983).

Wordsworth and Hoskins share a common contradiction. They both believe strongly in a democratic and populist means of expression; Hoskins made a huge commitment to disseminating his message to weekend and extra-mural classes when many of his academic contemporaries stood aloof. Yet this very populism meant that their beloved English countryside was overrun, in Wordsworth's case by the vulgar multitude disembarking from the railways, in Hoskins's case by his pet hate, the motor-car. For Hoskins this contradiction was particularly sharp, in that he got much of his vision and appreciation of the English countryside across – and at the same time managed to communicate his hatred of modernity – through pieces written for the guides sponsored by the Shell petroleum company (see for example Hoskins 1980). Many of Hoskins's hated motor-cars were driven through the formerly peaceful countryside by families clutching Hoskins's words in the form of the Shell guide in their hands.

There was also a tension in gendered understandings of landscape. Hoskins was careful to explain in his "how-to" guide *Local History in England* that "throughout the rest of this book I shall refer to the local historian as he in default of any simpler way of saying what I mean; but I am not unmindful of the fact that women form a large proportion of local historians at work today" (1983:1). There are echoes of Dorothy Wordsworth in Hoskins's fulsome acknowledgement of "my wife for producing the domestic conditions in which continuous writing is possible, almost a luxury in these hard-pressed times" (1960:v), or in his observation that "as regards the length of time these [Anglo-Saxon land] charters take to work out, that in all cases we are referring to the spare-time activities of busy professional men (or busy housewives)" (1967:37). Wordsworth said the poet was "a man speaking to other men," and this is what landscape archaeologists and historians are also, by the affirmation of some of their leading authorities both male and female. According to Joan Thirsk:

> Women are not often asked to write on the subject [of landscape history], and, from choice, they seem to prefer to make it a background, often memorable, to fiction. Perhaps it is because people are as important to them as the natural features, and essays on landscape tend to leave them out of sight. On the other hand, menfolk excel when writing about large landscapes, assembling the features that bring them together and create a unified impression. (Thirsk 2000:10)

Where does the link between Wordsworth and Hoskins come from? It might be argued to have come from the intellectual and cultural milieu in which Hoskins worked, for it has to be acknowledged that English Romanticism was a vibrant force in Hoskins's England. The British neo-Romantic artists worked between 1918 and the 1950s, most notably the artist Paul Nash, who aimed in his paintings to evoke "genius loci" or "spirit of place" (Woodcock 2000:1; Riding 2005). The films of Powell and Pressburger (most obviously the anti-materialist and mystical celebration of the English landscape, *A Canterbury Tale*, which has an archaeologist at the centre of the plot), the fiction of John Cowper Powys, and the art of John Piper (who illustrated Wordsworth's *Guide through the District of the Lakes*: Wordsworth 1951) also fall into this category. The reconstructions of castles and prehistoric sites by the artist Alan Sorrell are classic examples of the genre, and excited much critical comment at the time (Pitts 2005). However, there is little or no acknowledgement of this work in Hoskins's texts, or of the writers H. J. Massingham or H. V. Morton, whereas quotations from and allusions to the Romantic poets abound. It is difficult for a reader of his books to believe that Hoskins showed much interest in the neo-Romantic movement.

The literary critic Alan Sinfield traces a direct line between Romanticism and the 1950s, the decade in which Hoskins wrote many of his most important works. Sinfield is interested in literature and culture rather than historical writing as such, but his description of English "middle-class dissidence" is an uncanny portrait of much of Hoskins's intellectual frame and its cultural context:

> Since the late 18th century, when enclosures, the factory system and urbanization helped to provoke the Romantic movement, the middle class has thrown up a dissident fraction partly hostile to the hegemony of that class. The stance is particularly attractive to intellectuals, who find their concerns slighted by aggressive commerce . . . it runs through the aesthetic movement, Fabianism, Modernism, Bloomsbury, 1930s public-school communists, Leavisism, and the New Left-CND nexus. Dissident middle-class intellectuals may be right-wing, left-wing or liberal . . . The consistent feature is hostility to the hegemony of the principal part of the middle class – the businessmen, industrialists and empire-builders. (Sinfield 1989:41)

In my view, the link between Hoskins and Wordsworth is much more simple and direct. Hoskins loved Romantic poetry and spent much of his leisure hours reading it. *Devon* itself was dedicated to the lesser-known Hope Bagenal, "poet and topographer" (1954b:iv). Reading many of the Romantic poets for the first time, in connection with the research for this book, I found phrase after phrase that was vaguely familiar to me. This is because Hoskins had recycled them in the body of his text, in a rhetorical and allusive style, without overt reference – "the eye to see and the heart to enjoy"; the lark spiralling overhead (1954b:29). It is very difficult to read Hoskins's description of his own childhood, and the reasons why he came to want to understand the landscape, without hearing echoes of Wordsworth's autobiographical poem *The Prelude*. Hoskins himself justified composing *Devon* in Leicester by referring to Wordsworth's statement in the preface to *Lyrical Ballads*, where poetry "takes its origin from emotion recollected in tranquillity."

Hoskins's Contemporaries

It is easy enough to "explain" Hoskins by setting him in his context. There is a burgeoning interest in the influence of nationalism, class, and gender on the scholarship and popular writing of the 1930s to 1950s, and Hoskins fits neatly into many of the narratives promoted by David

Matless (1998) and others. In particular, Hoskins fits alongside a series of scholars whose task lay in instructing ordinary people in how to look at the landscape, and in particular in how to fit the landscape they saw into a post-war national narrative and sense of identity.

The archaeologist and curator of the National Museum of Wales, Sir Cyril Fox, from 1923 onwards had established a way of thinking about the British Isles as a whole, explaining peculiar regional characteristics in terms of their place within a broader national pattern. He used the terms "Highland Zone" and "Lowland Zone" to characterize these areas, and the way in which these two zones mirrored the geology of the British Isles, with the Highland Zone following the older rocks of the northern and western uplands, was very apparent. As a result, Fox's thinking has sometimes been characterized as representing a geographical or geological determinism to regional cultures; additionally, the south and east of the British Isles has simply been seen as more "progressive" due to its proximity to London and Continental Europe (see for example Barley 1961:4). His original texts, however (1923 and 1938) are more subtle. For our purposes, it is important to note, first, that Fox showed how different regions and localities of the British Isles fitted together in a broader pattern: regions might be different from one another, but they formed a national pattern nevertheless. Second, he showed how that pattern had very ancient origins. Both these points were taken up in Hoskins's work, though there is little overt reference to Fox in his books.

Fox's work can be compared with that of the architectural historian Nikolaus Pevsner. Fox addressed the identity of the British Isles through geology and physical geography; Pevsner also addressed the relationship between region and nation, but in terms of architecture and aesthetics. Pevsner arrived in England as a refugee from Germany in the 1930s and conceived of the idea of a series of county guides to architecture, which were started in 1945; the guides to Cornwall, Nottinghamshire, and Middlesex appeared in 1951 (Cherry 1998). Pevsner's guides are now a national institution. They tell the reader how to look at buildings in the landscape, in the sense that their descriptions and evaluations both make aesthetic judgements about the value of a building and implicitly set it in the context of a progressive, national narrative of development:

> Pevsner teaches us that to appreciate English architecture we must comprehend the diversity of provincial England. His books may prove to be a last memorial to the shire counties . . . In the introductions, Pevsner was adept at . . . piecing together a nation's culture from the raw material

of its architecture. . . . His reticence in [ignoring passing items of history] could be infuriating: the parallel Shell county guides are a necessary companion to a Pevsner. But to him the history of England lay in her buildings and her buildings alone. To know them is to learn a different island story from that of Macaulay or Trevelyan [two great "national" historians], a more intimate and more vivid one. (Jenkins 2001:57)

Pevsner related his detailed county guides to a passionate and ideologically loaded conception of the national imagination (part of which he characterized as middle-class rationality) at the same time as *The Making of the English Landscape*, in his book *The Englishness of English Art* (Pevsner 1956).

Hoskins claimed his approach was pioneering, and there is no doubt he was sincere in this, but in fact he brought together a series of elements that were "pioneered" by others (some of whom subsequently made sniffy remarks about this process). I will highlight just some of these. Chandler (2000) makes the point that Hoskins was pre-dated by Darby's edited volume *An Historical Geography of England* (1936). It was arguably from Darby rather than Hoskins that post-war British historical geography took its cue. Carl Sauer (1963) and the "Berkeley school" of humanistic geography were exploring similar terrain, though references to this work are hard to find in Hoskins's writings. Hoskins himself cited Maitland, who wrote that "two little fragments of the original one-inch Ordnance Survey map will be more eloquent than would be many paragraphs of written discourse" (1897:39) and also used the palimpsest analogy (for which see below: Fisher 1911). Maitland wrote suggestively: "a century hence the student's materials will not be in the shape he finds them in now . . . Instead of a few photographed village maps, there will be many; the history of land-measures and of field-systems will have been elaborated. Above all, by slow degrees the thoughts of our forefathers, their common thoughts about common things, will have become thinkable once more" (1897:596). The reference both to empathy and to the notion of a male-centred ancestry – "the thoughts of our forefathers" – is particularly striking here; it is extended by Hoskins when he writes of the historian "trying to enter into the minds of the first men to break into a virgin landscape" (1955:18).

Joan Thirsk (2000:12) has pointed out that *Stanford's Geological Atlas of Great Britain and Ireland* indicated features that could be seen from railways, and that in 1913 Hilda Sharpe and her pupils at Edgbaston High School for Girls added a photographic supplement. The use Hoskins makes of place-name evidence was also building on a previous generation of work; the English Place Name Survey was started in

1923 (Mawer and Stenton 1929). One might also point, as Thirsk has done, to a much longer tradition of rural writing stretching back to Izaak Walton, Jefferies, White, and John Clare (Thirsk 2000). Finally, Hoskins's work shares parallels with Vidal de la Blache's concept of *genre de vie* or way of life, which dominated much of 20th-century regional geography (Claval 1993); though again it is difficult to find any explicit acknowledgement of Vidal de la Blache in his writings. He does quote "the great French geographer Demangeon" in terms which suggest a deep appreciation of the French approach (1983:15).

However, the most profound influence on Hoskins, at least as far as his writings on landscape were concerned, was arguably the work of the field archaeologist O. G. S. Crawford.

Hoskins, Crawford, and Palimpsests

In his great book *Archaeology in the Field*, O. G. S. Crawford brought together an appreciation of air photography, the use of the Ordnance Survey map, and the use of documentary and place-name evidence, and codified these into what he called "field archaeology" (Crawford 1953). Crawford outlined a form of archaeology that did not involve excavation as the principal or primary mode of archaeological research and concentrated on the locality and its immediate questions. His method was to start in the local Record Office: he examined the six-inch Ordnance Survey map, and followed this by exploring, both through documents and by walking across the landscape. Crawford was quite explicit that this whole method was "a modern, and primarily a British invention" and went on to suggest that field archaeology as he had defined it "is an essentially English form of sport," in part due to the presence of "persons of means, leisure and intelligence" living in the country. It was a method that was highly local and particular in its focus – it "assumes that one has plenty of time to devote to a region that may comprise no more than two or three parishes. It is perhaps a programme more suited for a permanent resident than a temporary visitor" (Crawford 1953:52–3, 208). Mark Bowden's paper in *Landscapes* (2001) alludes to the close relationship between Hoskins and Crawford, and their admiration for each other. Hoskins included *Archaeology in the Field* in the select bibliography of later editions of *Making of the English Landscape*. Both shared the urge to get their boots muddy, and both shared negative feelings about the cultural and social elitism of Oxford University.

However, Hoskins chose to borrow some things from Crawford and not others, and his choices are revealing. He absorbed Crawford's thinking on identification of field monuments, and also on landscape as palimpsest. He also implicitly repeated Crawford's methods for doing research on a local landscape. However, nowhere in Hoskins's work is there any mention of much of the discussion that forms an important element of Crawford's book. Crawford discussed the use of ethnographic material to understand the archaeological record, drawing on material from North Africa, Australia, and Asia. For Crawford, this material was included to help him understand how we might take archaeological observations and turn them into interpretations of the prehistoric past. For example, plates 9a and 9b of *Archaeology in the Field* show two abandoned huts from Darfur in Sudan, and are annotated "how a hut circle is formed", and chapter 22 is entitled "Living 'Prehistory' in Central Africa" (Crawford 1953:220).

It is not therefore an oversimplification to suggest that what Hoskins borrowed was Crawford's work on the field identification of landscape elements, and what he chose to leave out was the means of turning these identifications into statements about the past.

For Hoskins, this omission did not matter. First, he was not interested in procedural questions of archaeological observation and inference, for he was resolutely anti-theoretical. This was partly as a result of his encounter with the discipline of geography. I suspect that Hoskins came quickly to associate theory with "unpalatable jargon" (1955:19), the use of abstracted spatial models (most famously the Thiessen polygons beloved of that generation of geographers: Boots 1986) which he found sterile and inhumane, and his own acute sense of being marginal to more established "scientific" disciplinary genres. He wrote in typically acerbic fashion later in his career that

> I once wrote a book with the simple title of *The Making of the English Landscape* but I should have called it *The Morphogenesis of the Cultural Environment* to make the fullest impact . . . A new title for one's subject, a glossary of jargon, and a computer, and one has the most lethal combination for academic advancement conceivable. One would then qualify to work in some shiny academic palace . . . [but] the scholar and the library are the real foundations of a university. (Hoskins 1966b:21)

I think that one of the reasons Hoskins was impatient with the theory he mocks with his "fake" title was that he felt that he did not need theory to help him make his data speak. This was because he already had a strong story to tell. It went something like this: later medieval economic changes left the middling sort, including his own Devon yeoman forefathers, better off than they ever had been before. They consolidated their position through the changes of the Reformation and the agricultural improvements of the 16th to 18th centuries. It all came to an end with enclosure and industrialization in the latter half of the 18th century.

Charles Phythian-Adams has noted this guiding theme and quotes from Hoskins's unpublished notebooks:

> I have the theme now: the old pattern of life slowly built up – describe at length – then the disintegration of the pattern, shattered beyond recognition. The old peasant tradition when men and women were "at home" in the world, rooted in place that had meaning and significance for them, among their own people, embedded in an ancient mode of living and conduct. They "took care of a few fundamental things", not nobly or beautifully perhaps, but they took care of them nevertheless. Attached to a place, and to a family and neighbours, the strongest cement a society can have. And gradually we can see the attachments being loosened, the cement crumbling, and the walls of that old society falling into ruin – the visible signs in the ruined church of St Wistan, the silent watermill, the tumble-down cottages in the village . . . (Hoskins's notebooks, late 1940s, cited in Phythian-Adams 1992:176)

Even if no formal theory was to be had, however, Hoskins had a very strong metaphor: that of text. The landscape was there to be read – we simply had to learn the language. In particular, both he and Crawford used the analogy of a palimpsest, or old document that had been written over and erased again and again. This metaphor has proved exceptionally strong: it is used over and over again, for example by Richard Muir (2000:xiv) though its underlying theory has been questioned by Cosgrove and Daniels (1988:8).

The metaphor of material culture and landscape as a form of text has subsequently been discussed to exhaustion in archaeology and related studies. The influence of linguistic thinking on anthropology and folklife studies has been profound, and through these influences many archaeologists, including this author, have found the textual metaphor a powerful one. Most famously Henry Glassie has talked of folk housing as a form of language, while both myself and Glassie have constructed "grammars" to help understand how the plans and forms of traditional buildings were generated from a simple set of base rules (Glassie 1975; Johnson 1993a). Partly in response to the perceived difficulties and limitations of such grammatical analysis, there has been widespread critique of such models, and an insistence that the textual metaphor is both problematic and limited (Hodder and Hutson 2003:204–5). There has also been an insistence that the metaphor of reading, apparently such a simple one, is desperately complex when considered in the context of the social history of the activity of reading (Smith 1992).

Hoskins and Crawford obviously did not intend to engage with linguistic theory; they were using the analogy of text in an (apparently) far simpler way. Rather more simply, I suggest that the metaphor of the palimpsest was almost *too strong*. Its power as an image, its facility and pedagogical power in helping the student to understand how to look at landscape, led the reader away from the question of what, once that structure had been correctly observed and described, the words and sentences inscribed on the landscape actually meant.

Prehistory and History

The question of how to interpret landscape evidence was arguably quite apparent for prehistory; once one had identified prehistoric field monuments and archaeological elements of landscapes such as field boundaries and lynchets, and how they fitted together in terms of phasing and dating, the wider interpretative work had to begin. Without documents, the prehistorian had to ask: what kind of society, what forms of human relations, produced these traces? And these were questions that the archaeologist had to address explicitly and using a distinctively archaeological set of conceptual tools.

The necessity of asking interpretative questions was not so clear for the field record of historic periods. Here, even for Crawford, it meant immediate and unreflective translation into classifications derived from the documentary record. Mark Bowden (2001) has drawn attention to the early use of the palimpsest analogy, pointing out that Crawford (and before him the English medieval historian Maitland) used it before Hoskins. But it is instructive to look at the entirety of Crawford's quote:

> The surface of England is like a palimpsest, a document that has been written on and erased over and over again; and it is the business of the field archaeologist to decipher it. The features concerned are of course the roads and field boundaries, the woods, the farms and other habitations, and all the other products of human labour; these are the letters and words inscribed on the land. But it is not easy to read them because, whereas the vellum document was seldom wiped clean more than once

or twice, the land has been subjected to continual change throughout the ages. The existing pattern, which is that we see on the six-inch Ordnance Map, was formed very largely at the end of the 18th and the beginning of the 19th centuries, when the medieval field-system was swept away by the enclosures. That system . . . was introduced by the Saxons . . . To revert to the analogy of the palimpsest – the writing was completely erased twice, by the Saxons and by the authors of the enclosures, and there were several alterations of letters, words and whole sentences within those periods. (Crawford 1953:51–2)

So Crawford follows his explication of the palimpsest analogy by isolating two archaeological horizons which are immediately equated with historical events – the enclosure movement, and the coming of the Saxons. The simplicity and integrity of the former horizon has now been partly dismantled by modern scholarship, the latter entirely so – but the method, of seeking to explain the archaeological record in terms of the circumstance of documentary history, remains intact.

In other words, the more archaeological evidence was assembled, the more its interpretation bifurcated. For prehistorians, reading the landscape led very quickly to a radical empirical revision of Hoskins's views: a recognition that in fact much of the landscape was of pre-Roman origin. But this empirical point led on to theoretical reflection, to a need to think about the traces revealed – the barrows, the field systems – in explicitly theoretical and social ways (Fleming 1988 is an excellent account of such an intellectual process in one region). However, historical archaeologists took a very different turn. The meanings of the words and sentences to be found in the landscape were not to be found in interpretation of whatever theoretical stripe: rather, they could be assigned documentary meanings: "tofts," "crofts," "assarts," "enclosures," "woodlands," "forests," "manorial sites." The archaeology of the landscape became *secondary*, a passive product of historical action to be explained by the historical/documentary record rather than in its own terms as a piece of archaeology (Table 3.1).

And so, paradoxically, the tremendous success and growth of historic landscape archaeology, as opposed to prehistory, conspired in this disciplinary subordination. The more archaeology expanded into historic periods, the more the secondary nature of archaeology was confirmed. This point was accurately and infuriatingly noted by the landscape historian H. P. R. Finberg:

I shall say nothing about Archaeology, because although it enjoys a large and flourishing establishment of its own in several universities, any claim it may have to be regarded as an independent study rests upon a concept

The interpretative divergence between prehistoric and historic
dscape archaeology. Both observe and interpret features in the landscape:
prehistorian interprets these in social terms, the historical archaeologist
ntifies and translates into entities defined in advance from the documents.

Prehistory

Field observations	Identification	Social Interpretation
"Fields"	Coaxial field systems	"Chiefdoms"
"Henges"	Reaves	"Territoriality"
"Barrows"		"Social power"
"Dykes"		"State formation"

Historical Archaeology

Field observations	Identification	Translation into named historical developments
Ridge and furrow	"Open field systems"	"Assarting"
Humps and bumps	"Tofts", "Crofts"	"Manorialization"
	"Deserted villages"	"Depopulation"
		"Champion landscape"
		"Parish formation"

which archaeologists themselves now repudiate as obsolete. It was plau-
sible only so long as they were supposed to confine their researches to a
past remote beyond the reach of written records, a past ending if not
before Ancient History began, at any rate well before the dawn of
Modern History. Today no one thinks of their function in those terms.
We find them busy excavating the sites of English villages deserted in
the 15th century, while others search out early monuments of the
Industrial Revolution. But in thus immensely broadening its range,
Archaeology has revealed itself more plainly as the ancillary discipline it
really is: in other words, as a combination of highly specialised techniques, the true and ultimate function of which is to illuminate the
subject-matter of History. (Finberg 1964:5)

Finberg has just claimed in this same text that his views are indistin-
guishable from those of Hoskins. The critical point here is the disjunc-
ture – the fact that there is more archaeological evidence does not
mean that more account is taken of it, if one is working within a
traditional, inductive historical model. The more the archaeological
evidence of historic periods is assembled by archaeologists, the more

archaeologists' ancillary status is confirmed. This ancillary status was explicit for Finberg, and, I shall go on to argue, implicit for landscape archaeology and history today.

The New Archaeology

The problem, then, with such a model is that the amount of data gathered does not have any necessary relationship to the accuracy of the story one is telling. This is a very basic point which was at the heart of the initial critique of the New Archaeology of the 1960s, when it insisted that rather than use an inductive or historical model for the accumulation of data, archaeologists should try to test their ideas within a scientific framework of hypothesis and deduction. New Archaeology in its earlier years was, of course, an intellectual movement largely driven by prehistorians (with some exceptions, for example Jope 1972).

David Clarke and others pointed out that the inductive method tended to place the archaeologist in the position of Alice in the looking-glass, of having to run harder and harder to stay in the same place: in a famous passage, Clarke poked fun at the archaeologist who "by dint of furious activity, can just maintain his status quo against the constant stream of data" but whose understanding of the past does not progress beyond "the maintenance of a relative status quo and a steady flow of counterfeit history books." Instead, Clarke proposed an agenda of disciplinary independence:

> archaeology, is archaeology, is archaeology . . . Archaeology is a discipline in its own right, concerned with archaeological data which it clusters in archaeological entities displaying certain archaeological processes and studies in terms of archaeological aims, methods and procedures. We fully appreciate that these entities and processes were once historical and social entities but the nature of the archaeological record is such that there is no simple way of equating our archaeological percepta with these lost events. We must certainly try to find out the social and historical equivalents of our archaeological entities and processes but we should not delude ourselves about the simplicity of these equivalents or our success in isolating them. (Clarke 1968:1, 13)

The relevance of New Archaeology is very apparent here. If, for the landscape archaeology of historic periods, archaeological evidence was being inductively gathered and used as illustrative material for a historical narrative, it would never be able to test that narrative, or modify

and make it more accurate in any significant way. Landscape archaeologists would be for ever running harder and harder to stay in the
same place.

This concern was raised in part by Hoskins's colleague H. P. R.
Finberg himself in relation to the writing of local history:

> Our first duty . . . is to propagate a reasoned conception of the subject.
> Local history still suffers from a lack of theoretical discussion . . . Far too
> many people still find themselves in the position of the amateur who
> wrote to me some weeks ago to ask for guidance. He explained that for
> five years he had been accumulating notes on the history of a Wiltshire
> village, but he was quite at a loss to interpret his materials or put them
> into shape; and he concluded by saying, with cheerful pessimism, that
> his collection now lacked only the detailed genealogies of the lords of
> the manor to make it quite ready for the dust-bin. (Finberg 1964:16)

A second basic point that was dear to New Archaeologists is also
relevant here. A critical understanding of variability is central to the
foundations of our knowledge. In other words, if we do not know
how "typical" our examples are, they will remain simply anecdotes,
little stories that may or may not be illustrative of some wider process.

Hoskins inaugurated a classic genre of writing about landscape, especially apparent in *The Making of the English Landscape* and *Fieldwork in
Local History*, of argument from example. One talked about medieval
villages and then discussed the history and archaeology of two or three
examples; one then turned to desertion, and again discussed two or
three examples. The differences between, say, the Midlands and the
West Country could again be illustrated by a few examples. This
technique of explication was easy to follow, as it focused on specific
case studies that were often in themselves little vignettes of interesting
local landscapes. It was also, apparently, very empirical: it resulted in
books whose pages were stuffed full of the minutiae of village plans
and air photographs. Yet it was actually quite unverifiable, since no
obvious handle was offered to judge how "typical" the examples were.
One simply had to trust the authority of the storyteller – one asked about
whether they were "respected" (by whom?), the density of the references cramming their texts, how muddy their boots were. This manner
of inductive argument was and remains common, not just in landscape
archaeology, but in areas such as castle studies (Johnson 2002:14–15).

A third point raised by New Archaeology was the need to be more
anthropological. This assertion had several dimensions, one of which
was very simple: that the society one was studying was not "just like
us." Cultures long dead had different social rules, different relations of

power, different habits of living and dying, different ways of looking at the world, different common senses. In studying them, then, we cannot take anything for granted, as even "commonsensical" things such as the layout of farms, rubbish disposal, and attitudes to heat, cleanliness, and dirt will vary from culture to culture. This point was obscured in Hoskins's view of landscape as the whole source of its interest lay in the fact that these were our ancestors. For Hoskins, and for succeeding generations of landscape archaeologists, it was an all too easy slippage from ancestry into the proposition that the men and women of the past were "just like us." They were Christian, they had petty disputes, they sought to maximize their grain yields, they made homes in "virgin" uncleared woodland. The landscape was familiar to Hoskins and to the English landscape archaeologist – they wandered around it every weekend; the mud on their boots from such wanderings was not yet dry as they wrote – and it was an easy, almost imperceptible, further step to the assertion that the people who created that landscape were familiar too.

Hoskins and his Contemporaries

At the time that Hoskins was producing his most influential work, the intellectual and practical foundations of historic landscape archaeology were being laid. Hoskins was present at the famous 1948 meeting at the deserted medieval sites of Knaptoft and Hamilton which established the presence in the landscape and the importance of deserted medieval villages, and the potential results to be gained from fieldwork and excavation of them. Indeed Hoskins and his Leicester students put some trial trenches through the deserted village of Hamilton, a few miles from Leicester (see Figure 1.3 above). The Society for Medieval Archaeology had its inaugural meeting in 1957, and the unpublished archive of correspondence from those years shows Hoskins connected with the leading figures of that nascent society. University departments of archaeology were founded and expanded in an accelerating pattern through to the 1970s. Many of the new appointments made during this time were made in the fields of both early and high medieval archaeology, though appointments for periods after 1500 were slower in coming. Finally, the Royal Commission on Historical Monuments continued and expanded its work on medieval and later settlements and buildings, while the Archaeology Division of the Ordnance Survey systematized its record from 1947 onwards (Gerrard 2003:114, 122).

Hoskins did not necessarily directly influence and prefigure all these developments. I have focused on his work, as one of a constellation of individual scholars at that time, for several reasons. First, Hoskins has become a metaphorical father-figure. He continues to be routinely cited as an ancestral figure in landscape history and archaeology. Robert Dodgshon's preface to Della Hooke's edited volume *Landscape: The Richest Historical Record* (Hooke 2000) places Hoskins in the role of the central and controlling figure in landscape studies. The editorials of the journal *Landscapes* posit Hoskins as an absolutely central figure in the appreciation of landscape. John Chandler says of Hoskins: "I have lived in his shadow all my adult life" (Chandler 2000:133). Mick Aston chose a quotation from *The Making of the English Landscape* to open one of his recent books and makes the notion of palimpsest central to his explication of the method of understanding the landscape (Aston 2002:2, 23). Tom Williamson chooses to end *Shaping Medieval Landscapes* with a quotation from Hoskins, adding in words of his own the classic Hoskins-derived sentiment: "modern urban, industrial society has become dangerously divorced from the realities of food production and the natural world" (2003:199).

Joan Thirsk, Hoskins's successor as Reader in Economic History at Oxford, cites a *Sunday Times* survey of 1991 in which Hoskins is listed as one of "a thousand makers of 20th century opinion" and suggests that as a direct result "Britain may be said to lead the way in Europe in telling the history of its landscape" (Thirsk 2000:11). Writing almost half a century after the publication of *The Making of the English Landscape*, Thirsk goes on to describe the project of understanding the landscape in terms that are virtually identical to those of Hoskins, discussing both its field methods and its wider justification and appeal:

Some shallow-brained theorists would doubtless call [the promotion of local history] "escapism", but the fact is that we are not born internationalists . . . We belong to a particular place and the bigger and more incomprehensible the world grows the more people will turn to study something of which they can grasp the scale and in which they can find a personal and individual meaning (Hoskins 1983:6–7, first published 1959).

Everyone walking our countryside today has the chance to enter in imagination into the local history of a place they know well. They may then go further, and link otherwise disparate observations with others, for as we understand things better, we ought, without being too dogmatic about such things, to be able to construct a few more general theories, inserting another cornerstone into the general landscape history of the whole kingdom . . . Such an enquiry could be an unexpectedly satisfying experience in a world that is being made more and more impersonal by technology. (Thirsk 2000:15–16)

The use of empathy, the inductive/empiricist approach in which smaller studies can be aggregated into a "cornerstone" of "general landscape history," the linking of features in the landscape with people in the archives, and the equation of wider generalization with national rather than international characteristics are all classic features of the Hoskins tradition. Only by working within such a tradition could scholars see midland and eastern England, an area less than 300 kilometres across, of a gently undulating height entirely between 200 metres and sea level, subject to a temperate climate, and virtually all suitable for a combination of arable and pastoral farming, as "a bewildering variety of landscapes" (Williamson 2003:25).

This repeated citation of Hoskins as an ancestral figure shows that he has become a talisman, a central reference-point among students of the landscape for certain ideas and patterns of thought that are habitual and emotional as well as strictly intellectual. In this respect Richard Muir's reaction to David Matless's analysis of Hoskins is revealing – he takes exception to Matless's criticisms, believing that his critique reduces Hoskins to a "Captain Mainwaring figure," in other words a comic Little Englander from an old British situation comedy. Elsewhere, in a book devoted to scrupulously objective review of many differing viewpoints on landscape, Muir loses patience and chooses to respond negatively just once, for a short but very revealing moment when Denis Cosgrove talks of Hoskins's "affective meaning" (Muir 1998:218; see also Matless 1998; Muir 2002).

Such a reaction is typical of many to whom I have presented the material: an attempt to look critically at Hoskins and his generation, to place them in historical context, is greeted with hostility by a certain kind of reader, since it seems, for some reason, to touch something very close to their soul. Matless's critique cannot reasonably be characterized as one of ridicule; it does look objectively and dispassionately at Hoskins, and in the process *historicizes* him. In other words, Hoskins is treated by Matless not as a titanic ahistorical figure whose genius is ineffable, but rather as a product of his times who thought and wrote within a changing context. In this sense, Hoskins is similar to the literary figure Philip Larkin, who was under-librarian at Leicester at the same time as Hoskins was there. The contradictions of Larkin's legacy, as a Great English Poet (often referred to as an unofficial Poet Laureate) and a blinkered misogynist and racist are routine fodder for the chattering classes and the Sunday papers. It is difficult when reading discussions of Larkin to avoid the feeling that one is not really discussing the man, but actually reading a coded and implicit discussion of the supposed values of "Englishness" that he is held to represent (Jardine 1994:109–13). In its coded and implicit nature, the way in which such debates are played out is characteristic of English intellectual culture (Easthope 1999; Johnson 2003). Hoskins's contradictions are less painful and have been the subject of far less overt discourse, but they follow a similar pattern. I will address the question of why Hoskins provokes such affection and such a passionate defence when I consider the social and political context of his writing in Chapter 6.

Second, it is generally accepted that strictly academic work does not take place in a vacuum, but is always undertaken within and responds to a framework of popular consciousness (Johnson 1999:167–8). This observation is particularly true for the Hoskins/Crawford tradition of landscape history and archaeology. As we have seen, much work in this area is undertaken by bodies of amateurs, who are often part of the extramural and continuing education classes that are taught by "professional"/academic landscape scholars. Hoskins's own understanding of the landscape was shaped in part by the 1930s evening classes he taught at Vaughan Working Men's College, and he spent much of his subsequent career organizing and giving conferences and papers to a generation of teachers who took the message back to their classrooms. (Many times, in the course of writing this book, I have talked about what I was doing to a retired or senior teacher, and have seen their eyes light up with warm recollection of these conferences and how Hoskins opened their eyes to landscape.)

These amateurs are often drawn to the subject both by their love of the English countryside and of the localities that they live in or visit every weekend and also by books and television programmes, either by Hoskins or in the Hoskins tradition. *The Making of the English Landscape* succeeded in riding upon a wave of popularity through the book clubs, Hoskins's articles in *The Listener* (1954a), and the "paperback revolution" from 1935 onwards. It may therefore be the case that historians of landscape studies might insist that this or that specific technique was actually the innovation of O. G. S. Crawford or Harry Thorpe. I would argue that nevertheless those amateurs were drawn to the subject in part by Hoskins's vision and succeeding visions, and it remains Hoskins's vision that articulated an emotional and intellectual horizon for landscape history and archaeology, and for landscape appreciation in general. Christopher Taylor (2000), for example, talks of Hoskins's impact on the outstandingly successful popular British television archaeology series *Time Team*, while Fiona Reynolds, director of the National Trust, in an interview for the British Broadcasting Corporation, gives Hoskins's *The Making of the English Landscape* as her preferred book to take on a desert island (alongside the compulsory Shakespeare and Bible: Reynolds 2002). Reynolds's favourite recordings to take with her to contemplate amid the sand and coconuts include a classic of English landscape appreciation – a recorded reading of Wordsworth's *Lines Composed above Tintern Abbey*.

The discourse of landscape embodied by Hoskins in this way is much deeper than specific theoretical orientations. It is difficult for example to see the postprocessualist Mark Edmonds writing about landscape in the following way without his legacy: for Edmonds, the landscape "is a surface inhabited over millennia, variously worked and changed by people. Lines of hawthorn and ash follow the edges of medieval tracks and fields, enclosing land where old furrows survive as soil marks. Other hedges are the imprint of more recent hands, boundaries set in the last two centuries. There are other traces too. Seen from the air, the land is etched with the marks of prehistory; places of settlement and ceremonial and of dead long forgotten; sites revealed when the plough brings its varied crop of pottery and stone to the surface" (1999:3).

Third, though I have concentrated on Hoskins's writings, much of his pattern of thought can be held to be typical of a whole generation of scholars. For David Matless (1998), Hoskins was one of a diverse and culturally powerful set of discourses set up in opposition to what was seen as a rampant and all-consuming modernity. These discourses were articulated by politicians of both the left and the right, for example in the "Back to the Earth" movement. Hoskins was not so naive as to advocate an active rejection of modernity in the form of a genuinely alternative mode of living: he saw that the "England of the scientists and military men" was here to stay, and in his work as a document-based historian he charted rural poverty and hardship many times (Hoskins 1964a, 1964b). As a result, what seems to us to be a rather negative political quietism when he urges us to turn away before all is lost to the vandals could be seen more charitably as a more sensible and less sentimentalized attitude than some of the contemporaries discussed by Matless.

Finally, while I have argued here that many of the intellectual tenets of English Romanticism were refracted through Hoskins's writing and thus inscribed in the discourse of English landscape history and archaeology, there were also other streams and currents of thought which translated Romantic patterns of thought into archaeological practice. In other words, Hoskins may have been the prime exponent, but the traditions of English Romanticism I have identified are common to a wider set of scholars. The previous chapter identified how English Romanticism contributed to a strand of left-wing thought that carried through in the 20th century to a brand of reformist socialism that owed more to reformist and libertarian thought than it did to Karl Marx. Hoskins was a political liberal, but many of the figures involved in the genesis of post-war landscape archaeology were socialists in this tradition, part of the upsurge of reformist socialism that also produced the post-war Labour government. The excavators of Wharram Percy, Maurice Beresford and John Hurst, in particular fit into this tradition. It is not going too far to say that part of the impetus behind the recognition of and research into the deserted medieval village and the historic landscape beyond was for many a desire to uncover the ways of life of ordinary people, as opposed to the kings and princes of conventional political history, even if this aim was implicit rather than explicit in what was published at the time (Gerrard 2003).

Conclusion

I have argued that, although Hoskins's writing conditioned a generation of landscape archaeology, there was a gap where the archaeological method and theory should have been. This gap was apparent to, and was rapidly filled by, practitioners of prehistoric landscape archaeology through the use of explicit theory, but it was not so perceived by archaeologists of historic periods. What Hoskins set up, and what was taken forward by contemporaries and followers, was not an archaeological research agenda, but rather a set of techniques for historical *reconstruction* of past landscapes and communities in which archaeological evidence played an ancillary role. Moreover, the role of archaeology became supplementary and supportive to a text-based narrative rather than oppositional and critical. Thus Hoskins and his contemporaries showed that late medieval desertion was something that needed to be explained, and that the archaeological remains of deserted villages were suitable evidence. Or that if we wanted to understand medieval assarting, maps and field boundaries were suitable evidence.

Now, as a result of these factors, I suggest that the link between archaeological facts and historical interpretations was, by definition, entirely unexamined in the genesis of historic landscape archaeology. Data were not brought to bear on theory in such a way as to test the rigour of the interpretation being offered; data illustrated rather than confronted theory. *Instead landscape archaeology provided a series of illustrative anecdotes which referred to a grand underlying story about the nature and development of the English landscape.* And this reference was implicit, untheorized, and subsequently unexamined.

As a literary composition, as a statement of English and regional identity, and as a governing narrative for the use of ordinary people visiting the landscape to help them make sense of what they were looking at, texts such as *The Making of the English Landscape* had and continue to have immense and enduring emotive and pedagogical power. As the basis for coming up with better scholarly understandings of the archaeology of landscapes, of moving archaeological knowledge forward in a systematic and indeed scientific manner, they were quite problematic. In the next chapter, we shall explore the history of landscape archaeology in England over the fifty years following the publication of *The Making of the English Landscape*, and show how these problems have become increasingly apparent.

Chapter Four

THE LOSS OF INNOCENCE

> Thus as he ponder'd what to do,
> A guide post rose within his view:
> And, when the pleasing shape he spied,
> He prick'd his steed and thither hied;
> But some unheeding, senseless wight,
> Who to fair learning owed a spite,
> Had ev'ry letter'd mark defac'd;
> Which once its several pointers grac'd.
> The mangled post thus long had stood,
> An uninforming piece of wood;
> Like other guides as some folks say,
> Who neither lead, nor tell the way.
>
> *(Combe 1812:10)*

The Tour of Dr Syntax in Search of the Picturesque (Combe 1812) is a satirical, book-length illustrated poem whose target is a certain form of Romanticism. Written by William Combe and accompanied by engravings by Rowlandson (Figure 4.1), it tells the story of the Reverend Doctor Syntax, who in mid-life crisis conceives a desire to travel the landscape in search of picturesque scenes. However, Dr Syntax's desire is for Combe misconceived, with crudely hilarious results. Before long on his journey, all sorts of unpleasant indignities befall him: he is beset by robbers, tied up, and his faithful and long-suffering if rather mangy horse Grizzle stolen. Later, stepping back to acquire the perfect view of a ruined castle, he falls into the mire (Figure 4.2).

Syntax's encounter early on in his travels with the defaced sign, the "uninforming piece of wood," encapsulates many of the discontents of Romanticism. The poem was conceived at the time as a specific mockery

Figure 4.1 Dr Syntax and the "uninforming" sign (from Combe 1812)

Figure 4.2 Dr Syntax falls into the mire, with Grizzle looking on (from Combe 1812)

of the picturesque artist and theorist Thomas Gilpin, whose Romanticism was focused on an appreciation of a rather artificial conception of the picturesque; he regarded it as perfectly acceptable to move landscape features around in his landscape compositions if nature herself had not deigned to place them in a suitably picturesque way. Wordsworth criticized Gilpin too in his 1793 *Descriptive Sketches*: he took issue with

Gilpin's attempt to restrict aesthetic appreciation to "the cold rules of painting" in what Wordsworth saw as an excessively formulaic and generalized manner (Bermingham 2000:105). However, I want to suggest here that the lessons of Combe's satire might usefully be heeded by all those working within the Romantic tradition, whether in literature or in landscape history and archaeology.

Indeed, I am going to stretch the metaphor a little and argue that Dr Syntax's "uninforming piece of wood" stands for the central problem, not just in historic landscape archaeology, but in archaeology as a whole, and even beyond to all disciplines that explain patterns found in the present by reference to processes that occurred in the past. The piece of wood is clearly evidence, and it is clearly physical or material in nature: with apologies to Dr Johnson, kick the post and it hurts. But *what it means* is completely unclear. For the piece of wood, some "unheeding, senseless wight" has defaced the letters.

To put it another way: the past is dead and gone; all we have left are traces surviving in the present (Binford 1987). Those traces (field boundaries, buildings, archaeological sites, artefacts, or for that matter documents or the geological and environmental record) are habitually explained by scholars of all disciplines by reference to processes that happened many centuries or even millennia ago, in other words in the past. The past processes that are inferred from this evidence may be very simple, everyday, and small-scale (the digging of a pit and the discarding of rubbish into it, the building of a field wall, the ploughing of a field) or long-term and abstract ("state formation," "manorialization," "Saxon settlement," "enclosure," "lordship," "response to climatic change"). However, the modern archaeologist can never directly observe these past processes; neither the digging of a medieval pit nor "manorialization" will ever actually be experienced directly by the modern scholar.

The problem goes further than this. Many of the patterns archaeologists see have a number of different processes that might account for them. At a basic level, a ditch might be the result of a single event or of many generations of recutting. More fundamentally, the apparently "regular" layout of the property boundaries of a village might or might not be the result of conscious "planning"; and if it is the result of planning, it might be planning by one of a number of parties working in a number of different possible ways (the lord imposing his will? the peasants working cooperatively?). Other landscape features may or may not be "human" in origin: thus lynchets might be the result of natural processes or deliberate construction.

What archaeologists do, then, in practice, in the face of all these possible processes that might account for the patterns they see, is to adopt a series of assumptions about how to translate present into past. These assumptions often appear obvious and commonsensical to the extent that archaeologists do not even put them into words or consciously think about them when they are being used. However, many were not so obvious to previous generations of scholars. For example, geologists, geomorphologists, and physical geographers habitually interpret the geological record in terms of long-term, gradual processes of deposition and erosion that we can see around us today; this is second nature. But when first proposed in the 19th century, such observations were highly controversial and part of an intellectual revolution in geological thinking (Rudwick 2005).

One of the central elements of the New Archaeology of the 1960s, in particular in the work of Lewis Binford, was the examination of our assumptions about how to link evidence and interpretation, in other words how to move between the observable traces in the present and the processes that created those traces in the past. Such an examination was motivated by the insistence that links between the two were made clear, rigorous, and explicit (Binford 1983, 1987; see also Johnson 1999:48–64, and Leone and Crosby 1987 for its application to historical archaeology). At the same time, New Archaeology wanted to couple this new rigour with new ambitions. It proposed new and exciting ways of saying things about the past – it wanted to move beyond what it saw as a dry, traditional stress on dating and diffusion to look at all aspects of social, economic, and cultural systems. However, it rapidly became clear, as New Archaeologists moved from polemic to practice, that the optimism was not fully justified. It became clear that the link between present observation and inferences about past processes were more complex and difficult to understand than appeared at first sight – one could not simply "read off" past processes and structures in a simple and straightforward manner from the archaeological record.

This growing recognition of the difficulty of linking pattern and process became known as the "taphonomic retreat" in archaeology. Taphonomy is the study of how the archaeological record comes to be created, or more specifically how we might understand the attrition of artefacts and ecofacts – the mangling and defacing of Dr Syntax's wooden sign – before and during the depositional process. It can be a profoundly depressing topic. We find that dogs gnaw at and destroy bones in gatherer-hunter camps, ruining any chance of a clear profile of economic activity at the site; different patterns of grain processing produce completely different kinds of residue, differences that give a misleading impression of what and how much people were actually eating. In other words, archaeologists retreated from the convenient but mistaken assumption that one clear pattern indicated one clear process in the past (Albarella 1999:872; Lyman 1994; Huntley and Stallibrass 2000).

In this chapter I will argue that the landscape archaeology of historic periods has undergone a similar kind of "taphonomic retreat." In the last chapter we saw how Hoskins's method was to treat the landscape as illustrative evidence for a wider historical and moral story, and how, following the lead of Wordsworthian Romanticism, in the process of composing this grand story the link between archaeological evidence and archaeological interpretation was not clearly considered.

Hoskins and his contemporaries treated features in the landscape as clear and unambiguous signs. However, on closer inspection many of these signs have turned out to be uninforming pieces of wood, not capable of providing a single unambiguous indication of what actually happened in past landscapes. The result, as we shall see, has been a steady erosion of our confidence in making the landscape tell us anything clear and unambiguous about what actually happened in the past.

Translating Landscape into History

Wasn't this simply because Hoskins did not understand archaeology? A common statement made in landscape archaeology is that Hoskins, having had a primary training as an economic historian, did not understand archaeological method, or that he was either not very good at it or never did it – the assertion, often repeated verbally, that he never actually physically placed a measuring-tape against a building, or that he did not understand basic archaeological principles such as stratigraphy. This lack of practical training and understanding of the mysteries of archaeological method led, it is further alleged, to his greatest error – the belief that there were relatively few vestiges of large-scale prehistoric land use and settlement, and that, after the end of Roman Britain, Anglo-Saxon migrants came to a land that was still in large part uncleared.

Such allegations are in my view only partly true, and do him an injustice. Hoskins did look closely at elements of the archaeological record such as buildings. We have, for example, the testament of the archaeologist M. W. Barley in the acknowledgements to his great book *The English Farmhouse and Cottage* (1961): "One of the pleasantest, as well as the most profitable, parts of the long task of collecting material took the form of visits to Devonshire and Somerset farmhouses in the company of Mr A. W. Everett, Sir Robert de Z. Hall and Dr W. G.

Hoskins" (Barley 1961:xvi). Hoskins's description of how to do a survey of a house suggests that Barley's experience is not an isolated example (1983:171). Hoskins visited many deserted villages, even if he did not necessarily understand fully what he was looking at (in our humbler moments, what archaeologist can ever claim full understanding of the humps and bumps we lovingly record?). However, he made these visits at a very early stage in the study of deserted medieval settlement, and his alleged oversights were shared by many of his contemporaries who were trained as archaeologists. When a meeting took place at Knaptoft, those present included Postan, Steensberg, Hoskins, Beresford, and Grahame Clark. It is not at all clear from accounts of that meeting that those present who had been trained as archaeologists had a significantly different understanding of what they were looking at from Hoskins. Elsewhere, Hoskins shows an archaeological appreciation, and a willingness to turn aside to examine the unexpected, when he relates his "discovery" of a Roman villa site while on a walk with a friend to see a deserted medieval village (1983:151).

It is, I feel, demonstrably untrue to suggest that Hoskins did not understand stratigraphy. Stratigraphy in its simpler forms is an implicit backdrop to even the simplest statement about landscape. By recognizing the lines of fields as 18th-century enclosures running across the earthworks of a deserted medieval village, Hoskins was understanding and applying principles of horizontal stratigraphy. In any case, stratigraphy is not strictly or properly a specifically archaeological technique: it was developed in 19th-century geology (Trigger 1989; Winchester 2001). Hoskins had a detailed appreciation of the fundamentals of geology, and handles geological observations with apparent detail and command in his books, for example *Devon* (1954b:14–21). Finally, stratigraphy is itself not a simple or commonsensical tool that one either does or does not understand. The underlying assumption that stratigraphy is beyond theory is itself empiricist. Gavin Lucas has recently shown how the concept is theoretically bounded and has evolved, even to the extent that its classic proponent, Mortimer Wheeler, had a delimited view of it (Lucas 2001:36–43).

It is also worth remembering that if Hoskins was not primarily trained as an archaeologist, this was also true for many of his generation of researchers on the landscape. The teaching of high medieval and later archaeology at British universities did not expand significantly until the 1960s, and consequently there was no cohort of trained archaeologists, or for that matter a set corpus of techniques distinctive to medieval and later archaeology (Gerrard 2003; see also the discussion of Finberg below). Where early students of historic landscapes did use stratigraphy, it was partly the result of training in historical geography, and behind that training lay concepts and assumptions derived from geology, rather than archaeology as such (Gerrard 2003:130).

It is instructive to look at Hoskins's treatment of archaeological evidence in one of his finest books, *Devon* (1954b), which was favourably reviewed by, among others, the historian A. L. Rowse and the architectural critic and poet John Betjeman (later to be appointed Poet Laureate) in the *Sunday Times* and *Daily Telegraph* respectively (Hoskins 1953:flyleaf). *Devon* is a large book, consisting first of a series of synthetic chapters covering the natural and human history of the county, followed by gazetteer entries on particular places.

Devon is a particularly significant example in this context because we now know that the upland landscapes of Devon, in particular Dartmoor, contain a great deal of evidence for prehistoric land use and settlement, in the form of reaves, other land divisions, and habitation sites. These have been brilliantly explored in a subsequent programme of fieldwork and interpretation by Andrew Fleming and others (Fleming 1988; see below, and Figure 4.3). Why did Hoskins not recognize these landscape features, which might have led him to take more seriously the evidence for widespread prehistoric settlement of the landscape? Is it because he was a bad or untrained archaeologist, or were there other and different factors at work?

In Hoskins's day, there were two prehistoric sites in particular on Dartmoor that had been recognized and which merited attention: Standon Hill and Grimspound. Hoskins's description of Standon Hill is revealing:

> It is difficult for any but prehistorians to feel a passionate interest in the visible remains of the hut-circles on Dartmoor, which are the walls, or the ruins of walls, of dwelling-houses, store-sheds, and cattle-sheds. Nevertheless, certain sites are impressive even to the layman and give him some sense of kinship, however dim, with his prehistoric ancestors . . . [after an extensive description of the panoramic view from the site he goes on:]
>
> In the silent Bronze Age village in which we now stand, among the tumbled walls, with the wheatears jerking from stone to stone and the larks spiralling overhead, we are among the oldest houses that we know . . . Standon village contains the remains of over seventy hut-circles, some of them with substantial walls still in situ and standing to a height of three or four feet. Some, however, appear to have been rebuilt to form modern shelters for sheep and shepherds [Hoskins at this point footnotes the *Victoria County History* and the journal *Devon Archaeology*] . . . There are corn-plots of early Bronze Age date. (Hoskins 1954b:29)

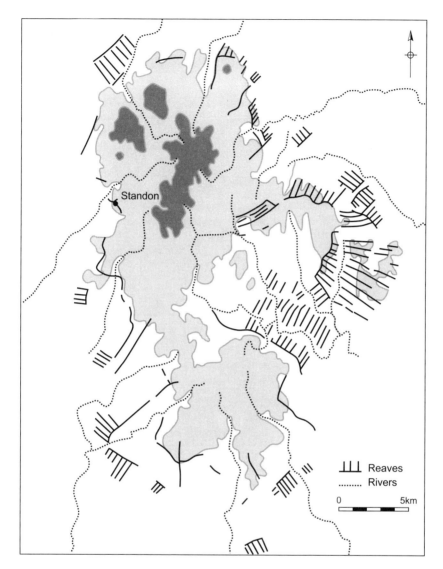

Figure 4.3 Reaves and other prehistoric settlement remains on Dartmoor (after Fleming 1988:54)

The use of Romantic imagery is of course to be expected (most obviously, the spiralling lark is borrowed from Shelley); but note here the careful observation of the archaeology. Hoskins knows enough about what he is looking at to identify modifications to buildings and also manages to observe and identify surrounding prehistoric "corn-plots," albeit guided by other writers.

It is also striking that the more sweeping statements to be found in the early edition of *The Making of the English Landscape* about uncleared woodland are not to be found in this more detailed study of a specific county. Later in *Devon* Hoskins shows his understanding and appreciation of landscape evidence when he notes that "the eastern side of the Moor was considerably more populated than the few remains of pottery at present suggest," and he goes on in succeeding pages to note the existence of 1,330 hut circles on Dartmoor, "not all of which are yet marked on the Ordnance Survey maps" (1954b:30) and predicts further discoveries. Later in his career Hoskins was happy to acknowledge "the extent to which prehistory and the Roman period underlie our modern villages and their fields" (1983:7).

But note the first sentence of our quotation: Hoskins could see the prehistoric archaeology; he just *was not particularly interested in what he was looking at*. Why not? Also note the use of the word "silence." In what sense is this site silent, as opposed to, say, a medieval parish church or a 17th-century farmhouse? Partly in the sense of being ruined and no longer in use, but also in the sense of being from a prehistoric, or pre-literate, period, and therefore incapable of being slotted into Hoskins's historical and document-based narrative. When Hoskins wants to make prehistory relevant, he does so by suggesting a lineal descent to the present through "our prehistoric ancestors." On page 28 of *Devon*, he does this by claiming that prehistoric migrations were "the first of many such cross-channel migrations down to the Breton 'onion-boys' who used to make their cheerful and loquacious way from house to house in Exeter before the war," a memory he clearly recollects from his childhood. It is striking that the relative proportion of distant views from above in the plates of *The Making of the English Landscape* decreases rapidly once Hoskins's narrative moves from prehistoric to historic periods (compare plates 1–10 to plates 11–30).

I am suggesting here that Hoskins's alleged deficiencies spring not simply from a supposed lack of skills, knowledge, or training, but from much deeper theoretical roots. In particular, they stem indirectly from a Romantic view of the past, in which emotive kinship and empathy with the people of the past is primary – when we can be "linked in feeling" to the people who produced the monuments and landscapes we are looking at (1954b:39). *Feeling* is the link here between present and past, a fine poetic sentiment that comes to us directly from Wordsworth and the other Romantics. "Feeling" is a sentiment that does not fit well with the pretensions to science and objectivity of many modern archaeologists, and it is an area of experience whose contribution to archaeology has often been under-acknowledged (Tarlow 1999). However, an untheorized "feeling" is not necessarily suitable as a central, guiding interpretative principle for a scientific archaeology, however defined.

Being "linked in feeling" is an idea whose difficulties are clearly apparent when considering prehistory and its remains. The men, women, and children who built and lived in the huts at Standon Hill and Grimspound, we can be sure, had feelings that were quite different from ours. They had belief systems and patterns of thought that were utterly remote; cultural anthropology teaches us that people from other cultures cannot be judged or interpreted by the standards of 21st-century Western culture, and this goes also for people in the past.

But the difficulties of being "linked in feeling" are still there, albeit less apparent, when considering historic landscapes. There is no *a priori* reason why medieval peasants are any more or less "linked in feeling" to the modern world than prehistoric settlers. To suppose that they were, one would have to posit some extremely simplistic form of evolutionary theory in which the mentality of human groups becomes "more like us" the closer to the modern world one gets. This might just be a sustainable position, but it is not an argument that that I have seen made anywhere in the work of the English land-scape tradition.

Translating Landscape into Literature

Hoskins's *Devon* is also interesting in its attitude to literature. He admires the historical novel *Westward Ho!* in terms which again evoke the contradictions of Wordsworth:

> Even now one cannot fail to be moved by [*Westward Ho!*], one of the greatest and most satisfying historical novels in the English language. One can only pity children who are more interested in jet engines and train numbers . . . Blackmore's *Lorna Doone* (1869), another of the great English historical novels, does the same for the Exmoor country, but like *Westward Ho!* had, too, the incidental effect of destroying the beauty and solitude of the natural landscape by making it too widely known. (1954b:284, 285)

There is one book, however, which eludes Hoskins. A powerful description of Dartmoor, and a detailed description of the prehistoric hut circles (which play a key role in the plot), is to be found in Conan Doyle's famous Sherlock Holmes novel *The Hound of the Baskervilles*. Hoskins finds no space for even a mention of Conan Doyle, despite the immense fame of the book and its complex and disturbing evocation of the dark fells and prehistoric remains around Baskerville Hall. In Conan Doyle's account, the concept of kinship is implicitly ridiculed. The local amateur archaeologist is subjected to legal action by a litigious eccentric, having excavated a series of Neolithic burials without asking the permission of the next of kin. Holmes himself turns up in one of the Neolithic huts (Figure 4.4).

The fictional Baskerville Hall, we are told by the estimable Dr Watson, is 14 miles from Princetown, a place which also gets little mention in Hoskins's guide. Princetown is mentioned only twice and then incidentally in the synthetic chapters; in its gazetteer entry (it is actually to be found not by name, but under Lydford) it is described as a "grim little town . . . with an abominable climate of fog, snow, wind, and more than 80 in. of cold rain" (1954b:429) followed by a brief description of the history of the prison. It is hardly surprising that Hoskins does not like Princetown prison; we have already noted his dislike for what he saw as alien intrusions into the landscape. What is surprising is that the prison is given extensive treatment by another anti-modernist, H. V. Morton, in his classic celebratory and semi-mystical text *In Search of England* (1927); one might expect Hoskins and Morton to share similar prejudices in this regard.

The Hound of the Baskervilles evokes a Dartmoor landscape that is sublime, in the Romantic sense of the term – it is terrifying, dangerous, vertiginous, and alien. The concept of the sublime is one element of Romanticism that hardly enters into Hoskins's work (one of the most famous sites of the Romantic sublime, Lydford Gorge, with its waterfalls and swirling eddies, gets only a passing mention and that in a geological context: Hoskins 1954b:20). Hoskins's favoured landscapes are peaceful, unmoving, stable, human in scale; he instinctively turns away from the sublime and the chaos and void it is taken to represent in Romantic thought.

I suggest, therefore, that the idea that Hoskins was a "bad archaeologist" is at best an oversimplification and at worst positively misleading. Behind his alleged archaeological errors lurk deeper theoretical attitudes, preferences for certain periods over others, an

Figure 4.4 "There he sat upon a stone outside . . .". One of Sidney Paget's original drawings illustrating *The Hound of the Baskervilles* for *Strand* magazine

aversion to the sublime, and an implicit prioritization of documentary evidence over the material and archaeological, a Romantic imagination, and an empiricism in which the facts were held to speak for themselves.

Empiricism

I argued in the last chapter that Romanticism led directly to an empiricism in which the facts were held to speak for themselves, without the benefit of intervening theory. This empiricism also endured.

Enduring empiricism is often expressed as a gut feeling, even when all rational arguments have dropped away. It is particularly strong in British landscape studies, in part because of its presence as an enduring discourse within national culture stretching back to the early 17th-century writing of Francis Bacon (Easthope 1999). Empiricism, being implicit, is most apparent not in overt explication but in passing comments. More than one practising landscape archaeologist has said to me, using different forms of words, that "all this theory is all very well, but when you get out into a muddy field and look around you, you just *know*." Others, in conversation, refer to the act of looking, of direct observation, as somehow ineffable or beyond critical analysis or deconstruction, and certainly superior to a thousand technical aids (Fleming, personal communication). It is this process of looking that is referred to when scholars see technology and Internet advances as unimportant compared to "the observational skill and field-craft discipline of the fieldworker, developed over several centuries but particularly refined in the last 30 years" (Ainsworth et al. 1999:3).

Such empiricism can also be seen in the concentration on technique as opposed to theory in many explications of historic landscape archaeology. If the past can be held to speak for itself, all we have to do is list or describe the remains of that past. As a result, there has been very little explicit theoretical reflection on the field techniques of landscape archaeology, in contrast with excavation processes (Hodder 1999; Lucas 2001; Edgeworth 2003) or with fieldwork in human geography (Driver 2000, 2001; Cloke et al. 2003). Thus, when Mick Aston asks "how we know what we know" in landscape archaeology, the answer is phrased exclusively in terms of the sources of archaeological and documentary information. Implicitly, the task of getting from this information to finding out what we want to know about the past is not seen as problematic (Aston 1985:13–20; contrast Lewis Binford's answer to the same question, outlined above).

This gut feeling appears to be based in common sense and everyday experience, with all its potential and problems. Behind ideas of "common sense," or even the notion that all one needs to understand the landscape is a countryman's eye and a good pair of boots, the English landscape tradition makes one cardinal and central assumption: that the past peoples we study were essentially like ourselves. Common sense, therefore, far from being theory-free or somehow opposed to apparently more "sentimental" approaches, is complicit with Romantic sentiment, since it implies some form of being "linked in feeling" with the past. As such, it formed a powerful rhetorical tool. "History in the form of feeling – ancestral, aesthetic and moral – was a conventional form. It resolved the puzzle of instability by turning it into the bedrock of certainty" (Taylor 1994:200).

In itself, being "linked in feeling" is not necessarily a bad or politically objectionable sentiment: without the notion of some form of common human feeling, one could argue, the student of the past cannot really do anything, and additionally the moral assertion of human rights would be undercut. This is the position adopted by R. G. Collingwood in his work on the philosophy and methodology of history, when he argues that whatever they claim is their method, historians actually work through empathy, the re-thinking of the thoughts of past historical actors. Collingwood's method has been convincingly argued to apply to archaeology also (Collingwood 1946; Hodder and Hutson 2003:145–51).

However, being linked in feeling runs the risk of a denial of *otherness* in the past. We saw the epistemological difficulties with such a notion raised in the last chapter; it is politically problematic also. The assertion of "common sense" is an insistence that there is *one* way of understanding landscape, that there is *one* way of living, that is obvious and again beyond critique. Anyone who does not act according to the rules of "common sense," in this view, is simply being irrational or mystical.

It is to state the obvious that our common sense and everyday experience are not necessarily those of the past. The modern student of landscape comes with a mindset and system for perceiving and understanding the world that is a modern, 21st-century product. Many of the elements of that system that are labelled "common sense" actually vary from culture to culture. Cultural anthropologists insist as a primary principle that apparently commonsensical attitudes to the land, to domestic comfort, to heat, smell, and cleanliness are themselves variable from society to society and cannot be assumed in advance (Sahlins 1977, 1995; Vigarello 1988). The inner certainty one feels, then, derived from the wind in one's face, the smell of manure, and the muck on one's boots is completely illusory. Indeed, inner certainty through raw experience is a classic construct of modernity.

It may be illusory, but it is exceptionally powerful in its rhetorical appeal to some deep-seated elements in the national consciousness (Easthope 1999). In particular, a stress on the ineffability of the experience of the land also goes hand in hand with a Romantic attitude to landscape. Wordsworth tramped across the landscape, made observations, but then just gathered it up into his heart and it became a poem.

Landscape archaeologists in the Hoskins tradition tramp across the landscape and get their boots muddy, collect their facts carefully, and then just gather up their material and it becomes a closely argued article. The facts speak for themselves, because however objectively they appear to be presented they refer implicitly to the grand story that Hoskins was telling.

An introductory course on the philosophy of knowledge establishes very quickly that an empiricist position of this kind appeals to the emotions, but is simply not a seriously tenable position. From the time when philosophy advanced beyond early 17th-century empiricism, it has been clear that facts do not speak for themselves. The data only "speak" when they are interrogated with a specific idea or hypothesis (Gower 1997). We have seen that Hoskins got away with this partly through the implicit nature of the theoretical assumptions underlying the scholarship of his time, and partly because of an implicit borrowing of Romantic notions, but also because the grand story he had to tell about the formation and dissolution of the landscape was already there for him. The phrase from his notebooks – "I have it now" – refers not just to his intuitive grasp of the story he wished to tell, but also to the revelation of the method by which he was to tell it.

For the present generation, the underlying empiricism of traditional landscape archaeology and the problems raised by that empiricism are also hidden behind the emotional and aesthetic appeal, and apparent power, of three of its most basic techniques: the map, the air photograph, and the hachured plan. All three of these techniques offer a way for the scholar, whether professional or amateur, to easily access and appreciate elements of the historic landscape, and all three need relatively little training to achieve that appreciation (though all three are highly specialized and need decades of experience to do really well). Each could be argued to be a technique of empiricism, in that each makes claims to be a true and objective record of what is "really there" that speaks for itself. However, each is, I will argue, complicit in a Romantic view of the world – each invites the observer to gaze down on the landscape like Wordsworth in the Lakes, at the ant-like figures of human beings scurrying busily below. All three inscribe the gaze as an all-powerful tool for understanding the landscape. It is striking that, with all three techniques, there is much "how-to" discussion of their use in the literature, but very little discussion of their underlying discursive assumptions. What little discussion there is has occurred in cultural geography and in prehistory, both areas that have been much more informed by postmodernism than the traditional study of historic landscapes (Thomas 2004). I will discuss each in turn.

The Powerful Gaze: Maps

It is now well established that maps purport to embody an objective description of the landscape, but actually represent "reality" selectively and are anything but objective, a point made most obviously in the way that traditional projections of the globe onto a flat surface have habitually prioritized the "West" over other areas (Cosgrove 2000; Harley 2000). As such, the maps used by the landscape historian are not neutral tools, but play a central role in inscribing ways of thinking on to the landscape.

It is difficult to communicate to a non-British observer how deeply a familiarity with the Ordnance Survey map is embedded in the consciousness of the British landscape archaeologist, and of anyone, professional or amateur, walking across the landscape as a whole. Its most common forms, the "one-inch" (actually now one-and-a-quarter-inch) and "two-and-half-inch" to the mile, are a basic element of familiarity with the landscape; one could say that they are old friends to the archaeologist and to the walker in general (Figure 4.5; Owen and Pilbeam 1992). Knowledge of the conventions of the Ordnance Survey map and an ability to read it are a requirement for all English schoolchildren under the government-prescribed National Curriculum (Rawling 2002).

It is a mark of status to have an Ordnance Survey map that is well thumbed and stained with the mud and spilt coffee from a thermos flask of a thousand visits to the countryside, much as a well-worn trowel is a status symbol for "circuit diggers" (Edgeworth 2003). Most students of the historic landscape have a shelf-ful of such maps occupying a prominent position in their studies. The contours, symbols, and colours of the Ordnance Survey map are thus deeply ingrained in the consciousness and affections of the British landscape archaeologist to the extent that the action of "map-reading" is second nature; one might make similar comments about the French IGN series of maps and other European series.

Historical geographers have argued that the 18th- and 19th-century development of Ordnance Survey maps was bound up with the need of the ruling classes to control and dominate the landscape. This need was originally a specifically military one – English armies needed a reliable guide to help them patrol the Scottish Highlands after the 1745 rebellion; in this respect they were following the more advanced examples of the military academies of France and Prussia (Bermingham 2000). The British army's Board of Ordnance had a Drawing Room located within the labyrinthine corridors and offices of the medieval Tower of London.

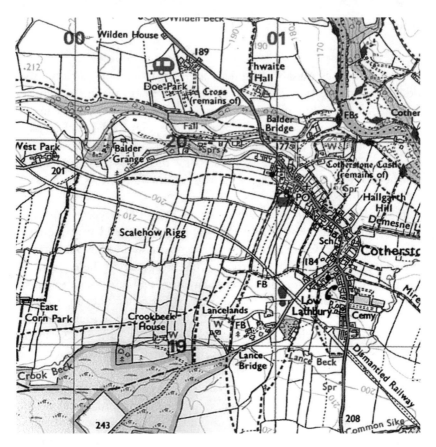

Figure 4.5 The modern "two-and-a-half-inch" Ordnance Survey map (2.5 inches to the mile) for the village of Cotherstone. The field patterns suggest traces of earlier field systems; horizontal stratigraphy can clearly be traced, most obviously in the line of the now dismantled railway cutting across the fields; monuments such as Cotherstone Castle and a medieval wayside cross are indicated in Gothic script; names suggest function and date (a medieval "demesne" is a lord's farm or estate; "Thwaite" is of Scandinavian origin). *Reproduced by permission of Ordnance Survey on behalf of HMSO. © Crown copyright 2005. All rights reserved. Ordnance Survey licence number 100044559*

The mapping of Scotland was complete by 1755. The 19th-century mapping of the rest of Britain and Ireland followed (Angela Smith 2003).

Today, one of the first steps any landscape archaeologist will take in familiarizing him- or herself with an area is to consult the first-edition Ordnance Survey map, issued at different dates from the early 19th century onwards and made on a scale of six inches to the mile. (Roberts and Wrathmell's recent survey of England as a whole is based on a more rapid and larger-scale observation of the first-edition one-inch maps: see Roberts and Wrathmell 2000, 2002). By doing so, he or she can mentally "peel off" the accretions of the last century and a half. A standard technique is then to work backwards through time, mentally or physically removing later features from the map – for example railway lines, areas of industry, forest plantations, and 18th-century landscape parks. In this way, traces of earlier patterns and linear features "come to the surface." Tom Williamson's argument for the early date of whole systems of field boundaries in East Anglia, for example, was based on this process, working back through the removal of railways, parks, and other post-medieval features to reveal patterns of field boundaries interpreted as coaxial systems that were Roman or prehistoric in date (Williamson 1988, 1998; Figure 4.6).

The map, of course, has been subjected to critique (Harley 1992, 2000). Postcolonial theorists have asserted that it was one of a series of technologies that were part of a colonial apparatus to assist the administrator and the army man. In the process of "objectively" defining and creating space, the map acted to erase "native" understandings of the landscape, based on customary usage and often spiritual in nature, and to replace those understandings with "Western" modes of naming and hence control. Maps showed "unexplored" areas as empty spaces, *terra nullius*, and thus legitimated their conquest and control; under the presentation of Mercator's atlas, the projection served to present Europe and European environments as central to the world.

In Ireland, the work of the Ordnance Survey led to an attempted erasure of much of the native Irish understanding of the landscape. In earlier centuries, the colonial nature of mapmaking was understood by colonizer and colonized alike. The attempted reorganization and "plantation" of the Irish landscape and the production of maps were closely related enterprises. The topographer and mapmaker Bartlett published his *Generalle Description of Ireland* in 1603, after the attempted plantation of Munster and before that of Ulster. The reaction of the native Irish was to ambush and behead Bartlett (Johnson 1996:95; see also Angela Smith 2003). Two centuries later, the Ordnance Survey brought techniques perfected in Scotland to the mapping of the Irish landscape. This was, in part, the culmination of a colonial project that brought maps and imperial acquisition together across the globe (Carter 1987).

It is very difficult for a student of the English landscape to look at the much-loved symbols, contour lines, and folds of the Ordnance Survey map and see them simply or solely as elements of a colonialist enterprise. For students of landscape, and for those walking and touring

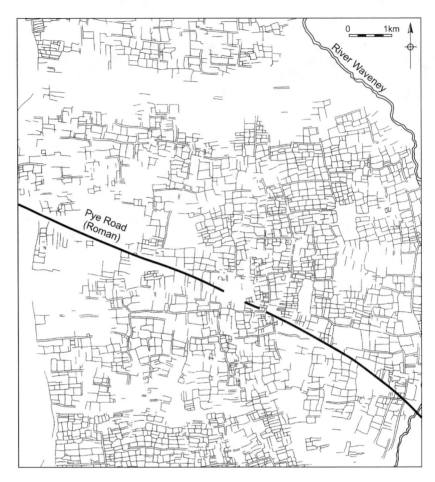

Figure 4.6 Williamson's tracing of the "Scole–Dickleburgh field system" (after Williamson 2003:42)

the English countryside more generally, such maps are in part enabling. Most obviously, they encode and enshrine property rights, and conversely act as a record and confirmation of public rights of way and, after recent legislation, areas where the public are free to roam. Antiquities are marked on the map, in different scripts; medieval and prehistoric sites get Gothic lettering, while Roman sites get capitals. This inscription of archaeological sites on to the standard map owes much to the work of O. G. S. Crawford, who in the years after the First World War worked for the Ordnance Survey (thereafter, the Ordnance Survey had an Archaeology Division, which was eventually absorbed into the Royal Commission on Historical Monuments in the early 1980s and from thence merged along with the rest of the Royal Commission into English Heritage: Gerrard 2003).

Interestingly, given the interest in such topics in postmodern human geography, there has been relatively little discussion of the field experience of map-handling. David Matless has discussed how the educational movements of the 1930s instilled a sense of consciousness of the cartographic project; the map took its place alongside the "good companions" of the rucksack and hiking boots, and the covers of early Ordnance Survey maps feature pictures of the map-user "stationed on a hill overlooking a valley. A church-focused nucleated village nestles below. Unfolding the map unfolds the country. A sense of survey satisfies" (1998:76–9 and figs 17–20).

The action of map-reading has been argued to be a gendered one in terms which inscribe a Romantic prioritization of the masculine into everyday practice. Crawford felt that women were unsuited to the practice of map-reading (1955), while the popular perception that "women can't read maps" has been given academic credence by popular sociobiology (Pease and Pease 2001).

The Powerful Gaze: Air Photographs

The second technique, that of the air photograph and its interpretation, had increasingly been used in archaeology since the work of O. G. S. Crawford in the 1920s. As editor of *Antiquity*, which he founded in 1926, Crawford published an air photograph in every issue; amongst the earliest were of medieval lynchets. His book *Wessex From the Air* (Crawford 1928) was the pioneering work in the subject (see also Crawford 1955). After the Second World War air photographs became a classic means of identifying and understanding medieval sites. This was most obviously true of deserted medieval villages, but other such sites included moats, linear boundaries, prehistoric and later lynchets, complexes of fishponds, areas of mining, and roads (Beresford and St Joseph 1978). Part of the appeal of air photographs lies not just in their obvious utility but also, I suggest, in their aesthetic appeal. The front covers of the journals *Landscapes* and *Journal of the Medieval Settlement Research Group* are almost invariably adorned with a particularly beautiful air photograph; David Austin describes one selection of air photos as "mouth-watering" (see the front cover of Ainsworth et al. 1999; Austin 1996:341).

Such a photograph, like the Ordnance Survey map, answers Wordsworth's need for an elevated position from which to survey and command the landscape where no mountains are conveniently available. From the air photo, human beings are either tiny, beetling figures or non-existent. Instead the pattern of the landscape dominates and is shown off in a manner that subtly suggests that it is independent of human agency. Indeed, part of the attraction of many aerial photographs is their complex and multi-layered nature. Like a difficult puzzle, they need decoding; this can be characterized as a craft every bit as complex and full of its own lore as excavation or indeed map interpretation (Frodeman 2004 discusses field geology in similar terms).

I do not know of a single discussion of the air photograph in historic landscape archaeology that makes the very elementary point that, before the invention of the balloon, people would have had a very different view of their landscape. Mick Aston notes how "the air view has only been accessible for a very short time in human history" but does not explore the implications of this remark (2002:8). David Austin, reviewing a standard Royal Commission volume on Dartmoor, makes the point that of the many plans and photographs in the monograph, not a single one is taken from the ground – all is the plan view and the air photograph (1996). Part of the reason for this abstraction is the specialized nature of air photo interpretation: Wlodzimierz Raczowski has discussed the interpretation of air photographs, and has observed how after Crawford's death aerial archaeology and academic archaeology went their separate ways, leaving a theoretical vacuum in air photo interpretation (Raczowksi 2002).

Instead of complementing the air photograph with an account that was "on the ground," that is, written in human terms, scholars came instead to translate archaeological features into historical entities. The example of the geographer Harry Thorpe is classic in this regard. Thorpe took the air photograph of Wormleighton, a deserted village and landscape in Warwickshire (Figures 4.7 and 4.8). Gerrard points out that this photo and its "key" were used by Continental scholars as an illustration – a selected anecdote – to exemplify the development of the English landscape (Gerrard 2003:152–3; Chapelot and Fossier 1980:176–8). But what Thorpe does with this picture is revealing. Different features are picked out and their stratigraphic relationship implicitly alluded to (thus the 18th-century Oxford Canal cuts through the medieval moated manor site). An implicit narrative is alluded to also – the moated fields, medieval manor(s) and fish ponds come first; after depopulation, there is agricultural improvement in the form of water-meadows, paddocks, and closes. Further, Thorpe's annotation

Figure 4.7 Aerial photo used by Harry Thorpe to illustrate the evolution of the English landscape (Thorpe 1975: fig. 6). *Cambridge University Collection of Air Photographs*

presumes a fair amount of background knowledge. The reader is expected to know that stewponds, for example, are for breeding fish, that crofts are medieval property boundaries, and that depopulation is a phenomenon (according to the thinking of the time) that marks the end of the Middle Ages and the beginning of the modern period.

Air photos are thus anecdotal – they tell a little story – and in terms of the expected background knowledge of the reader were treated historically rather than archaeologically. The identified features become mnemonics – that is, they act as identifiers and reminders for wider historical processes that are already part of the consciousness of the

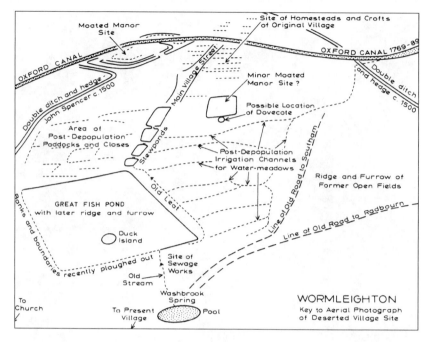

Figure 4.8 Thorpe's explanatory key to Figure 4.7 (after Thorpe 1975: fig. 9)

intended audience, who, it is assumed, are already familiar with the wider theme or story of the creation and dissolution of the English medieval village. These mnemonics are then referred to through extended figure captions which act as explications of the air photo (for example Morris 1989:454–66, or for that matter in my own writing on the historic landscape: Johnson 1996:48–53).

The classic text in this regard is *Medieval England: An Aerial Survey*, by Beresford and St Joseph (1978). This book still offers a wonderful selection of photographs to examine and text to study, and its images have a powerful pedagogical role – they are perfect for the task of teaching students about the elements of medieval landscapes; a favourite exercise of many teachers, including this author, is to give each student in a class a single illustration to describe and explain to the others. But its methods of explication follow the method already exemplified by Thorpe. It consists of photos arranged thematically into "the fields and villages," "the towns," and "industrial and other remains." Each photograph is the subject of a small essay. The essays give historical detail, thus for example: "between the pond and the road in the left foreground are other soil-marks. These seem to correspond in position to houses shown on the 1680 plan . . . thus we have an area outside modern Leighton where houses have disappeared since 1680" (1978:15). So what it does is to use the photos as illustrative material for a larger story about the English landscape that is essentially told from the documents. The pattern set by Beresford and St Joseph has been followed by many other books both academic and popular (for example Aston 2002).

As with other elements of landscape archaeology, then, the aesthetic appeal and pedagogical power of the air photo – its use in enhancing students' appreciation and understanding of landscape archaeology – and also the sheer beauty and complexity of what is revealed, and the intellectual exercise of attempting to decipher the puzzle, to make sense of what may be at first a confusing jumble of elements, obscures some of its deeper discontents. It foregrounds the larger pattern in both space and time; in space, the view from above privileges the larger pattern, while in time, we are shown changes over many centuries and even millennia. Somewhere in these larger scales the human realities of small-scale movement on a human pattern are lost.

The air photograph, then, is another artefact of Romanticism. As with Romanticism in general, we are seduced by the aesthetic appeal of the scene laid out before us in our elevated position, and turn it into a spectacle rather than regard it as an arena for human action. Human beings are either absent entirely, or become ant-like figures in the background; their homesteads and crofts have either been destroyed long ago, or only survive in the fine detail.

The Powerful Gaze: The Hachured Plan

At a smaller scale, and often working directly from air photographs, scholars have transcribed the humps and bumps littering the English landscape on to plans. Typically, though, for the English tradition, this technique has involved a craft-like element of interpretation right from the start. In many parts of the world, the habitual way to record earthworks is through a contour survey. Within the English landscape tradition, fieldworkers often prefer to do a hachure survey. This uses a feature derived from Ordnance Survey maps – the hachure or "tadpole" – to indicate patterns of earthworks (Figure 4.9).

Producing these maps takes an incredible amount of time, and to the untutored eye they appear to show little more than is apparent on a good air photograph. Yet they are a major element of landscape archae-

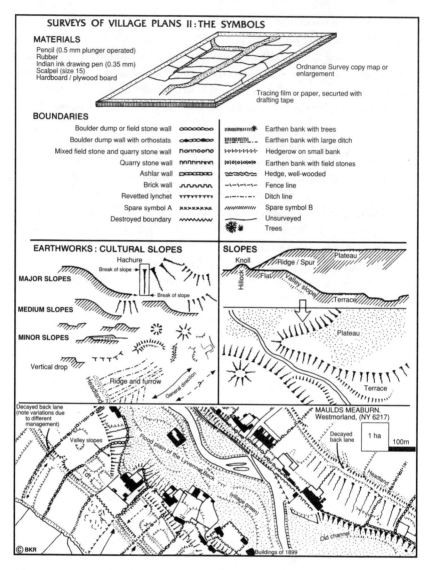

Figure 4.9 The use of hachures in village plans (after Roberts 1990:9)

ology, and indeed the sight of such a plan prompts a similar level of affection and emotive affinity among landscape archaeologists as the Ordnance Survey map. These plans are partly and self-consciously inter-pretative. Part of the value of drawing them up is not in the final product, but the discipline they exert on the fieldworker to observe and interpret in the field. Many scholars will state that they do not feel that they have properly "looked" at a landscape until they have been forced to render its subtleties in the form of a plan, and to make a concrete decision about where each hachure should start and stop, where a line of hachures should tail off, and where one line of hachures enters into a stratigraphic relationship with another by running "over" or "under" it.

Christopher Taylor, in his how-to guide *Fieldwork in Medieval Archaeology*, published in 1974 as landscape archaeology was maturing but before some of its later doubts grew, described the method of laying out hachures and in particular the unavoidably subjective element in their denotation:

> Even more difficult is where to fix the top or bottom of a bank or scarp. One can usually see the feature clearly enough but when one comes down to determining exactly where a low bank on a gentle natural slope ends it is possible to vary the point considerably. To prove this to a group of disbelieving students, the writer once made four separate groups plan a small and simple medieval sheep paddock . . . Every plan showed the correct shape and layout of the site, with its entrance, bank and ditch and all the minor internal features correctly drawn. But they all varied in up to a metre in places where the ditch and bank were not sharply defined. (Taylor 1974:40)

Taylor, writing before the advent of Geographical Positioning Systems, goes on to state that the hachured plan is nevertheless preferable to the contoured plan, as it is much simpler and less time-consuming to prepare. He could also have added that a well-executed hachured plan is far more aesthetically pleasing, an object of beauty, which like the air photograph inspires affection that masks its status as a form of interpretation.

It is worth reflecting on the way in which the hachured plan selects certain features as worthy of note. To state the obvious, it is another technique which prioritizes the plan view over that of the ground-level observer. Hachures, especially on medieval sites, tend to elevate and enshrine property boundaries – the edges of tofts and crofts, tenement lines. They are relatively quick to do, and as such are again a technique that is relatively accessible to the generalist or amateur. Taylor sees one of the decisive advantages of the hachured plan or the contour survey as being its simplicity, lack of necessary technology and ease of use. However, plans share the same discontents as air photographs: they "give schematic 'birds-eye' views that in no way capture how a place was set in the land, or how it was approached, or how it worked at a human scale" (Edmonds 1999:162).

Intractable Material

So far, I have argued that the apparently very empirical techniques of landscape archaeology are actually deeply theoretical. To clarify, the map, the air photograph and the plan are all "data." They bear the stamp of the muddy boot of painstaking fieldwork. The creation and the interpretation of the patterns contained in them is a skilled craft. Yet at the same time they are also anything but objective records of what is really there. Each, through its texture, the background knowledge it assumes, the way it is "read," its use in the field, its selection of features, the specific viewpoint taken, enshrines theoretical preferences from its inception.

There is nothing inherently unusual or wrong in the way such techniques are theoretically embedded. It was a basic insight of postprocessual archaeology that all techniques that were apparently "theory-free" were in fact theoretically loaded from the start; this was Ian Hodder's famous "interpretation at the trowel's edge," though it is revealing that most postprocessual discussions of such issues concentrate on excavation rather than other forms of fieldwork (Hodder 1999; see also Lucas 2001). The issue I am raising here is that of, on the one hand, the *reality* of the theoretically embedded set of techniques in which the data are seen through a series of complex filters, and on the other, the Romantic *rhetoric* of the data speaking for themselves. Insofar as landscape archaeology remains a largely empiricist field, its techniques have implicitly made a claim to be objective and commonsensical that simply cannot be sustained.

However, I now want to look at this argument in reverse. The theoretical preferences taken in the development of historic landscape archaeology were not simply abstract choices. They were also conditioned by the grain of the material. In other words, behind theoretical decisions to take a certain attitude to the data – to draw up a hachured rather than contoured plan, to select a parish for study rather than employ a randomly generated set of sampling squares – were very powerful "practical," organizational, and operational reasons for adopting certain methods and techniques of research.

If behind the presentation of apparently "raw data" lie certain theoretical attitudes, the converse is also true: there are empirical reasons for the selection of certain ways of working. Scholars find certain ways of working and thinking about landscape normal and natural, in part because their everyday field habits and day-to-day experience of working with different forms of archaeological and documentary material lead them in that direction. We might comment that if the data are theory-laden, then theories are also data-laden — their form is constrained by the empirical phenomena they are seeking to explain.

Selecting a Landscape

I return to the Romantic notion of emotional kinship, that we are "linked in feeling" to "our" historic forebears as we tramp across the countryside or stand amongst the humps and bumps of a medieval village. Such an idea is not simply a theoretical proposition in the abstract. It was encouraged, even turned into a taken-for-granted fact, not simply by theoretical fancy but by the empirical realities of doing landscape archaeology. This process began right at the start of the research process, in other words at the moment of selection of a particular area to study.

In North America, this selection of an area to study is constrained in part by the sheer scale of the terrain. Stand in the middle of the desert of the American Southwest and the need for techniques such as random sampling becomes all too clear — an archaeologist seeking to follow the Crawford/Hoskins method of building up an intimate knowledge of a small area of landscape would rapidly find him or herself knowing about a tiny, even utterly insignificant, piece of territory, without the density of traces of past human settlement to produce a meaningful account or narrative on that scale. Perhaps more fundamentally, many if not most of the political boundaries that run across such territory — between different states, or between federal and privately owned land — are largely contingent, being laid out as part of 19th-century Anglo settlement of the area, and manifestly unconnected to past historical traditions of Native American cultures.

Further, there is a relative lack of obvious political or territorial boundaries running across this terrain. Sites reveal themselves in the main as scatters of dots within a "blank" terrain. Some have argued that this perception was itself partly ideological, that it reflects the doctrine of *terra nullius* discussed above. Thus, "Anasazi" sites (Anasazi of course meaning "the vanished ones") were treated as effectively prehistoric, occupying a space in a blank space/time matrix rather than being Ancestral Pueblo places that were part of a continuing tradition that is also materialized by the rituals and practices of contemporary indigenous peoples. Ancestral Pueblo sites were also frequently linked by roads, paths, and trackways. However, it is undeniable that it is less obvious or intuitive to see the North American pre-contact landscape as divided up into entities comparable to the medieval parish, township, and manor.

In England, by contrast, the "natural" unit of analysis of landscape is often one defined by pre-existing political and ecclesiastical boundaries. These boundaries are familiar to both the scholar and the modern inhabitant of the landscape. Moreover, they have often existed spatially in their modern form for a thousand years and more – the parish, the township, the hundred, the county. These units are habitually used as the basic unit for selecting a region to study. The use of sample squares or "random" selection of areas for study at a regional level is almost unknown in historic landscape archaeology in England or indeed Europe. These pre-existing boundaries have a long and complex history. Many were set up at some point in the first millennium A.D., as the basic structures of ecclesiastical and political administration were created, though these in their turn often followed both natural and humanly made features of much older date. The reintroduction and spread of Christianity brought parish and diocesan boundaries in its wake as the early Church sought to impose an order and structure on people's religious experience, while the territorial and subsequently feudal political organization of the Middle Ages brought the boundaries defining the edges of townships, manors, hundreds, counties, and so on.

Scholars have engaged in complex and often tortured arguments about the antiquity of these boundaries (Griffiths 2003). Both Hoskins and Crawford devoted much time to the discussion and elucidation of Anglo-Saxon estates, taking the contemporary written descriptions of them to be found in charters and retracing these through the physical action of walking the boundaries, looking for the landmarks – barrows, hills, woodland – mentioned by the Anglo-Saxon writer of the charter. It is clear now that many political and territorial boundaries have their origins in the Roman period, while others may well be of prehistoric origin or at the very least follow the lines of prehistoric features such as roadways and defensive ditches. That debate need not detain us here. What is important about these very long-lasting and ancient boundaries is that they often came to define civil and ecclesiastical administration, as well as the identity and self-perception of modern communities.

These boundaries are more than merely physical: they also classify and condition the documentary record. Most historical documents are organized and classified place by place, parish by parish for example, rather than distributed across a "neutral" spatial grid. These documentary materials are not simply the ramblings of the literate elite: although often drawn up by those in the upper echelons of society, they often bear very directly on the lives and experiences of people of all social classes (Tate 1969). If I want to study, for example, the archaeology of 17th-century agricultural practices, then an obvious source of documentary information is going to be the wills and inventories of 17th-century farmers, which list personal possessions such as farm tools, horses and oxen, and harvested crops. But such inventories are classified by parish; they are listed in indexes by their parish name – often the original document will not even contain any clue as to which farmstead or specific location in the landscape it relates to. It is methodologically intuitive and even easy to use such material to compare this parish with that parish, or this group of communities with that group of communities, but conversely counter-intuitive and methodologically very difficult to compare this arbitrarily defined and/or randomly selected square with that one.

The record offices where these documents are stored are themselves part of local and national government, and as such themselves often relate to political entities of medieval or earlier origin – "Hampshire Record Office," "Archives of the Diocese of Lincoln." The relationships generating the documents under study could be quite complex and are themselves worthy of attention. Thus, for example, farmers who died in the county of Suffolk needed to be of a certain wealth level to require their wills and probate records to be "proved" or legally certified. According to how wealthy they were, this would be done at a church court in Bury St Edmunds or Ipswich, a court in the diocesan capital of Norwich, or in the London courts. A researcher has to have the training and experience to be aware of this, and to rethink the thoughts of the 17th-century Church administrators, if he or she is to conduct systematic research into this area, starting with visits to the four different offices.

These record offices are often the first port of call for a researcher starting work in an area; one of the best ways to start a project is to get talking with their staff, who are often invaluable sources of local "inside knowledge." The information stored in such record offices is not simply documentary. Lists of local historic buildings are kept, for example; it is a statutory requirement that all buildings still standing in a reasonable state and dating from before 1700, as well as buildings of "architectural merit" from later periods, have a description on file. Similarly, sites and monuments records are classified by county and locality as well as by grid reference (Tiller 1992).

The theoretical implications of this organization of empirical material are profound. A landscape archaeologist setting out to study "the landscape of Devon" or "Babergh hundred" or "the parishes north of

Wansdyke" is not selecting a neutral or arbitrarily defined area. He or she is already "linked in feeling" with the medieval and post-medieval past, as important elements of the framing of the material and the perceived landscape are shared between scholar and object of study. And when he or she comes to the task of ferreting out relevant documentary information, how much more convenient it is to search through the materials parish by parish rather than a more arbitrarily defined area.

The structures of knowledge and power of which these units are artefacts, then, are taken not as cultural creations to be studied, but as "obvious" and "self-evident" in their meanings. The way Maya or Ancestral Pueblo cosmology was mapped on to the landscape clearly needs to be explicated to an academic audience. (Such a statement clearly raises ethical and ideological issues of the academic study of the archaeology and history of indigenous peoples, which will be discussed in Chapter 6.) However, in the post-war view of the English landscape "everybody knows" about villages, fields, and churches and the way they work, and hence for example that the parish, ostensibly a religious entity, was also and continues to be a political one. Occasionally this assumption of familiarity led to problems in the early years of landscape archaeology, for example in the assumption that the term "vill" in early documents equated to a village, or that "wasta" or waste was in some sense unused or unexploited land.

Now there are some very obvious points to be made about parishes. First, they are of uneven size, and it is not easy to go to a convenient reference point to discover their size in terms of acres or hectares. As a result, quantification of, for example, density of sites between parish and parish can be very difficult to achieve. Second, their boundaries are wiggly, quite unlike the straight lines and grids of the North American surveyors in the 18th and 19th centuries (Linklater 2002). Each parish boundary is full of endless twists and turns, each one not quite like the next. Third, though parishes are ecclesiastical units, their boundaries may have been set up for a variety of non-religious reasons relating to politics, land ownership, economy, or topography. Fourth, they have a very long and often politically contingent history. This means that genuine comparisons between parish and parish in the way that might answer standard "processual" questions are very difficult. Relative density of settlement between parishes; survival rates of buildings and other landscape features; statistical measurement of nucleation versus dispersal – all of these questions are methodologically straightforward when dealing with the ideal of prehistoric sites scattered across a flat plain so beloved of the New Geography, but are very difficult when the material has already been divided into uneven and wiggly blocks.

So our landscape researcher has selected his or her area for study. The next task for the scholar is to look at the material itself. The documentary background characteristically will involve tax records, parish records, household inventories, wills, and a stack of other documentary material (Tate 1969; Currie 2004). To read this material, our researcher must have skills in palaeography. He or she will also find Latin useful, but not just classical Latin – many documents relating to feudal and Church administration in Europe, particularly before the Reformation, are written in variants of bureaucratic medieval Latin rather than the classical form. Studies of eastern Mediterranean historic landscapes have been hampered by the fact that not only are the relevant documents stored far away in the centre of the Ottoman empire, Istanbul, but they are written in a highly specialized bureaucratic language which only a handful of historians can understand (Faroghi 1999). Finally, some knowledge of place-names and their interpretation will be helpful – a particularly specialized area where specialists are not slow to highlight and condemn what they see as the "catastrophic misunderstandings" of archaeologists (Gelling 1997: unnumbered page).

An archaeologist will find the acquisition of these skills a difficult and time-consuming task, and he or she will find that the corpus of pre-existing scholarship in fields such as palaeography and "diplomatic" is exceptionally traditional in scope and approach. To take on the study of old documents is, very often, to take on a mindset that, for better or worse, is steeped in traditional values of learning for its own sake, is particularist in emphasis and outlook, and is averse to explicit discussion of theory of whatever kind. Consequently, the basic language and conceptual tool-set of the study of this material makes it very difficult to ask anthropological questions, in the sense of treating the past as another culture.

Landscapes of Patriarchy

A good example to illustrate the difficulty of taking an anthropological approach is that of patriarchy. It is an anthropological commonplace that male domination is not "normal" or "natural," but a problem to be studied in its own right (Moore 1988). We might expect, then, any discussion of the human relations embedded in the landscape to begin with questions of gender. Yet studies of the English landscape almost always take patriarchy as an accepted given. Thus, it is taken for granted in most discussions of this material that the head of household is normally male. When "landlord–tenant relations" are discussed, the gendering of both as male is assumed rather than argued through. Take the following definitions of specialist terms, taken at random from a standard "how-to" book on landscape history:

> Manor. An estate held by a landlord . . . who himself was a tenant of the Crown or of a mesne lord . . . The lord of the manor retained part of the land, called demesne, for his own use, while the rest was tenanted or else used for common or waste . . .

> Bondage. A service given by a tenant to his lord as an obligation of his tenure.

> Service. A general term for a duty, obligation or due resulting from a tenant's occupancy of land or buildings belonging to a manorial lord . . . [a tenant] might also pay various other dues, such as a fine when his daughter married, or when his son went to school. (Richardson 1986:34, 49, 51)

Only occasionally do gender relations emerge in such discussions as problematic, and then they are characteristically seen in terms that take as granted the male perspective: "Childwite. A fine paid for fathering an illegitimate child. The fine was regarded by the lord of the manor as compensation for cheapening the value of the woman to the manor" (Richardson 1986:49).

When the landscape historian then takes the pattern of thinking embedded in such terms and makes an apparently straightforward, descriptive, atheoretical statement about the past, active agency is seamlessly transferred to the world of men by "common-sense" assumption. This does not mean that individual women are absent from such an account, or that historical study of women's lives in the English countryside has been absent (see for example Hanawalt 1986, Bennett 1996, and Olson 2003, and from earlier generations Stenton 1957 and Power 1924). But it does mean, as a generation of feminists has pointed out, that constructions of patriarchy tend to be the accepted backdrop against which historical studies of men's and women's agencies are played out, rather than being contingent structures that are made and remade by that agency (see for example Jardine 1996).

I would argue that attempts at social reconstruction in the historic landscape often suffer from an impoverished notion of power, not just in terms of gender, but along other social and cultural dimensions as well. Historical archaeologists see power in the landscape, but almost exclusively in juridical, rather than social, terms. To put it another way, discussions of power and conflict in the landscape are full of references to legal obligations and duties of tenure, service, rent, and so on. This is hardly surprising, in that the documentary evidence is by definition a series of legal documents and records detailing people's formal obligations and imposing sanctions when those obligations are not met (see Faith 1997). Much effort has been spent in using these juridical records to reconstruct patterns of "multiple estates" (Jones 1971) and in exploring lordship as "the power to command goods and services from the population of an area" (Faith 1997:10).

All these aspects are of course of the utmost importance. However, power in the landscape was, self-evidently, much more than juridical or legal in two senses. In the first place, "Lordship," in reality, was a whole series of social practices ranging from the military and economic through to the social and even the theatrical, in the sense of the staging and presentation of social status; warfare, with religion the central component of feudal ideology, embraced all these spheres (Johnson 2002: 12–14). What made somebody a lord, and what maintained the lord in that social position, were not simply legal sanctions backed explicitly or implicitly by force, but also their self-presentation through dress, the architecture of their dwelling, and so on, and the "lordly" activities they engaged in such as riding and hunting. Second, a juridical notion of power tends to concentrate on the apex of society. A recent book on "the archaeology of power" discusses palaces, great churches and civic buildings, and town walls and halls; yet the everyday exercise of power, for example between husband and wife within and outside the walls of the peasant house, is not mentioned (Steane 2001). Power is exercised in the most mundane transaction between people of the most humble social level. It extends right through any social structure, from the actions of a king down to the everyday habits of husband and wife, father and child, master and servant. To take one of many examples: using ethnographic data, Nadia Seremmatakis (1991) has explored how, in the southern Peloponnese area of Greece, the construction of the landscape was gendered: women built walls and cairns as an active strategy in the construction of male and female domains. It is difficult to see how such a subtle making of the landscape can be captured through a juridical account.

The basic vocabulary of landscape history is also compounded by the traditional use of sexist language. The critique of such usage (Spender 1980; Dunant 1993) is now well established and need not be repeated here; only the most traditional and unreflective accounts (of which it has to be said there are a still a few in landscape history and archaeology) still use "man" and "he" to refer to all humans. What is interesting here is that, in this area, the reasons for the sexist use of language are not simply philosophical or political. Rather, the historical reasons for the evolution of such language lie, in part, in the very fabric of the perceived make-up of the English landscape and the constitution of property and other rules concerning it.

English "common law," which dates back to the first millennium A.D., states that the husband and wife are one, and the one is the husband. It takes as a given the unit of the household, and that the head of that household is male. Behind this bald yet ambiguous assumption lies a great deal of complexity; historians have shown how, in terms of the transmission of property between generations, there was great variability in practice between different households and regions. It has also been suggested that the medieval and early modern periods saw a conflict and fusion between different forms of law, from which "common law" (and with it the subordination of women's property and other rights) emerged victorious. It is these historically contingent processes, wrapped up as they are with power over the landscape and over other human beings, that form part of the story of landscape evolution, and which should be part of any story of landscape change in the medieval and early modern periods. It is a story that has been told by Amy Erickson (1993), and which has implications for our understanding of activities in the landscape at a very basic interpretative level. For example, concepts and definitions of "housework," and its definition as non-productive and private in relation to productive and public (male) labour outside the house and in the fields, only emerged at the end of the 17th century; yet such a classification underpins the driest, most descriptive statement made by modern scholars about what does or does not constitute productive activity, for example farming, in the past (McKeon 1992:299). The feminist critique of such relations and insistence that they are historically changing is hardly new (Myrdal and Klein 1956 is one influential early study; see also Sinfield 1989: 201–9, and Graham 1997 for women's work in the fields). Yet, rather than look at the landscape in terms of this struggle, traditional landscape archaeology and history tends to take the common-law view as natural and given.

The end result of all these researches is that the unwary archaeological researcher is caught up, like a fly in a spider's web, in the traces of the cognitive world that produced these documents. The Romantic "emotional kinship" with the medieval peasant is in this sense not an overarching theoretical concept or ethereal ideology but a hard, practical, working reality for someone engaged in this research. As a result, the grain of the material, and of the secondary scholarship one must master in order to understand it, leads one to take for granted rather than set up as a problem the social relations and practices that created it. An anthropological approach to English historic landscapes, in the North American sense of the term, is thus very difficult.

It should be noted that much of the discussion above is only partly or arguably true for the prehistorian. The parish and other boundaries in the landscape may have some relevance, particularly where they can be taken as evidence of much earlier territorial units or where they follow prehistoric linear earthworks. However, this link may well be tenuous and have to be argued through rather than being self-evident.

To summarize thus far: ideas of empiricism, of common sense, and emotional kinship are deeply embedded in the discourse and habits of thinking of English landscape archaeology of historic periods. I have tried to show how these ideas impose theoretical restrictions on the construction of new forms of knowledge of historic landscapes. I will now turn to two case studies, to show how, in practical terms, we have come to be able to say less and less that is meaningful about historic landscape archaeology.

The Origins of the English Village

The classic example of the taphonomic retreat is that of the debate over the origins of the medieval English village. One of the key achievements of Hoskins's generation, particularly in the immediate post-war period, was to identify, classify, and interpret the remains of literally thousands of deserted settlements in the English landscape. Field visits, air photography, and documentary research by Maurice Beresford (1956) showed up the number and extent of these deserted settlements. Regional survey and identification of sites – not only villages, but also their attendant field systems, as well as hamlets, moated sites, and other elements of the medieval landscape – was a core preoccupation of English landscape archaeologists from the 1950s onwards. At first, this fieldwork was undertaken through a series of disparate groups, which eventually coalesced into the Medieval Settlement Research Group (Gerrard 2003).

In the 1940s and 1950s archaeological study of the village involved identifying these thousands of sites, surveying and classifying their features, and equating them with words or phrases "known" from the documents. "Tofts," "crofts," "messuages," "tenements," and "manorial sites" were all identified in the humps and bumps that were recognized as deserted village sites during this period. Most (though not all) "parish churches" survived as standing and functioning buildings and thus needed no fieldwork to identify, but slotted into this pattern alongside the other elements with a ready-made historical tag. The ridge-and-furrow earthworks in the fields beyond were similarly equated with the strips in the medieval open fields (Beresford 1948). At the time, this exercise was conceived of as a technically difficult but theoretically commonsensical one of attaching historical labels to archaeological features (Beresford and Hurst 1971). However, I suggest that these labels are actually what Binford might call middle-range propositions. That is, they related patterning in the archaeological record in the present, on the one hand, to inferred dynamics or activities in the past, on the other.

Much of the development of the study of medieval villages was hammered out through a single project – the survey and excavation of a single medieval village and its context. Wharram Percy is a deserted medieval village on the Yorkshire Wolds in northern England (Figure 4.10). It was first studied and excavated in 1950–1 by Maurice Beresford, who shared Hoskins's profile of a trained economic historian with landscape interests, and who with his students dug into the tofts in order to demonstrate that the site was indeed a medieval village and to attempt to date its desertion. The involvement of a trained archaeologist, John Hurst, changed the excavation methodology and broadened the aims at Wharram to look at the life of medieval peasant farmers as a whole. Through the 1960s and 1970s the aims of the project broadened still further – into an exploration of the village and landscape as a whole, including the church, burial ground, dam, and mill, and the evolution of the landscape before and after the Middle Ages (hence the change in title from Wharram Percy, its name during the Middle Ages, to the more "neutral" and multi-period Wharram: Beresford and Hurst 1990).

For forty years a large number of volunteers (over a hundred people at its height) would descend on Wharram for a period of three weeks each summer. The project became an institution, whose social history is an important element in understanding the development of medieval archaeology – many archaeologists, including myself, took part in the Wharram project at different stages of their career and were profoundly influenced by the experience; a quarter of a century on, the kindness of the Wharram community is still very fresh in my mind. It is important to understand that the Wharram community of archaeologists was a

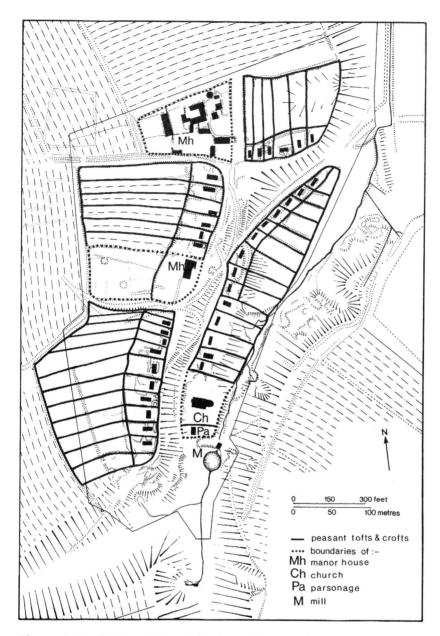

Figure 4.10 Hachured plan of the deserted village of Wharram Percy, with the "grid" highlighted (after Beresford and Hurst 1990)

close and mutually supportive one, in part conditioned by the rather isolated location of the site – close intellectual and personal relationships were formed over evening walks around the village and to neighbouring sites, or on the long walks to and from the local pub.

The intellectual history of Wharram, as has been made clear by Beresford and Hurst, has been one of increasing questioning of the easy assumptions and interpretations that were made at the start of the project. The pattern of three-week field seasons followed by eleven months of thought, plus the very long timescale of the project, meant that Wharram's story became that of the intellectual development of historic landscape archaeology writ small. It is a commonplace to note that the initial excavations at Wharram started with largely historical questions in mind to do with the date of desertion, but rapidly broadened out into a wider study of peasant house forms and patterns of life. However, although wider questions were raised, it is not at all clear that they were answered.

At the outset, a simple view of village development was assumed. Wharram village had grown up around the area of the church, and extended outwards from this single focus. Excavations rapidly showed that such a single initial focus did not exist. Instead, the process of nucleation at Wharram seems to have developed out of a dispersed landscape. The formation of the grid of peasant tenements (Figure 4.10) gives every indication of having been a single episode in the life of the community. However, as Chris Taylor indicates (1992:9), it is still an open question as to what the social processes were behind this episode.

So there was a retreat into uncertainty over settlement evolution at Wharram, just as there was in the study of medieval rural settlement in general. Hoskins himself came to see this, observing gloomily that the archaeological discovery of settlement evidence simply meant that "more problems have been raised than solved" (Hoskins 1979:157). Perhaps the wittiest and most perceptive account of this retreat was Chris Taylor's account of his researches into the origins of the village he lived in at the time. Albeit on a much smaller scale than Wharram, here was the Hoskins/Crawford method par excellence: an intensive study combining documentary, fieldwalking, and map information, carried out by a local inhabitant. Yet, in Taylor's account the study seemed to go backwards: from a clear understanding and a simple model of settlement evolution, Taylor's view of the village became more and more qualified. The article ends not with a conclusion but with a best guess, itself contradicted in the final line of the paper by fresh discoveries (Taylor 1989:226).

Increasing Uncertainty

What Taylor was finding, I suggest, was that the easy middle-range links between traces on the ground and processes in the past could not so easily be assumed. This story can be repeated over and over again in landscape archaeology. Here are four middle-range links that have been increasingly questioned over the last thirty years:

Moated sites equate to the sites of manors, or of secondary settlement. The phenomenon of moated sites, and their medieval date, was recognized very early on. Many moats were seen as straightforward artefacts or relics of "manorial" sites. Where there was no documentary reference, and/or where the moat was at or near the parish boundary, the moat would be seen as a farmstead of more humble origins, established as part of the expansion of medieval rural settlement in the 12th and 13th centuries (Aberg 1978). However, in the decades since, it has been shown that these explanations are too simple. Many moats do not seem to have had attached dwellings at all, or to have had buildings of any kind on or adjacent to them. In other cases, the dynamic and easy assumption of "secondary settlement" has been questioned. In short, we can engage in a field identification of the monument, but what it means is now much less clear.

Place-names can be dated and equated with distinct ethnic migrations/historical events. Traditionally, the end of Roman Britain and the succeeding archaeology and history of the early Middle Ages was told in terms of successive waves of ethnic migration (Anglo-Saxon, Scandinavian, Norman). The influence and extent of these migrations, it was held, could be seen through the presence or absence of ethnically distinct place-names in an area. Conversely, an individual settlement could be dated by reference to the ethnic ascription of its place-name. Thus, for example, *-ingas* names were held to be indicative of early phases of Anglo-Saxon settlement, while the name Swaffham might be equated with the Suebi, thought to be Germanic mercenaries in late Roman Britain (Hills 1979; Myres 1986). There is no doubt that at a very broad level place-names do tell us something about the nature and history of settlement: the predominance of, for example, Scandinavian place-names (*-thwaite, -thorpe, -side*) in upland areas of the north of England is clearly telling us something. However, it is equally clear that the simple equation made by earlier scholars between place-name, ethnic group, and date of settlement simply does not work, as Hoskins himself realized towards the end of his career: he noted in one of his latest published pieces that "we used to have a more or less standard account of the evolution of villages in this country" but that the demolition of place-name evidence in particular had left "everything in a state of flux" (Hoskins 1979:157; see also Gelling 1997; Gelling and Cole 2000; Hills 2003:54–5). Roberts and Wrathmell comment that "there are often indications that a given word may change its meaning during its period of use" (2002:21), while Hooke comments that "confidence in a chronology of place-names has steadily been eroded" (1997:27). Place-names continue to be an invaluable source of information, particularly in the topographical information they provide (Gelling and Cole 2000). However, another middle-range link between present and past has been shown to be fallible.

The size and appearance of churches is a reflection of the size of the settlement/community they served. The classic instance was the series of plans of Wharram church, which appeared to grow and then contract in size as the settlement around it grew and contracted. Church archaeologists, however, became more and more aware that there was no direct link between size of church and size of settlement. This was because church building and rebuilding often had more to do with the level of wealth of particular individuals within the parish, and their inclination to pour money into church fabric, or with liturgical factors. Thus, the vast naves and towers of the famous "wool churches" of late medieval Norfolk actually served settlements that were much smaller in population size than those of earlier centuries. As Hoskins himself noted (1983:87), the form of churches is testament to the fortunes of sheep farming and of the cloth industry and has no direct link to population growth and contraction (Morris 1989).

There is a correlation between population density and different landscape types. Tom Williamson has reviewed the evidence for such a supposed link and concluded that "in spite of what is still often asserted, there is no correlation between variations in population density, and the distribution of different forms of field system or settlement . . . this lack of correlation is, to say the least, surprising"; for example, in documentary records such as Domesday Book, there is "little obvious relationship between [population and] recorded densities of woodland" (2003:35, 56).

This steady lessening of confidence in our ability to interrogate the archaeological record in a way that leads to inferences about the past was summed up in a brilliant, and to my mind under-acknowledged, article by Christopher Taylor (1992). Taylor drew on his lifetime's experience in the study of medieval settlements to trace a pattern of early intellectual confidence in a model of medieval landscape which opened with Anglo-Saxon migration from Continental Europe, followed by expansion, culminating in the mid-14th-century crisis and the phenomenon of desertion – the model which in broad terms was conveyed by Hoskins. Taylor then traced the steady abandonment of belief in this model as excavations at Wharram, Riseholme, and other sites failed to find evidence of Anglo-Saxon cores. He concludes:

> The last 30 years' work in medieval rural settlement in England has not produced any clear pattern. Indeed, matters have become increasingly complex and confused. Nowhere is this more clearly demonstrated than in the late Saxon to early medieval period. All the recent work now seems to indicate that the English landscape was torn apart at this time and largely rebuilt over a period of perhaps 300 years. However . . . there remains one more basic problem which at the moment appears to be insoluble. This is the understanding of the mechanism by which all the changes to the landscape at this time were actually effected . . . how, in detail, nucleation was achieved, settlements replanned and even field systems reorganised, remains quite unknown. Archaeology, as always, is useful in explaining what kinds of changes to settlement occurred and when, but not why, how and especially by whom they were carried out. Historians in the last few years have attempted to tackle this problem but have come up with no agreed solution. All that has developed is a politically influenced dialogue between historians whose understanding of past societies is inevitably coloured by their own and contemporary society's attitudes and perceptions. (Taylor 1992:9; see also Taylor 2000)

Taylor's article ends with a great surprise. Having detailed precisely how and why we have reached an intellectual dead end in the study of the medieval village, he gives five case studies to show how quickly ideas can change. The article then simply finishes. I remember reading it for the first time and turning the page, expecting to find a set of suggestions for the future to complement the masterly demolition of existing models given in the first part, and finding instead . . . the title page of the next article. In my view, Taylor's despair at the excellence of the techniques we have so lovingly assembled to understand the landscape (the map, the hachured plan, the air photograph), coupled with our growing inability to use these techniques to tell a coherent and convincing story about the medieval landscape, parallels Lewis Binford's complaint about paradigmatic debates, and Dr Syntax's worried scrutiny of the uninforming sign.

Confirmation of Taylor's gloomy views came five years later with the publication of *Village, Hamlet and Field* (Lewis et al. 1997). This was a closely argued, scholarly report on a study of the east Midlands landscape, with the central research question of understanding the processes that lay behind and accounted for the present pattern of nucleated versus dispersed patterns of settlement. The scholarship was detailed and careful, and the amassing of documentary and archaeological evidence was to the highest standard. The observation, for example, that there were areas of dispersed settlement within otherwise "nucleated" areas was a valuable refinement of our picture of patterns in the present. Yet it was difficult to see the link between these observations and a new understanding of processes in the past. At the end of the exercise the reader was no wiser as to the *causes* and underlying *processes* of settlement variation than before. Population rise, commerce, dependence on arable farming, "territorial friction," lordship, were all cited as part of a "model," but how these related to each other was unclear and there was occasionally a statement of the obvious: "the precise form that villages took had a basis in ideas and attitudes – contemporaries planned and constructed villages according to clear notions of what a village should be" (Lewis et al. 1997:233). Tom Williamson commented that in this study "the principal explanations for settlement nucleation . . . remained much as in earlier studies" (2003:17).

Studies in this genre are held back in their attempt to explain landscape variation not by the care with which they amass evidence, but by the same theoretical gap that we observed in both Wordsworth and Hoskins. Wordsworth tramped across the fells, observed the landscape, and just gathered it up into his heart and produced a poem. Hoskins tramped across Devon and Leicestershire, pored over the Ordnance Survey map, gathered up his observations and wrote a historical narrative. Contemporary landscape archaeologists walk the fields, gather scatters of pottery, prepare hachured plans of earthworks, collate the sites and monuments record, and then gather this material up and expect it to become an understanding of past processes. The link is unexamined, then, between the settlement remains observed in the present and the processes archaeologists were trying to infer or understand in the past. Lewis et al. see much more clearly than many of their contemporaries that such links need to be made when they write: "The settlement is an artefact which gives us some help in understanding medieval ideas and culture. The more regularly planned villages indicate an ordered society, anxious to measure and allocate land rationally, yet the wandering lanes and irregularly arranged tofts in both nucleated and dispersed settlements, speak of a distinct approach to the organisation of space, and a different balance between private and public access to resources" (Lewis et al. 1997:8). However, these links are not obvious or self-evident at all: each phrase in this quotation is a middle-range link that can be questioned. Regularity does not necessarily imply planning; rationality is not necessarily the same as measurement; "private" and "public" are modern concepts that are not unproblematic in their application to the early Middle Ages; and so on.

The many amateurs on extramural classes, and the willing volunteers of Wharram, are the Grizzles of landscape archaeology. They have borne the brunt of the work; they have carried their masters hither and thither. But whether at the end of this we have moved progressively forward to a better understanding of past landscapes is another matter.

The Great Rebuilding

A second classic case of the taphonomic retreat is the post-war history of vernacular architecture studies. Studies of vernacular architecture went back to the pioneering work of S. O. Addy (1898) and Innocent (1916), but the post-war period saw a rise in studies of vernacular buildings that paralleled that in studies of historic landscapes as a whole. Much of this work, again, was carried out by enthusiastic amateurs, though the survey of occupied buildings meant that the muddy boots had to be left at the door.

Hoskins himself gave intellectual shape and theme to this emergent field of interest with a key 1953 article in *Past and Present* entitled "The Rebuilding of Rural England 1570–1640." He asserted that

> between the accession of Elizabeth I and the outbreak of the Civil War [that is *c*.1560–1640], there occurred in England a revolution in the housing of a considerable part of the population . . . There was, first, the physical rebuilding or substantial modernisation of the medieval houses that had come down from the past: and there was, almost simultaneously, a remarkable increase in household furnishings and equipment.

To prove his thesis, Hoskins looked at evidence for rural housing county by county, and used a combination of evidence from different sources. The physical evidence of surviving houses was cited county by county, from Cornwall to Lancashire and from Herefordshire across to Suffolk (1953:44, 48; see also Figure 4.11). Hoskins also cited the evidence of probate inventories, indicating wealth levels, movable goods, and house size. Finally, Hoskins cited a series of contemporary commentators. The most notable of these was William Harrison's comments on housing standards and levels of furnishings.

Figure 4.11 Hoskins's photograph from *The Making of the English Landscape*, intended to illustrate the Great Rebuilding. The caption reads: "Colly Weston: Northamptonshire. Like a great number of English villages, Colly Weston was largely rebuilt in the late sixteenth century and the early seventeenth. Above is shown a typical yeoman's house of about 1620, built of the local oolitic limestone and roofed with the famous Colly Weston stone slates." (Hoskins 1955:120)

What were the causes of this rebuilding? Hoskins cited population rise and a rise in wealth levels among "the bigger husbandmen, the yeomen, and the lesser gentry" (1953:55). From 1540 onwards this group was in the happy position of having fixed expenses and rising selling prices for their agricultural produce. More fundamentally, Hoskins alluded to a growing sense of privacy that had its origins in the Renaissance and which filtered down the social scale to middling groups.

The "Great Rebuilding Thesis" rapidly became accepted as a coherent story. It stood as a national narrative alongside a plethora of more detailed regional studies. The model for these was Sir Cyril Fox and Lord Raglan's three-volume opus *Monmouthshire Houses* (Fox and Raglan 1951), which came to represent a kind of template for the execution of a regional study of vernacular architecture – select an area, more often than not a county; record a selection of standing vernacular buildings within it, often through the local amateur or extramural group or the Royal Commission on Historical Monuments; discuss with reference to appropriate documentary material, most obviously probate inventories; and write up in a narrative mode with attendant gazetteer giving the "raw data" in the form of a house-by-house inventory (see for example Pearson 1985; Alcock 1993; Smith 1993). This work was ideal for extramural classes and other amateur groups meeting at weekends, coordinated by a tutor who was often a committed, charismatic, and inspiring figure, and some of the volumes resulting from such work are classics (for example Machin 1978; Harrison and Hutton 1984). So, as with studies of the landscape, regional studies complemented the national picture; each could not be made sense of without reference to the other (Johnson 1994).

Over the next thirty years, vernacular architectural studies underwent a taphonomic retreat. In this case, the easy assumption to be questioned was that impressionistic assessments of numbers of houses of particular dates as seen in visits to the countryside, or (apocryphally) as seen from the window of Hoskins's train travelling across the English Midlands from Leicester to Exeter, automatically equated to phases of building and rebuilding in the past.

There are several problems with such a position. In the first place, Hoskins's data (and the data of many succeeding scholars) were never rigorously quantified. Hoskins's original article is made up of a series of qualitative statements, county by county – "a great number of examples" in the south-west while "the evidence is . . . striking" for Essex and Suffolk, in each cased backed up by references to odd houses and localities. This, as we have seen, is the use of anecdote: a standard mode of agreement in landscape archaeology; empirical in the sense that masses of data are cited, yet unverifiable in that no rigorous quantification is ever attempted. Such a quantification is actually quite easy to do. As mentioned earlier, it is a statutory duty of local authorities to compile and maintain lists of buildings of architectural merit, in particular of all buildings dating from before $c.1700$ and still in reasonable condition. These lists are available for consultation in any local record office. At the same time, there are various records from which the number of houses standing at particular moments in the past may be estimated. Most obviously, the hearth tax returns of the 1670s list how many houses stood in a parish, and how many hearths each house had. Problems and biases exist with these lists: the modern lists can often vary according to the whim of the researcher and do not always reflect a fully rigorous internal survey of the building, while earlier tax records were not always accurate, for example for reasons of the corruption of officials (Husbands 1985). However, the central point remains that an estimate, however rough, of relative survival rates of buildings and how these vary from locality to locality can be easily made. Yet such a task has rarely been attempted: scholars of vernacular architecture rightly prize the craft of detailed observation and survey of a building, and expend great time and effort in this craft, yet show much less concern in assessing the historical value in terms of what New Archaeologists would term the variability of the information so carefully gathered.

As a result, the basis for Hoskins's proposition, and the basis for a subsequent generation of regional studies in vernacular architecture, is highly questionable. I have argued elsewhere (Johnson 1993a) that one of the reasons it was so readily accepted was that it fitted in with the emerging historical orthodoxy of the dates. Hoskins's dates for the Great Rebuilding were, whether by chance or design, coincidental with the great socialist historian Richard Tawney's dates for the rise of the gentry classes in early modern England (Tawney 1941). The work of the Marxist Christopher Hill and others from the 1950s onwards established the idea of the English Civil War of the 1640s as the "English Revolution," that is, a bourgeois revolution led by the "middling sort" akin to the French Revolution over a century later (Hill 1964). As a result, interpretations of the preceding period which stressed the rise of the yeoman and gentry classes, and in particular their growing economic power and cultural and political self-confidence, "fitted in" to the prevailing historical orthodoxy. Hoskins's choice of the journal *Past and Present* was surely no accident: *Past and Present* had been founded by this group of Marxist historians and wore its political colours in its subtitle, "a journal of scientific history," an orientation and subtitle abandoned after 1958 (Elliott 1999).

Of course, when the Marxist view of the English Revolution came under attack by "revisionist" historians from the 1970s onwards, this revision left the thesis of the Great Rebuilding vulnerable. It is not a coincidence, I think, that the first serious questioning of Hoskins's thesis came in 1977 when Robert Machin reassessed the numbers of dated houses. Machin found that if we were to define such a rebuilding, its peak should rather be towards the end of the 17th century. Interestingly, his conclusion was arguably prefigured by Hoskins himself. In a passing comment on Exeter, he notes that "the opening up of brickfields in St Sidwell's parish by 1690 probably reflects what must have been a building boom in the closing year[s] of the century" (Hoskins 1957:xiii); while on a visit in 1964 to a medieval cruck-framed house being demolished under archaeological supervision, he commented that the numbers of such medieval houses must be higher than he had postulated (David Hinton, personal communication; the archaeological investigation of the house was subsequently published in Hinton 1967). However, Machin's conclusion was rather that instead of a thesis of a Great Rebuilding at some specific period, we require a theory of building history which will explain . . . the Medieval preference for impermanent building, the emergence of permanent vernacular building in the 15th century, its extension and the successive rebuildings of vernacular houses from the late 16th to the early 18th centuries, and the replacement of vernacular by "polite" or "pattern-book" architecture in the mid 18th century. (Machin 1977:56)

The revisionist rolling back continued in 1988 when Christopher Currie modelled the attrition rate by fire on housing in a Cambridgeshire village, working from documentary records, and used these data to question the entire basis of the Hoskins-derived method of mapping waves of rebuilding in the countryside: "small differences in attrition rates can mean dramatic differences in final survival . . . Apparent waves of rebuilding may be illusory. The richest areas may have the fewest old houses. The earliest surviving houses in an area may not have differed significantly in construction and quality from their lost contemporaries and predecessors" (Currie 1988:6).

I am arguing here that the debate over the Great Rebuilding is another instance of the taphonomic retreat. In this case, the middle-range assumption made by Hoskins and his contemporaries was that the survival in the present of large numbers of houses of a given date in a given region could be used to infer past processes – wealth levels or other social and economic processes at work at the time of their construction. Currie's work in particular showed that such a link did not necessarily work.

Conclusion

The landscape archaeology of medieval and post-medieval England has given our picture of those periods much greater depth and detail. In many respects, it has made striking advances since the 1950s. Grenville Astill wrote in 1988: "the old landmarks do not seem so prominent – villages, particularly deserted ones, do not dominate the scene. The 'new' medieval countryside is a landscape: the settlements are still there, in a variety of forms – farms, hamlets and villages – but the fields which surround them, the tracks which join them and the buildings within them are much in focus" (Astill 1988:36). However, it has been less successful in its project of giving us a new picture of the patterns of human relationships and ways of life that created that landscape.

Instead, as Finberg so acutely observed (see Chapter 3), it has often been relegated to the role of an ancillary discipline to history. Forty years after Finberg made his damning comments, little has changed. His sentiment is repeated by Joan Thirsk, when she writes of landscape: "Historians retrieve this story through documents and archaeology, and sometimes artists assist them" (Thirsk 2000:22).

When the great Oxford historian Keith Thomas wrote a classic study of cultural attitudes to landscape, *Man and the Natural World*, he did not cite any landscape archaeologist, though he did make use of artefactual finds, such as witch-bottles, in his other work (Thomas 1983, 1971). A recent summary of medieval economic history (Hatcher and Bailey 2001) fails to mention a single piece of landscape archaeology; Wharram is not mentioned, and neither is any other deserted medieval village; not a single piece of ridge and furrow sullies its pages. A single footnote mentions one of Christopher Taylor's articles. The old injunction to the historians to get their boots muddy is here comprehensively ignored. What is worrying for the archaeologist is not that Hatcher and Bailey discount or denigrate their work, or seek to refute it, but that they get away with ignoring it. Hatcher and Bailey write as if all the surveys and excavations of the last fifty years had simply never happened.

Readers may disagree with the analysis offered here of why this is so, why it is that two commanding and well-respected figures in their field can get away with such an omission. However, they cannot deny that there is a problem here and an issue which historians and archaeologists need to confront. What should we do about it? That is the topic discussed in the next chapter.

Chapter Five

LANDSCAPE ARCHAEOLOGY TODAY

— What do you say, ploughman? How do you carry out your work?
— Oh, my lord, I work too hard. I go out at the crack of dawn to take the cattle to pasture, and I yoke them to the plough. No winter is so harsh, that I dare to hide at home, for fear of my master, but, the oxen yoked, share and coulter set on the plough, every day it is my duty to plough an entire field or more.
— Do you have anyone to help you?
— I have some boy, who herds the cattle with a prod, who is even somewhat hoarse from cold and shouting.
— What more do you do in the day?
— I certainly do more. I must fill the mangers of the oxen, give them water, and heave out the muck.
— Oh! Oh! What huge work!
— It certainly is huge work, since I'm not a free man.
From Ælfric's Colloquy (c.1005), 11. 1–35; translated from the Latin

Behind the evidence, whatever form it may take, one must strive to hear the men and women of the past talking and working, and creating what has come down to us.

(Hoskins 1967:184)

The last chapter concluded on a rather pessimistic note. The landscape archaeology of historic periods, it argued, has reached a point where it has less and less confidence in its ability to make meaningful statements about the past. That lack of confidence is shared by others, most notably traditional historians, for whom archaeology is often seen implicitly as an ancillary discipline.

However, I now want to turn the argument around. The Romantic legacy of Hoskins has carried with it certain intellectual flaws; but also and at the same time it continues to carry tremendous power, a power that can and should be harnessed in a reconstituted archaeology of historic landscapes. It might be possible to deconstruct the tradition in an intellectually pleasing fashion, but the fact remains that it does continue to inspire and motivate scholars, both professional and amateur. Arguably, it lies behind the personal and emotional inspiration for many archaeologists of all theoretical stripes. One of the most explicit discussions of personal motivation, Michael Shanks's *Experiencing the Past*, for example, is in many ways a classic piece of English Romanticism (Shanks 1992).

Complete rejection, then, is scarcely an option. In this chapter I will consider how to maintain and extend the best of the Hoskins tradition at the same time as moving it forward conceptually. I will further argue that, in the process, the English landscape tradition can break free of its rather insular and atheoretical perspective and contribute in a more explicit and exciting way to comparative and global debates about the constitution and perception of landscape. I will make this argument not by setting out a completely new theoretical agenda, but rather by demonstrating how many scholars working in this tradition are already aware of some of the issues raised in previous chapters and are working to address them in different ways, even if they might not accept the totality of the analysis offered here. Chris Taylor's critical evaluation (1992, 2000) was discussed in the last chapter; Tom Williamson has written that "our problem has not, for the most part, been a paucity of data. It has been our failure to interrogate it in the most effective way" (2003:27). My concern here is to place these various particular instances of work in the context of more general theoretical advances in our understanding of landscape.

I will take up Hoskins's injunction to listen to the men and women talking and working not in the last few lines of this volume but here, centre stage. I place at the centre of such an archaeology issues raised by the everyday experiences of ordinary human beings as they lived and worked in the landscape. Through their actions, humans constituted and reconstituted that landscape and left the material and documentary traces that we study. For these ordinary women and men, engagement with the landscape was hard work (Frantzen 1994). As such, it occupied a space that cannot be characterized either in terms of a modern definition of subsistence economics on the one hand, or as a "symbolic," disengaged experience on the other. It was hard work, in part, because practical engagement with the surrounding world is a social process. As a social process, it is situated in its time and to be understood in part within the values of its time; it is not one of a "real," commonsensical, modern "countryman's knowledge" nor of an "ideal" Wordsworthian aesthetics. We have seen how these two views, each apparently the obverse of the other, are actually complicit and fit together like lock and key. Not only should archaeologists reject the either/or of ideal and real; a stress on practice also leads understanding away from the false opposition between passive and active. People in the past were neither adaptive automata reacting blindly to either the requirements of soil types or the demands of the lord, nor were they the free (and implicitly masculine) agents of Romantic discourse. For Ælfric's peasant, his labour is hard work not just because of the length of time and the hardness of the labour, but because he is not a free man.

Fifty years ago New Archaeology, a movement that was strong in both North America and Britain but which achieved a more complete intellectual revolution in the former and in studies focusing on prehistory, outlined some very fundamental methodological advances in the field of archaeological research. New Archaeologists grouped their thinking around the themes of science – how we make our explanations better, more accurate and complete, not merely repetitive narratives in counterfeit history books – and anthropology – how we understand past cultures as functioning social systems that were different from our own (Leone 1972; Trigger 1989; Johnson 1999). I will consider the implications of "science" and "anthropology" in turn, before turning to the question of what such a specifically archaeological approach to historic landscapes might look like. Specific to such an approach will be the concepts of agency and practice, long familiar in other areas of archaeology, particularly prehistory, but hitherto rarely applied to historic landscapes.

Science

When New Archaeologists such as Lewis Binford (1962, 1964) and Kent Flannery (1976) in North America, and David Clarke (1968) in Britain, talked of the need to be "more scientific," they had, among other things, a very simple point in mind, a point concerned not with the amassing of facts, but rather with the relationship of those facts to interpretations. Archaeologists are adept at collecting evidence; we are very good at collecting surface scatters of pottery sherds or mapping humps and bumps. But how do we translate the material we collect into better understandings of the past, and how do we effectively evaluate one interpretation against another? And how do we then move forward, rather than simply maintaining a relative status quo in David Clarke's terms?

"Science" in this view is not about the use of impenetrable jargon, expensive machines, and white coats, and it is not about sacrificing what is best in the humanistic tradition. It is also most emphatically not about the amassing of facts or observations in themselves. The last chapter suggested that too often, in the wake of the Romantic tradition, landscape archaeologists had assembled their material in an inductive manner as a series of anecdotes or little stories. The nature of these anecdotes as case studies, and the extent to which they had a necessary or logical relationship to some wider argument, was rarely discussed. I made the point that the piling up of these anecdotes gave our stories an empirical sheen, in the sense of giving example after example. Each example was mired in mud and legitimated by the earthy feel of the Ordnance Survey map and the hachured plan rather than by airy-fairy theorizing, but it did not drive knowledge forward in the sense of developing better and better arguments. If we are to make the evidence we gather address our arguments about what that evidence means, we have to think through the link between data and theory in a rigorous and effective manner.

To do this, archaeologists must first have an understanding of variability – very basic questions of numbers, statistics, and proportions. As Margaret Spufford has noted with reference to local studies of "microhistory" (2000:xxii), we may have lovingly described our locality, but how do we know it is "typical"? How do we quantify what has survived – when we talk of there being "many examples" of this settlement type, how many exactly, and what proportion of this type as opposed to other settlement types? And what is a type anyway? When we talk of this area as "nucleated" and that area as "dispersed," what do we mean? How far is a selection of examples merely "innuendo," to quote Richard Morris's commendable frankness (1989:39)? Such a position is hinted at by Jones and Page (2003), who examine what they see as a "hybrid" landscape at Whittlewood in midland England; but I would extend their careful and cautionary discussion to a deeper level, to a questioning of the underlying concepts of region and landscape type itself. All too often the appeal is to the Romantic eye – just stand there and look long enough and carefully enough, and such commonsensical observational terms will make sense to you if you have acquired the right training and experience.

At the same time as historic landscape archaeology was developing the method outlined by Crawford and popularized by Hoskins into a set of concrete field projects, processual archaeology was developing a very different approach to the question of "regional field survey." It insisted that all survey was a form of sampling – that is, a decision about which data to collect. One of Lewis Binford's classic early papers defining the methodology of the New Archaeology concerned itself with field surveys. It insisted that "a cultural system is a set of constant or cyclically repetitive articulations between the social, technological, and ideological extrasomatic, adaptive means available to a human population," citing the anthropologist and proponent of cultural evolution Leslie White (White 1959; Binford 1964:425). To isolate such a cultural system, Binford proposed taking the "region" as a suitable sample area. However, Binford's "region" is utterly different from that of the English landscape tradition: it is the setting for a cultural system. Binford comments:

> As cultural systems become more complex, they generally span greater ecological ranges and enter into more complex, widespread, extrasocietal interaction. The isolation and definition of the *content*, the *structure*, and the *range* of a cultural system, together with its ecological relationships, may be viewed as a research objective. (Binford 1964:426; italics in the original)

It is difficult to think of a more different approach to the question of region and culture from that of Hoskins, both in content and in literary style.

What is interesting is that one can also tell the story of processual approaches in the 1970s and 1980s in terms of a taphonomic retreat. It was easy enough to insist on more robust links between data and theory, but much more difficult to actually create them in practice. However, it should be said in fairness that New Archaeologists recognized this problem and at least sought to understand what might be done about it. Michael Schiffer and his colleagues, for example, concluded in characteristically guarded terms that: "probabilistic sampling techniques (1) are not cost-effective under some field conditions, (2) do not facilitate cost-effective discovery or population estimation of rare or highly clustered elements, particularly small elements . . . but (3) do permit under favourable field conditions relatively good estimates to be made of nonclustered and abundant population elements" (Schiffer et al. 1978:1–2; references omitted). Models derived from cultural ecology such as optimal foraging theory and site catchment analysis were shown to be more complex than they appeared at first sight (Smith 1983; see also Sabloff and Ashmore 2001). Where early New Archaeology thought it could "read off" levels of social complexity from observation of settlement hierarchy, work rapidly showed that the objective definition of settlement hierarchy in the archaeological record was problematic. Attempts to randomly sample the landscape were shown to be fraught with problems: one "dummy" random sample, simulated across an area of the Valley of Mexico that had already been subjected to a complete survey, produced an alarming result: it managed to "miss" the largest and most stupendous site in the area, one that is arguably indispensable to any meaningful interpretation of the region, the city of Teotihuacán. Flannery (1976:132–5) discussed this apparent debacle, pointing out that its implications were more complex than simply a demonstration of the limitations of random samples; his carefully argued conclusion was not that random sampling should be abandoned, but that complementary techniques were needed.

This question of variability in the landscape, and the way in which we could or should come up with a measure and evaluation of that variability, has recently been addressed indirectly through the Historic Landscapes Characterization Project sponsored by English Heritage. The funding and impetus for this project sprang not from strictly academic or intellectual concerns, but out of the needs of preservation and management of the English countryside. English Heritage had become increasingly aware that its duty of selecting sites to be given statutory protection was not as well informed as it might be by knowledge of the landscape within which those sites were set. Brian Roberts and Stuart Wrathmell were set the task of providing "maps of England's dispersed and nucleated settlement patterns, to enable those patterns to inform the identification and selection of nationally important settlement remains in the course of the Monuments Protection Programme" (Roberts and Wrathmell 2000, 2002:viii). In other words, a basic mapping of variability in the landscape was needed in order to help English Heritage place particular sites and monuments in context when deciding whether or not to give them statutory protection.

Roberts and Wrathmell achieved this task through a national survey of first-edition Ordnance Survey maps of the sort discussed in the previous chapter. Settlements were graded subjectively, the guarantee of consistency being that the exercise was carried out by one person (Figure 5.1). They then adopted the technique of preparing and overlaying national distribution maps of different archaeological and documentary data. This technique threw up, according to the authors, unexpected patterns and correspondences, all of which pointed towards the great antiquity of three zones, each with its own characteristic landscape forms, that run across the English countryside. These zones were termed "settlement provinces." It is worth noting that Roberts

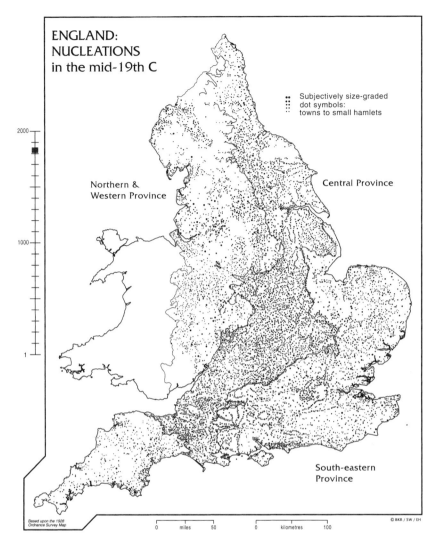

Figure 5.1 Roberts and Wrathmell's map of nucleations (after Roberts and Wrathmell 2002: figure 1.1)

and Wrathmell's achievement is the greater in that it stands in some ways in a complementary relationship to the Hoskins/Crawford tradition. The latter built up its general picture from particular areas or regions, though the implicit model was fuzzier and more recursive; as we have seen, Hoskins's celebration of region and place was dependent on a corresponding and implicit idea of nation. Roberts and Wrathmell start at the national scale and work down – though again many of their smaller observations are clearly informed by their research background in northern England.

There is a central issue with this exercise: Roberts and Wrathmell's settlement provinces are primarily defined by "measures" of nucleation and dispersal. However, these two terms are not defined in a completely objective manner. At the heart of the survey, settlement size and degree of nucleation were still graded subjectively – as stated above, an appeal is made to the reader to trust these drawings on the basis that they were all done by the same person. It is only fair to note that it is difficult to see how any other satisfactory course could have been adopted, given that the grain of the material militates against other approaches (see Chapter 4), and that such a methodology was arguably quite appropriate for the questions being asked about heritage management.

Roberts and Wrathmell's methodology for understanding pattern is well developed, with its biases and assumptions clear; however, that for understanding process is less so. In Binford's terms, it is difficult to see how the content, structure, and range of the system have been objectively defined; and it is that objective definition that for Binford is the "seat of process" (1964:426). Their mapping of a basic framework for the English landscape, then, is a quite stunning achievement, but what is less clear is their success in developing a framework to explain the variability thus presented. Just as the maps delineate some highly interesting distributions, so their diagrams map out some highly interesting possible trajectories; but in the end, rather than refer to underlying process, they are driven back to a reference to "cataclysms" precipitated by contingent historical events (the Norman Conquest and "harrying of the north," for example) to explain patterns of change in the archaeological record. Consequently, impressive – and beautiful – as Roberts and Wrathmell's maps and diagrams are, their translation into a processual account is more complex than might seem at first sight.

The task Roberts and Wrathmell set themselves verges on the impossible because, as noted in the last chapter, an attempt to work in such a processual way cuts across the grain of everyday practice in landscape archaeology. Such methods have also encountered militant hostility from other practitioners when they have been suggested. In the early 1980s the new Professor of Archaeology at York, Philip Rahtz, became involved in the Wharram project, bringing his students into the field alongside the Wharram volunteers. Rahtz was enthusiastic about the development of a processual agenda for medieval archaeology, and attempted to apply this to the Wharram project (Rahtz 2001; Gerrard 2003). Rahtz and his students encountered much informal opposition – as a 19-year-old volunteer at Wharram in 1982, I recall the snorts of derision at the suggested use of random sample squares and the rumour, probably apocryphal but nevertheless revealing, that Rahtz wished to rename all routes and trackways at the site as "linear movement zones." Rahtz's suggestions, according to his autobiography, "fell like a lead balloon." Rahtz comments that "Wharram Percy has escaped theory; but it will come into its own when all the data are synthesized in coming years" (2001:142). A second influence on New Archaeology came through Mick Aston's use of diagrams representing the functional interrelationships of different elements of the historic countryside (for example 1985: figures 1, 51, and 93). However, neither of these could be described as a seriously sustained attempt to write a processual archaeology of historic landscapes; Aston describes his diagrams in tentative terms (1985:153).

Anthropology

When New Archaeologists insisted "we must be more anthropological," they were referring to the habit of traditional archaeologists of understanding change in terms of "influence" rather than of a functioning social system (Clarke 1968; Leone 1972; Johnson 1999:21). Here, I want to broaden and deepen the point a little.

The Romantic gaze often reduced ordinary people to ant-like creatures, and tended to see them as objects of aesthetic appreciation. The Romantic vision was reinscribed into the practice of landscape archaeology through the map, air photograph, and plan. At the same time, relations between people – women and men, different social classes – were treated aesthetically rather than socially, and to an extent, I have argued, students of the historic landscape lost sight of ordinary men and women and their culture. Expressions of interest in ordinary people were made, but as a statement of belief rather than as a central element of an analysis, more often than not on the last page of a volume (see for example Hoskins 1967:184; Aston 1985). Studies of relations between people in historic landscapes, then, were attenuated. Archaeologists and geographers confined their attention to subsistence and agriculture, while historians, because of the nature of their source material, often confined their concerns to the exclusively juridical ("lordship," "manorialization") rather than asking broader questions about agency and social power. For many landscape historians and archaeologists medieval peasants beaver away, acquiring a little bit of land here, engrossing there, improving . . . the image is strikingly similar to the traditional documentary historian and topographer beavering away in the record office, accumulating little "facts," or more accurately anecdotes on index cards, and aiming to produce a holistic picture by the careful accumulation and ordering of those cards.

Part of the underlying set of assumptions behind the perception of the pre-industrial countryside was the view of its inhabitants as "our ancestors" which we have seen strongly present in both Wordsworth and Hoskins. There is a strongly ideological component in the idea of "ancestry" relating to traditions within European nationalism, the search for roots and a sense of place, competing claims over the land, and the marginalization of groups who cannot claim such ancestry, which will be dealt with in the next chapter. However, for our purpose here it should be noted that an idea of ancestry – that "they" were "our" forebears, that they were just like us – militates against the very first principle of cultural anthropology, namely that peoples and cultures are *different* from one another. People from other cultures do not simply wear different kinds of clothes and live in different kinds of houses: they also have ways of thinking, mindsets, that are utterly different from those of modern western Europe or North America. If, then, we are to make any headway in an attempt to understand people in the past, and indeed to make their lives appear rather more interesting than we have hitherto managed, we have to start by putting a question mark against an uncritical notion of ancestry.

Do other cultures really possess different mentalities that cannot be approximated to Western models, as some anthropologists suggest? A classic debate within cultural anthropology is over the question of the extent to which "other cultures" are "rational." Most classically it is seen in the formalist/substantivist debate between different schools of economic anthropology (Sahlins 1972, 1977). Formalists suggested that the principles of classical economics, developed to explain the behaviour of markets and economic actors in the modern West, could be applied to other cultures. Substantivists reacted by insisting that other cultures had other systems of economic rationality that cannot be assimilated to Western ideas. It has surfaced most obviously in the debate between Marshall Sahlins and Gananath Obeyesekere over the interpretation of "natives'" thinking about Captain Cook (Obeyesekere 1992; Sahlins 1995). Sahlins argued that Polynesian perceptions of Captain Cook, culminating in his killing, had to be understood in the context of their identification of Cook with a Hawaiian god. Obeyesekere denied this context, asserting rather that Polynesians were never under any illusions about the identity of Cook.

Sahlins's final point is especially pertinent here. He points out that when Obeyesekere invokes an empirical reality, he does so in characteristically Western terms. In other words, according to Sahlins, what Obeyesekere classifies as "reality" is actually the preference for one construct over another. What scholars see as "hard practical considerations" (Lewis et al. 1997:213) is actually a set of modern, Western-derived assumptions (Sahlins 1995). Both "social" and "environmental" views are actually a modern imposition, and as such are dialectically related: one constitutes and makes possible the other. According to the *Oxford English Dictionary*, the words "farm" and "farming" only take on their modern meaning in the later 16th century, and only arguably so even then; it could be argued that a truly modern conception of farming only emerged with the 18th-century ideology of improvement, in other words at the very moment that an unmediated environment in the form of Nature emerged in the Romantic imagination (Tarlow, in press).

The splits between nature and culture, mind and body, that underlie such a modern conception have very deep roots, for example as Sahlins argues, in the Judaeo-Christian tradition, but this does not mean that they are not cultural constructions (Sahlins 1996). A third view is possible, one which sees peasants as having an intimate understanding of the land, but within the terms of their own view of their own world. In short, "cow and plough" are important, but both would be nothing without the hand and mind of the peasant that drove the one and made the other.

A Romantic and empiricist view of past people obscures this very basic anthropological insight in two ways. First, it tends to impose an assumption of continuity in practices, particularly in the countryside. Part of the emotional appeal of the sense of locatedness and of place so central to both Wordsworth and Hoskins is an idea of the timelessness of structures that endure and persist at a level untouched by historical contingency and rupture. When linked to a condemnation of modernity as an alien set of practices bearing down on common humanity, the essential and invariant nature of common humanity comes to be taken for granted. Second, by constituting past people as "our ancestors," the ability to hear them talking in different ways is reduced, however much archaeologists might profess the need to do this.

The question of anthropological "otherness" is made more complex by the nature of the period under discussion. It is too simple to merely state that past peoples had other ways of understanding the world. Medieval and later landscape archaeology deals by definition with a period of transition between ways of thinking about and acting upon the world that were very different to ways that are "modern," however defined, and therefore familiar to us. The values and mentalities of prehistoric users of landscapes are clearly an issue up for debate; those of, say, Victorian industrialists are not so clearly alien. Medieval peasants, demonstrably engaged in market relations, and going to church, sit uneasily in this classification, as does the later historic reuse of prehistoric monuments such as barrows in meaningful ways (Whyte 2003b). Medieval agricultural treatises were an established genre of writing, and they did make extensive recommendations for improvement and maximization of returns; they related to the elite-controlled activities of demesne farms rather than the motivations of peasants, but they nevertheless constitute an important locus of discourse about the land, and much has been written about the involvement of medieval peasants in the land market and in commerce generally (Britnell 1996; Dyer 2002). Tarlow and West's edited volume on the archaeology of later historic Britain, *The Familiar Past?* (Tarlow and West 1999) placed a question mark in the title to address precisely this issue of whether or not we could treat the post-1500 period as one of familiarity. Somewhere between these two points of medieval otherness and modern familiarity lies the historical origin of modern views of the landscape. The lack of clarity, then, in specifying precisely when and in what terms this emerged muddies the question. Indeed, for this author the central interest of the late medieval and early modern period is that one can see different views of landscape fighting it out, with the ultimate victory of modernity (Johnson 1996). So it is not simply a question of "like" or "unlike" the modern world.

This does not mean that past peoples had an ethereal or exclusively "symbolic" or "ritual" view of landscape. Indeed, to assert such a thing is to reinforce the Romantic distinction between ways of thinking about landscape that would have been quite alien to the medieval peasant. This point is most pertinent when thinking about how religious experience intersects with landscape. If fields were not simply about a modern conception of farming, churches were not simply about religion: both field and churches structured everyday experience of the world and were the products of human agency.

The Landscape of Religion

An overtly religious perspective is very rare in landscape studies (Clark and Sleeman 1991 is a relevant example of the application of Christian belief to social geography, and Gorringe 2002 attempts a theology of the built environment). However, an assumption that religion occupies a specific, delimited space in the landscape, and that such a space is Christian, is rarely overtly articulated but is not difficult to find in the disciplinary assumptions of historic landscape archaeology. Closely related to this is an assumption that literate priests and elites have a complex set of theological views about the world, while illiterate people just get on with farming. One symptom of this radical division between the religious and the mundane is that we fail to see non-Christian significance in the landscape. Assertions of "primitive survival" of "pagan customs" by a certain school of folklorists, and by New Age and other pagan and fringe archaeologies, are rightly considered by scholars to be largely without foundation (Wallis 2003). This does not devalue the assertion that much of the behaviour of people in the landscape often has ritual elements to it that are not formally Christian. One of the most perceptive social and cultural historians of pre-industrial England, Ronald Hutton, has explored how vernacular understandings of the world were expressed in a series of ritual forms that were not necessarily Christian in form or content (Hutton 1994).

Where ritual forms were Christian, Christian behaviour could be approached anthropologically, as the beliefs and practices of a foreign culture. This strategy has been attempted before: Philip Rahtz asked of the gravestones at Wharram: "What would Martians make of them from first principles?" Rahtz's suggestions are mild enough, and he gave them a semi-humorous edge by writing under the pen-name of Rilip Phatz (1985), but it is revealing that they caused enough offence to prompt a leading medievalist to walk out of his conference presentation (Rahtz 2001:139).

Again, such a strategy cuts across the grain of the research materials. An understanding of medieval Christian belief and practice and the way it was mapped out across the medieval and early modern landscape involves a series of specialized skills. These skills range from a knowledge of medieval Latin to a deep understanding of Christian doctrine and theology. As a result, it takes a great deal of time and effort to become conversant with the material, and to be able to talk with facility of liturgy, baptism, the doctrine of Purgatory, the significance of the setting of the altar table-wise, as well as of their material correlates – rood screens, vestries, chancel arches, chantry chapels. Those who make the effort tend to do so for a personal reason, namely that they have a prior commitment to Christian belief in general, and to one or another view of Christian belief in particular. In a country where the monarch as Head of State was and continues to be also Defender of the Faith (a title, ironically, first awarded to the destroyer of the monasteries Henry VIII by the Pope before the split with Rome), different views of Christian belief are by definition also political views about the constitution of Britain. This congruity between religion and politics was even stronger when Hoskins was writing (see for example Coleman and Elsner 1999). Both of the premier religious historians of the 16th century, Eamon Duffy and Diarmaid Macculloch, are explicitly committed to Christian views of different denominations (Duffy 1992; Macculloch 1999).

There is nothing inherently unscholarly about such religious commitment, just as there is nothing inherently unscholarly about political commitment, but it does tend to militate against a more detached, anthropological view of behaviour in which ordinary people from other cultures, such as medieval peasants, lived their lives within a spiritualized world. By implicitly making the Church and spirituality coterminous, the parish church becomes the specific and exclusive location of "belief" and the wider landscape is rendered functional and mundane, outside the realm of "belief," by comparison. In Duffy's fascinating study of the 16th-century life in the small Devon parish of Morebath, peasants go to church on Sundays, even argue about theology, and lead rich lives within the sphere of organized religion; they then go back to their vernacular houses and get on with the everyday secular business of ploughing, eating, quarrelling, and sleeping. As a result, the religious and secular worlds are depicted so separately that Duffy's late Middle Ages are "lovingly idealised and charmingly depoliticised" (Aers and Staley 1996:24). It is revealing that, for Duffy, the best book ever written about Devon is Hoskins's *Devon* (1954b), which clearly confirms and reinforces a view of the world in which the religious and the mundane are kept separate (Duffy 2001:xiv).

It is no coincidence, then, that until 1989 the place of the church in the landscape was little discussed. Richard Morris's book *Churches in the Landscape* (1989) changed this. Its discussion – an account of the development of the structure of the church and its impact on the landscape, from the advent of Christianity in Britain through to modern times – was relatively traditional in format, but in the process raised a series of questions phrased in anthropological terms. For example: "many new churches are likely to have been byproducts of a much larger process. One result – or cause? – of this was the transfer of an individual's primary allegiance from kin-group to community" (Morris 1989:166–7). More recent work by Pam Graves has opened up the study of the parish church to a more social appreciation of its relationship with the cultural landscape (Graves 2000). For Henry Glassie (2000), the parish church is an act of collective sculpture carried out century by century, a representation of the community it serves and which created it; Glassie arguably underplays the unequal power relations that lay behind the fabric of the church, but his point remains valid. Nick Corcos has explored how a phenomenological approach of the sort practised by prehistorians can be applied to Christian sites such as Glastonbury Tor (Corcos 2001).

If we want to take seriously the experiences of ordinary men and women in the past, the landscape archaeology of religion is an obvious place to start. To state the obvious, the one thing all historic communities had was a church (in the north of England, for example at Wharram, several communities might share a church, but here one can see the church as materializing a larger community). Equally obviously, the church was a place where people began and ended their lives with baptism and burial. The whole community would come together once a week to worship God, which, as every student of Durkheim knows, is also and at the same time a celebration of the cultural forms through which God is constructed within a particular society. The working day of the peasant was constructed through the tolling of the church bell at specific times, and the working week through the structured interval of Sunday worship.

And none of these elements was ethereal or mystical or fanciful. They were direct, practical, hard-edged elements in the lives of ordinary people. And they are elements that have a very direct presence in the archaeological record: every village has its church, and every description in the "county Pevsner" (see Chapter 6) testifies to the way in which the fabric and memorials of that church act as a changing materialization of expression of community over the generations and centuries (Figure 5.2).

In a classic study the historian Margaret Spufford has described the centrality of the church to all aspects of the affairs of three communities in Cambridgeshire. Her thesis is that the ordinary men and women of these communities cared deeply about questions of religion, and further that patterns of belief and devotion shaped their lives. Her evidence is not just written testaments, for example the religious dedications found in wills and frequently dictated as peasants lay on their deathbeds, but also the physical fact that all three communities were dominated by their church. It is no coincidence, then, that Spufford's villagers emerge to a much greater extent as active agents making their own history than do those in many comparable "micro-histories" (Spufford 1974).

Figure 5.2 A typical parish church: Grinton in Swaledale, with a 17th-century house in the background and 18th- and 19th-century gravestones in the foreground. The different architectural elements and styles testify to the gradual accretion and modification of the church by each succeeding generation of the parish community

Archaeology

If past peoples must be understood on their own terms, so archaeologists must also come to terms with the intellectual integrity and independence of archaeology as a discipline. Without this integrity and independence, archaeologists cannot participate in interdisciplinary exchanges in an assertive and effective manner. One of the key perceived strengths of landscape history has been its claim to be interdisciplinary; that several different disciplines were married together in an equal relationship. My objection to this claim is not that interdisciplinarity is a bad thing: it is a good thing, and when approached in a theoretically informed manner it should be a central goal of all scholarship. However, interdisciplinarity in landscape studies often seems to be using the traditional common-law definition of marriage we saw in the last chapter, namely that the married couple are one and the one is the husband, the husband here being History. In other words, even as the value of archaeology as a *method* is applauded, so its subservience to the writing of a narrative in Romantic, traditional, and ultimately document-based terms is reinforced.

How is it that archaeology can simultaneously be hailed as an equal partner and yet subordinated in this way? One of the sources of this position goes back to the empiricist methods of local and landscape history. In an article in the journal *Local Historian*, Sheeran and Sheeran have related this empiricist bias to a language of reconstruction:

> local historians have no desire to engage in this debate [between postmodernists and empiricists], although it is obvious that they explicitly or implicitly side with the realists. The most they seem to have involved themselves in, theoretically, is the debate about the boundaries of the specialism and methods, rather than a philosophical questioning of underlying motives or thinking. The effect of this, we argue, is to place unnecessary limits on our understanding of the nature of our historical enterprise, as well as contributing to the marginalisation of academic local history. (1991:256)

Sheeran and Sheeran question "language such as 'recreate', 'recover', 'reconstruct', 'repopulate'" as being complicit with a methodological emphasis on "technique and fine-tuning of research methods in order to 'reconstruct' the past more accurately" (1999:261, 259). Their comments are echoed in Marshall (1997), who goes on to refer in disparaging terms to the activities of landscape archaeologists as little better than those of antiquarians; a harsh but revealing judgement. It is important to remember, however, that the range of responses to the Sheerans' arguments in the following issues of *Local Historian* from a variety of historians both professional and amateur was almost universally negative.

My gloss on Sheeran and Sheeran's arguments is not simply to point out the Romantic intellectual inheritance of this empiricism, but to indicate the way it prioritizes (traditional) historical forms of knowledge over the archaeological. Recreation, recovery, reconstruction, and repopulation are implicitly defined in terms of documentary variables – recorded number of taxpayers, named heads of household, numbers of births, marriages, and deaths as recorded in parish registers . . . Archaeology will only ever be able to approach such "reconstruction" in a flawed and imperfect manner because that which is being reconstructed is document-based. And its evidence will always be seen as more indeterminate and less direct than that offered by the documents for the same reason. This is why the most striking advances in landscape archaeology, and the more theoretically informed and intellectually adventurous work, has been in prehistory. Without the insistence that the "interdisciplinary" archaeologist contribute to questions defined in advance through study of the documentary record, two generations of British prehistorians have taken the prehistoric landscape on an exciting journey of empirical and theoretical progress.

Prehistory

For the generation of prehistorians after the Second World War, the recognition of the antiquity of whole landscapes via the Hoskins/ Crawford method threw up immediate and obvious theoretical challenges. Indeed, it can be argued that part of the impetus for New Archaeology in Britain, alongside influences from North Americans such as Binford and Flannery and from figures in "economic archaeology" such as Grahame Clark (Clark 1989), came from projects such as the archaeological survey prior to the construction of the western part of the M5 motorway and the work on the Thames Valley river gravels (Leech 1977; Jones 1984). In both these cases, extensive field survey and air photography prior to the destruction of entire landscapes gave a visible demonstration that, far from being isolated dots on a map, prehistoric features were densely packed on the landscape. These and other projects, such as Fleming's work on Dartmoor (1988), combined with the insights derived from the Hoskins/Crawford tradition, led, as noted in Chapter 4, to a powerful reassessment of the extent of the remains of the prehistoric landscape, and to a prompting of questions concerning the societies that created and used it. How do we understand the interrelationship of resources, territoriality, and social power in such societies? Were these prehistoric landscapes the products of chiefdom societies? What social forms were implied by the settlement traces they contained (Renfrew 1973b)?

The theoretical questions concerning the link between present and past, and the social questions about the kind of changing cultural systems that were responsible for these landscapes, were thus firmly at centre stage in British prehistory. It is no surprise, then, to observe that prehistorians were the first to move on beyond overly systemic and functional models; it was prehistorians who were the first to take the project of understanding everyday experience, and beyond that a phenomenology of landscape, seriously (Thomas 1991; Barrett 1993; Tilley 1994; Corcos 2001). Phenomenology is an explicit attempt to provide us with a way of thinking through movement across landscape, though

I would argue that insofar as phenomenology invites us once more to think through the body it owes more itself to Romanticist notions than it cares to admit (as has been noted indirectly by Adam Smith: 2003). One could also argue that the explicit modelling of the New Geography addresses this question, whatever doubts might be raised about the answers that New Geographers provided (Boots 1986). It is striking therefore that, while both approaches have been extensively deployed in archaeology, they have largely been applied to prehistoric periods. For the reasons noted above, they simply were not perceived as being needed for post-Roman landscapes. As a result, the more reflective work has been carried out in prehistoric landscapes, most obviously the work of Richard Bradley and Andrew Fleming (Bradley 1993, 1998; Fleming 1988, 1998).

This divergent development between prehistoric and historic landscape archaeology has led to a radical split between prehistory and history. There is a contrast, for example, between two attitudes taken to the landscape in Della Hooke's edited volume *Landscape: The Richest Historical Record*. As Richard Bradley notes, "the two approaches to landscape take little account of one another, with the result that the subject is fractured down the middle" (Bradley 2000:2). We can contrast Bradley's stress on the perception and phenomenology of landscapes with the medievalist Bond's more functional and mundane view of landscapes of monasticism: "What differences in management practices can be detected in the landscape between lay and monastic owners, and between monasteries and their tenants, and how did this change and evolve through time? To what extent were the monasteries pioneers in agricultural improvements and in the invention and application of new industrial technology?" (Bond 2000). Only recently has this split been questioned. John Evans wrote with irony that "by comparison with prehistory, the settlement patterns of the Middle Ages make sense. Villages are located close to water, in sheltered valleys . . . linked to each other and the market towns by tracks and roads. But this relationship with the practical world could be illusory" (Evans 2003:90; see also Corcos 2001).

The divergence between prehistory and history in the way landscape is treated in archaeological scholarship becomes quite fascinating in its intellectual implications when we consider cases where particular monuments might plausibly be assigned to either period. A notable instance is the dating and interpretation of chalk-cut figures in the chalk hills of the south of England (Figure 5.3). These figures were created by cutting away the thin layer of green turf to reveal the white chalk underneath; where they are not obviously modern, they have habitually

Figure 5.3   The Cerne Abbas Giant, as seen from the west

been interpreted as prehistoric. Recently, however, an alternative case has been made that at least two – the Long Man of Wilmington and the Cerne Abbas Giant – date in fact to the 17th century A.D., and are satirical comments on contemporary political events.

While classified in scholarly writing as prehistoric or of the Roman period, the Cerne Abbas Giant is mysterious, referring to a ritual world of pagan fertility gods. He both fits easily alongside the preconceptions of early 20th-century archaeologists, and slots easily as well into the writings of New Age and other mystics. Indeed, while professional archaeologists and "lunatic fringe" writers diverged in their writing styles, they shared the assumption that such an openly priapic figure could not possibly be the creation of a Christian society. However, Ronald Hutton (1999) has argued convincingly that it in fact sits alongside a 17th-century landscape of politics and conflict between king and Parliament.

Why can a certain kind of scholarship not allow the Giant to be historic? The reasons for this refusal reflect back on the assumptions of traditional landscape studies. First, it betrays the assumption of the primacy of documents. In this case, if the 17th-century construction of the Giant is not recorded, then surely it cannot have happened at that date. Hutton shows elegantly how documentary traces would have been erased by the chance accidents of archival survival. Second, though clearly ideological in some sense, the Giant is most certainly not easily appropriated into the traditions of the Church (Hutton 1999:116–18). Near the earthwork are the remains of a formal 17th-century pleasure garden; such gardens were habitually "symbolic" (Riley and Wilson-North 1999).

It is telling, I think, that the debate over the Cerne Abbas Giant led to one of the most interesting and innovative pieces of landscape archaeology in recent years – an open debate, held in the manner of courtroom proceedings in front of an audience in Cerne Abbas village hall, of three different views of the Giant's origins (Darvill et al. 1999). Three scholars each presented a courtroom-style argument concerning the origins of the Giant. Tim Darvill and Ronald Hutton were "orthodox" in their approach to the marshalling of evidence and argument, but in some ways the most interesting argument was made by Barbara Bender. Bender took up the questioning of "names and origins" discussed above, and argued that the specific date of origin of the Giant was not the real issue at stake. Whatever its ultimate antiquity, Bender argues, the Giant has to be scoured and re-scoured every generation; it takes its place, and its historical importance, as part of a continuing tradition that links the past to the present. To equate its meaning with its origins is, in Bender's view, to impose the dead hand of a linear history that would not be recognized by the community and the people more widely who find meaning in the Giant today (Bender 1999:126–9). Instead, she makes the case for a "living Giant" in both the present and the past. In arguing this case, she draws together material from both present and past, and from different genres, and makes a compelling case that the central question for scholars is not a precise point of origin, but the continuing use of a piece of landscape by different individuals and groups through the centuries.

Generalization

Part of the reason for the greater development of "social" perspectives in prehistory is tied up with the issue of generalization. New Archaeology insisted that part of the responsibility of a scientific and anthropological discipline was the development of general statements about the growth of human societies. This insistence was particularly marked in the early years of New Archaeology, the 1960s, and was often caricatured as the single-minded development of "cross-cultural laws" akin to those developed by natural scientists (Johnson 1999:22–5, 74). So, at the same time that Hoskins and his contemporaries were rolling out a programme of empirical research that had at its heart a Romantic celebration of the particular and the local, New Archaeologists were insisting on the value, indeed the necessity, of framing research in terms of an enquiry into the general characteristics of societies and "cultural evolution" (Flannery 1973 is one of many examples).

One of the most important of such general questions was that of the rise of social complexity, in particular "civilization" or "the state." Archaeology set itself the task of look for common processes in different contexts where "complex" or "state" societies, however defined, evolved – western Asia, China, and Mesoamerica. Central to an account of these processes were often questions of landscape change and the social systems and hierarchies that "managed" such change, most obviously in the "irrigation hypothesis" in which the development of systems of large-scale irrigation agriculture was tied, it was argued, to the emergence of managerial elites (Steward 1955).

New Archaeology drew back from some of the more mechanistic applications of general theories of this kind, and the postprocessual critique of the 1980s pointed out that the particularities of space and place remained important. However, the understanding of general processes and the development of ideas and models that can be applied across different cultures remains an important element of contemporary archaeology. Indeed, I would go further and say that the postprocessual critique was overstated. Ultimately, one of the central aims of scholarship must be the development of a general understanding of human societies, or more broadly of what it means to be human. In other areas of the globe and in prehistory, powerful general statements of the rise of complex societies have been made (Brumfiel and Fox 1994 and Earle 2002 are two examples of a vast literature).

An important element of landscape archaeology today, then, should be an engagement not just with celebration of place and space, but also a contribution to comparative and general debates. Indeed, the two elements should be complementary rather than competing. As we develop our understanding of the general processes of landscape change, we also understand better why this or that place varied in some particular way; conversely, any celebration of particularity is meaningless without an understanding of the general processes against which that particularity is played out. This very basic point, and a reassertion of the importance and value of generalization, has been made recently by Adam Smith (2003). Smith is writing within the North American anthropological tradition of the study of early states. As we have seen, in its earlier days, this tradition was explicitly generalizing and comparative. Scholars were interested in the origins of political complexity across the globe, and sought to develop generalizations about this process across space and time. We have seen that Hoskins reacted negatively to this way of thinking as it manifested itself in the New Geography; and it often seemed to the sceptical outside observer that many of the subtleties and nuances of local contexts got lost in this urge to develop a general political model. Mesopotamia, central America, and China were all lumped together on a scale that disregarded local particularity. Smith is conscious of this critique from other sources; part of his theme is to take it on board, and to stress that such a disregard for the local is in part a disregard for the importance of space and landscape. For Smith, places are different from one another, and as social scientists we need to take these differences into account.

It is clear that different currents within landscape studies today are grappling with the question of particularity versus generalization. A continuing concern within the "Leicester school" of English local history, taking its name from the Department of English Local History which Hoskins founded, has been to understand the origins and nature of "region" within the English landscape (Everitt 1970). Charles Phythian-Adams (1992, 1993) has developed this understanding into a systematic description, classification, and mapping of the regions of England, defined by river valleys and watersheds but also embracing community and kinship. His attempt was qualified by the insistence that "perception" was an important component of understanding of region by Marshall (1996). Clearly the issue here, as with Roberts and Wrathmell, is how to understand the general processes that lie behind the formation of "regions." As articulated by the Leicester school, however, this concern is primarily a historical one, led by questions of kinship, social networks, and patterns of farming defined and understood through the documents. Where historic landscape archaeologists have "contributed" to this debate, their contribution has again been one of the scholarly marshalling of the details of archaeological evidence to answer questions defined in advance through the documentary record (for example Jones and Page 2003).

Practice and Agency

I now want to introduce two concepts, closely interrelated, from recent trends in postprocessual and interpretative archaeology to pull these strands together: practice and agency. Both are now well inscribed into prehistoric archaeology, but both in fact are no less applicable to historic landscape studies.

Agency is a fashionable concept in archaeological theory; its concerns span different theoretical perspectives (Dobres and Robb 2000). At its heart is the very simple observation that the archaeological record is created by the actions of individuals. Those individuals have a cultural background or structure against which they operate – what Pierre Bourdieu called a *habitus* (Bourdieu 1979). Practice is closely related to agency; it is about the way in which the abstract structures and norms of "culture" are translated into actions on the ground (Barrett 1993). Practice is embedded in everyday life: the patterns of moving to and from the fields, the actions of ploughing and harrowing the soil, the everyday rhythms of individual, household, and community life. It is bound up with social ideas and values, in that practices embody and replicate expected ways of behaving. It is also bound up with social tradition and memory – the recognition that we do things this way because they always have been done this way "since time out of mind," to use a recurrent phrase from the written records of medieval peasant testimony.

It is worth stressing here yet again that I am not arguing for a view of the landscape as exclusively or overwhelmingly "symbolic." When I first put forward some of these ideas in connection with earlier work (1993, 1996) a common critical reaction was to claim that I was somehow seeing the landscape as a purely symbolic construct with little or no grounding in everyday activity. The a priori split between hard practical reality and cultural construct is repeated in one of the most influential books on vernacular buildings. Maurice Barley, in his seminal *The English Farmhouse and Cottage* (1961), wrote that traditional farmhouses and cottages

> remained in essence functional building[s], in which purpose determined plan and form, and ornament was subordinated to them. That the builder often achieved what an architect now consciously strives for – a satisfactory relation of forms, a harmony of structure and environment, a pleasing variety of finish and ornament – was incidental to his purpose of making a machine for living in. The archaeological approach, as distinct from the aesthetic, makes it easier to relate the form of an artefact, whether it is a flint implement, a pot or a house, to the culture which evolved it and the purpose for which it was made. (Barley 1961:xix)

The problem with this sentiment is not that houses are *not* machines for living in, or are *not* functional buildings. Of course they are. It is that, in the effort to get away from exclusively aesthetic approaches in which a house is a good or bad example of an architectural style, the divide between aesthetic and practical is not questioned, but is reinscribed. Such a split is repeatedly asserted by other writers, for example Muir when he separates "aesthetic" from other views of landscape (1998), and bemoaned by Spufford when she writes of the swing in fashion away from "economic man" to "social history man" (Spufford 2000:xxiii).

Engagement with the landscape was hard work for ordinary people in the past. Roberts and Wrathmell estimate that "if a standard holding of 30 acres is being tilled under a two-course rotation" then the ploughman must walk some 495 miles – "we must imagine the struggle with the stilts, or handles, to keep the plough in work, the battle with stones and mud, and the prodding of the recalcitrant oxen" (Roberts and Wrathmell 2002:40). The difficult and arduous nature of the work reinforced the peasant view of the world. Frantzen (1994) points out that, in the Middle Ages, the action of work bound the peasant into one part of a tripartite structure of the world (those who fight, those who work, and those who pray). Seen in this context, work was in itself ideological: every moment of the struggle with the plough, the battle with stones and mud, and prodding of the oxen, moulded and reinforced a particular kind of world-view or mentality. Ælfric's *Colloquy*, cited at the opening of this chapter, comes close to capturing this relationship between labour and world-view: the peasant's labour is great, but this is, in his own words, not in some modern gloss, because he is not a free man. In other words, the very real nature of the burden of work in pre-industrial societies is not set apart from the medieval mentality and structure of social relations in such a way that practice and culture can be opposed, but is instead part of it: the split between practice and culture is an unjustified modern imposition (Ruffing 1994:61–2). Both Frantzen and Ruffing are examining literary representations of peasant labour, but I would extend their arguments to the physical experience of the work itself. Indeed, Ælfric's *Colloquy* is itself not a piece of objective or authentic description of a medieval peasant, but rather a representation, produced with certain didactic and pedagogical motives, by a member of the literate elite, intended to be used in the schoolroom by other members of that elite, and framed with reference to a background ideology and culture (Garmonsway 1978). So engagement with the landscape was hard work, but it was an active engagement, not a passive one.

Some of the most exciting recent work on landscapes has been in the context of environmental archaeology, with the recognition that "environment" is created as much as it is responded to by human culture. The very mundane and everyday practices we see in the archaeological record, then, were active constructions. Similar points have been made about peasant farming and field systems in other con- texts. In Andean farming, for example, peasants responded to climatic and related changes in a variety of active ways. They are considered by Clark Erickson as "active and dynamic agents who not only respond to the challenges of . . . their environments, but also create, shape and transform these very environments" (1999:641). John Evans explores this point when he writes about such matter-of-fact topics as soil texture: "soil and land texture are important referents for social expression. Particular textures were understood and used not just for their functional attributes of fertility and knowledge but also as a means through which people communicated with each other" (2003:71). Such an active engagement is understood deeply by many historical ecologists. William Cronon, for example, has written on how the landscape of New England was constructed and responded to by English settlers and Native Americans (Cronon 1983). Carole Crumley has made similar points in her exploration of the Burgundian landscape (Crumley 1994).

Oliver Rackham's work on the English landscape, in particular on the management of woodland, has shown how human communities responded creatively to their perceived environment. Rackham makes strong rhetorical statements asserting a split between the objective study of the landscape and what he calls "attitudinizing" about it, and asserts the priority of the former (Rackham and Grove 2001:12). However, the very fabric of his close and careful analysis of both British and Mediterranean landscapes shows just how impossible it is to maintain such a split in practice. Through a detailed exposition of the fine details of the landscape and the plant and animal species that are "managed" in that landscape, ranging from British trees and woodland and hawthorn hedges to olive trees and terraces in Crete, Rackham insists that "it is not possible to say where Nature stops and human activity begins" (1994:6; Rackham and Grove 2001). What Rackham shows us throughout his work in both England and Crete (Rackham 1990; Rackham and Moody 1994) is that nature and culture are dialectically related – each creates and defines the other, and one cannot be made sense of without an understanding of the other. For example, Rackham shows us that behind the timber frame of a house lies a complex system of timber management, starting with the management of woodland over decades and even centuries. In doing so, he is showing us not a determinism of nature over culture, but the necessity of a deep and complex understanding of the mutual construction of both.

Practice, then, insists that people's actions are bound up with a "real world" but that this world is created by them; its elements are constituted through their subjective experience, their view of their world, not an explicit or implicit economic model imposed by a modern writer: "humans exist not separately from but rather within the mineral world as meaning-giving social organisms, who constitute their landscapes through acts of naming and dwelling, and who in turn are constituted by them in multiple ways that influence their cultural production" (Owoc 2004:220). The concept of agency leads us to insist that this practical engagement with the real world is an active one, though constrained by external structures that are often very powerful. In other words, Wordsworth's ant-like figures were actually real men and women who made their own history, though not in circumstances of their own choosing. The landscape archaeologist, then, is examining the effects of real people leading real lives, and, further, doing so in active ways.

Two commonly held assumptions tend to obscure this insight. The first is that peasants led purely passive lives, reacting to external changes, and had no history of their own. People in the past were often anonymous in the sense of their names being unrecorded; even in later historic periods, many ordinary people make no appearance or only a fleeting appearance in documentary records, particularly if they were women, children, or servants in a house with a male head of household. These people were often also illiterate. However, this does not mean that they did not have agency or that archaeologists cannot talk about their lives and experiences as human beings. If this were true, it would reduce prehistoric archaeologists to the role of mere antiquarians, in which comments on the social and cultural lives of the peoples they study would be completely out of bounds. The second assumption is the tendency to assume that recovering human beings in the past is the same thing as putting names to people, as argued by Thirsk when she writes: "In recovering features of past landscapes . . . we are not usually able to identify the individual people who put them there . . . But it is sometimes possible to get close" (2000:15). Thirsk goes on to equate the study of individuals to the task of putting names to people. Again, ruling the thoughts and actions of nameless people intellectually "out of court" would leave prehistorians in a very precarious position.

Social actors rarely impinge on the landscape as human beings in accounts written in the Hoskins tradition, as Thirsk has noted (2000:10). This may seem a strange statement to make, given that landscape history and archaeology constantly stress the importance of a humanistic approach. However, these men and women of the past are rarely heard to actually speak. Thus, we never see prehistoric actors: we are only tenuously linked in feeling to them, and as we have seen Hoskins, at heart, like Wordsworth, is not animated by an intrinsic interest in them. When we move to historic periods, writers are invariably thrown back not on accounts of human beings themselves, but on literary representations of them, representations moreover that are produced not by ordinary people in the landscape, but by a literate elite. The human beings Aston refers to on the last page of *Interpreting the Landscape* are actually *depictions* from the Luttrell Psalter. Michael Camille has recently shown how the representations in the Luttrell Psalter are composed according to a very complex set of values and meanings, and are the product of a complex set of agencies; they are anything but a direct, unmediated encounter with the realities of peasant life (Camille 1998:193–211).

As readers of landscape history and archaeology, we may know from other sources about how men and women did talk and work: of the richness and complexity of late medieval Catholic belief (Duffy 1992), or about the occurrence of ritual practices relating to witchcraft or other folk magic beliefs (Thomas 1971; Merrifield 1978). We also know of a wide variety of practices, reflecting a rich understanding of the social and material landscape, from writers in the folklife tradition (Ewart Evans 1960, 1966; Glassie 1982). Such practices, however, rarely figure in the writings of landscape historians. Traditions of writing on folklife and on landscape history and archaeology bifurcated in the mid-20th century: the methodological issues associated with folklife as a discipline, in particular its assumption of continuity in folk practices in the English countryside, were, in my view, one reason for this. As such, the discipline may well have fallen foul of the impatience of Hoskins with the "sentimental and formless slush" that characterized much landscape writing: we noted his implicit condemnation of mystical writers such as H. J. Massingham, who used material from folklife studies in many of their meditations (for example Massingham 1943). As a result, the "irrational" behaviour recorded by many such studies was written out of landscape archaeology, and only common sense remains.

Again, prehistorians see this issue with much greater clarity than historical archaeologists. The nature of their sources behoves them to find a way of talking about agency without reference to names, and they have done this with a large measure of success. The British Neolithic and Bronze Age, in recent accounts, has been successfully populated by thinking human agents with lives that made sense to them. These accounts are empirically rigorous and satisfying; in them, the everyday realities of making a living are not denied or glossed over, but rather embedded within a wider way of looking at the world (a few examples are Thomas 1991; Barrett 1993; Bender 1998; Edmonds 1999; Pollard and Reynolds 2002). The landscape, then, was actively created by ordinary people, and its form and appearance today are the result of their agency over thousands of years.

However, "historic" landscape archaeology is more "prehistoric" than it sometimes cares to admit. We have seen how the documentary record is largely the product of the literate elite, whose views and descriptions may or may not apply to the great mass of rural folk. Christopher Dyer points out that "the medieval village has left us virtually no records. The institutions that did produce documents, the manor, the central government, and the church, give us information about villages through the eyes if the landlords, the royal officials, and the higher clergy, people whose lives and experiences lay outside the village" (Dyer 1994:2). This problem changes its nature, but does not go away, with the spread of literacy down the social scale in the 16th and 17th centuries. The early modern period saw the proliferation of published advice books on the farm and household; the degree to which these ran into successive editions, and were plagiarized, suggests that they had some measure of success (Spufford 1981; Johnson 1996: 84–90). However, they were generally written by men of the gentry classes, and were addressed to men and women of the middling sort. They do not represent the direct testimony of those men and women of the middling sort. Where the words and actions of individuals from the lower social classes are communicated to us, it is characteristically through the medium of manorial and other court records, in other words via the mediation of certain forms of power and authority.

Back to the Evidence

Not only is a practice-based approach more coherent theoretically; it also corresponds with the strengths of archaeological evidence.

A practice-based approach leads us away from issues that are difficult to approach in the archaeological record, and back towards simple, direct, hard-edged observables. Archaeologists will never observe the rather ethereal and untestable category of the "village moment" (Lewis et al. 1997), but they can and do have direct evidence of what peasants did every day, week, and season, through the pathways of the village, the layout of the fields, and the location and structure of the church. It is a matter of record that archaeologists have found it exceptionally difficult to research "manorialization," but we are able to say with great precision what the views of the manor house were from the peasant houses, and what views of the village were from the manor. Ironically, such a move would represent a return to the early concerns of many of those working on landscapes and settlements in the 1950s, most obviously the aims of the Wharram research after they moved on from establishing the date of desertion but before they became wider still.

Archaeologists do not survey nucleation, manorialization, the dissolution of multiple estates, the formation of the parish system, the depopulation of medieval villages. These are historical entities, for which the correlates in the archaeological record can only be indirect. The raw material of the archaeologist's craft is much more simple and direct, and has a much closer relationship with the ways of life of ordinary peoples. Archaeologists dig up houses, survey fields, and draw churches. Houses, churches, and fields were the products of human labour, and framed the everyday lives of those who made them.

Of course, words were also the product of human labour, and the observation that both words and things are actively created, by real people, places archaeology not just in a position of disciplinary assertiveness in relation to history, but also in a position where archaeology and history can come together in a properly equal and mutually critical and beneficial manner (Moreland 2001). It can help archaeologists open up areas that were core to the taphonomic retreat, and look at them in ways that are fresh and new. A good example is place-names. It is to state the obvious to point out that the action of naming a locale is a social action. Human geographers have noted the distinction between space (abstract, Cartesian) and place (a locale with meaning, embedded in social memory); creation and identification of place out of space is implicit in the action of naming. The agency involved in the act of naming is most obvious when personal names are used, thus turning a locale in the landscape into a piece of social memory, or when names referring to tribal or ethnic affiliations are deployed. The point here is that, while confidence in the use of the "evidence" of place-names to help "reconstruct history" has been eroded, if we shift focus a little and think about the action of naming and what this is telling us about the nature of space and place in the landscape, the names can be used in more interesting and fruitful ways.

Such agency is most overt, and examples are most easily given, in the later historic use of naming in the action of compliment and commemoration. An extreme instance is that of the field names of

Halstock, Dorset, where the 18th-century landowner Thomas Hollis gave names to his fields that expressed his political and religious views, ranging from political theorists ("Aristotle," "Bacon"), tyrannicides ("Brutus"), places with Puritan associations ("Massachusetts," "New England"), political leaders ("Prynne," "Ireton"), and even virtues associated with Puritanism ("Education," "Reasonableness," "Settlement," "Toleration"). Popular reaction to such naming might be inferred from the complete disappearance of such names in the records of the area in the 19th century. At a more mundane level, unproductive fields would be tagged "Raw Bones" or "Devils," while remote fields were tagged "Botany Bay" or "Van Diemen's Land," reflecting the consciousness – and arguably the fear, among late 18th-century and 19th-century labouring folk – of the remoteness and rugged nature of Australian penal colonies (Field 1989:180, 280–1). In later historic periods, according to Keith Thomas, there was at least one phase when the action of naming was bound up with social power: when the language of countryside was "cleaned up" in two phases reflecting 18th-century Romanticism and 19th-century Victorian sensibilities (Thomas 1983).

The agency involved in the action of naming needs further exploration for earlier periods. Naming is a way of classifying the landscape which is not dependent on Cartesian techniques such as the map, but which offers choices of its own. In different cultures around the world, names can link kin-group with territory; act as a commemoration; invest the land with religious or ideological significance. Such actions were clearly also going on in the medieval landscape; this is what Gelling hints at, for example, when she talks of place-names betraying different attitudes to land (2000:131), or Andrew Reynolds when he looks at how Anglo-Saxon law was materialized in the landscape (Reynolds 1999).

The Archaeology of Historic Landscapes: A Research Agenda

In this chapter I have sketched out some of the concerns of historic landscape archaeology today. I have suggested that the response of archaeologists and other scholars to these concerns hints at a way forward for an archaeology of historic landscapes. How can these hints be linked up into a coherent programme – what, concretely, would an archaeology of historic landscapes written and practised in these terms look like?

First, it involves a clearer understanding of variability in archaeological terms, and a greater self-awareness of argument from example. This would mean a reluctance to use words like "typical," and more broadly "region," *pays*, and type, without rigorous and explicit definition in archaeological terms.

Second, it would encourage the development of a contextual account of the everyday realities of social life in the landscape. A close and careful consideration of context is the central and defining feature of archaeology (Hodder 1999). A description of peasant life: the houses and fields they lived and worked in, the church, the routes and trackways around the landscape. As we have seen, this was done in the early years of the Wharram research before the project widened its scope. Such descriptions should stress the physicality and textures of the architecture and landscape: the way "hollow-ways" were excavated and sunk in to the ground, the construction of the banks that defined tofts and crofts, the manuring of the soil as a transformation in its texture. And it should go on to delineate the everyday movements around that landscape – movement to and from the fields, the ceaseless up and down of the heavy plough, its oxen and their driver, activities around the house and in the yard.

Such a discussion should be arranged around the very basic parameters of space and time. In terms of space, it should look contextually at patterns of movement at different scales: within the house, between house and farm buildings, to and from other houses in the community, the fields, and church. Archaeologically, again, we have direct, practical, hard-edged evidence for the way the landscape delimited and organized this movement. The deep hollow-ways of Devon, the regular laying and relaying of the boundaries between strips in the Midlands open fields. The pattern of movement and work across the land was also a matter of texture: the spreading of rubbish and manure was an activity that linked the domestic and the agrarian realms. In terms of time, archaeologists should emphasize daily, weekly, seasonal, and yearly activities, about which we again have direct, practical, hard-edged evidence, rather than the more difficult question of absolute chronology.

All these very basic descriptions should be contextualized by an anthropological account of the social life they materialize. For example, when the observation is made that women swept out the houses at Wharram so often that the dirt floors became slightly dished in profile (Hurst 1984), this should be the start of an account of gender relations: what women and men did in the course of the day, the points in space and time when their lives intersected (dawn, the evening), the treatment of and attitudes towards children. The evidence of osteo-logy and environmental archaeology is critical here, particularly as much medieval economic history is actually biased in its sources towards the demesne farms and estates of the elite rather than the economies of ordinary villagers. Through such sources we see the dogs roaming the village, gnawing at odd bits of refuse for example (Albarella 1999), or women carrying heavy baskets back and forth (Sofaer 2006).

Archaeology has a proven record of discerning and exploring locales of power and memory in the landscape (Thomas 1991, 1996; Barrett 1993; and Bender 1998 are a few of many examples). The church is a critical element here, but other locales were important too: for ex-ample the early medieval use of prehistoric burial mounds in different ways, including boundary markers. In later historic periods, the loca-tion of features of political authority, such as gibbets displaying the decomposing bodies of executed criminals, were invested with more diverse meanings than their immediately obvious use as a deterrent might suggest (Whyte 2003a).

Having reached an understanding of a place at a particular point in time, an archaeology of changes that were brought to this pattern of life at various critical junctures can then be developed. Again, the emphasis would be on observables. What did the village look like, physically, before and after the Black Death? How many people crammed into the church at the height of the village's development, and would the church have echoed eerily in the empty spaces of, say, 1350? How might we picture the scene as a manor house is demolished, with the villagers looking on? Through such an examination of moments of rupture and how these were experienced by people of different social classes and genders, we can examine the interaction between the agency of the villagers and the agency of outside powers. If the tofts and crofts were laid out, the specific orientation and internal planning of the farmhouses was not. Nevertheless, the plans of houses erected at any one time are similar, even if their orientation is not (Gardiner 2000). What do these very simple observations tell us about their inhabitants' view of their world?

Study can then move outwards, to wider questions more familiar to landscape archaeology and history – issues of village and landscape planning, of the long term, of change and stability, of the degree to which material culture patterning is local, regional, or national in scope. However, we would be impelled to develop an anthropological defini-tion of social change and stability. In other words, such an analysis can identify and define social forms and cultural processes in terms that are comparable across cultures. Such an archaeological analysis could then take its place alongside other generalizing studies of state formation and agricultural process. For example C. Erickson (1993) discusses the social implications of raised field agriculture, while Cherry, Davis, and Mantzourani (1991) examine questions of nucleation and dispersal in the context of the Cyclades. The village planning seen archaeologically at Wharram is not to be explained in terms of "manorialization"; rather, debates over manorialization hint, through a glass darkly, at issues raised in other periods and contexts about how we explain social change and complexity in a generalizing and comparative manner. It is here that Adam Smith's (2003) work on the political landscape is especially helpful, in that it offers a bridge between an understanding of place and a generalizing account of political process.

It is also at this point, having done what it does best in terms of the basic stuff of the discipline (space, time, material patterning) and having engaged with the work of other archaeologists across the world, that archaeology can seriously engage with other disciplines. It can raise simple and obvious questions about the social actions that generated both village plans and the documentary record. John Evans notes the "complementarity between the strewing of pottery on the land and the intensity of document-making" in early medieval Brittany, a point that could be extended to the understanding of the material and documentary world in general (Evans 2003:132, also 160–71).

Such a proposal is not a rejection of the best of Romanticism. In looking at ordinary patterns of life, and in much of Bender's work for example, the influence of Romanticism is very clear. Empathy with the experiences of ordinary people in the past is still a strong element. It is also not a rejection of history. Rather, both the archaeological and historical "records" emerge as products and mediators of social action, rather than "evidence" about a past to be "reconstructed."

Reforming the Landscape

I will attempt to illustrate these points further by returning to the critical period isolated by W. G. Hoskins in his thesis of the Great Rebuilding in rural England between 1560 and 1640. As we saw in the last chapter, Hoskins's thesis derived its power from its congruence with prevailing ideas and interpretations in documentary history: the Great Rebuilding became illustrative material for the rise of the middling sort. And its power lessened and confidence in the Great Rebuilding retreated as, first, "rebuilding" was seen as a much more continuous process spanning the 14th to 18th centuries, and, second, the equation of numbers of surviving houses on the ground now to past phases of rebuilding was shown to be problematic as a middle-range assumption.

I suggest we can make two very simple moves to reopen and re-vivify the Great Rebuilding debate. I have discussed these different elements at some length on several other occasions (Johnson 1993b, 1996). Here, I want to stress how these moves correspond to the basic empirical strengths of archaeological enquiry, of context, form, and dating, and how they also open up issues of agency and practice.

Context

The archaeological context of change in the form of houses was change in the landscape as a whole. This change, in 16th-century England, was often sudden and dramatic in form. Change can be isolated in two areas in particular: the agrarian and the religious landscape[s].

First, we see transformation of the agrarian landscape, in the form of desertion of settlements and of enclosure of the open fields. In many local communities across England, the old system of medieval open fields came to a sudden and abrupt end. In some cases, this was the deliberate action of landlords, evicting the few tenants who remained in a village that had contracted in preceding centuries, and turning the area over to sheep pasture, often "fossilizing" the remains of peasant houses and the open fields in the form of earthworks that survive today (see Figures 1.3 and 4.10). Depopulation, as the deliberate destruction of a village community, was a very basic rupture in the physical and cultural fabric of the rural landscape. The reaction of the time was one of opposition at the level of both popular protest and of the state, which feared the weakening of the Commonwealth. Historians have stressed how contemporary perception of depopulation was overstated – how most depopulated villages were already shrunken, and/or how numbers were exaggerated (Dyer 1994). However, the complaint was itself a social action rather than a piece of evidence: when seen as such, complaints about depopulation serve to highlight how important the perception of rupture in the landscape was for contemporaries. In other places, enclosure of the landscape was a much more piecemeal and drawn-out process, often unfolding within the interstices of earlier field systems rather than simply destroying them (Figure 1.4).

The second transformation was the reformation of the "religious" landscape. The destruction and transformation of major elements of the landscape was not confined to agrarian change. As 16th-century peasants saw the agrarian world around them transformed, often very

Figure 5.4 The ruins of Binham Priory, Norfolk, dissolved in the 1530s. The survival of the "stump" of the nave is due to its continued use of that part of the structure as a parish church

dramatically and suddenly, so they also saw their religious world changed. First, the great monasteries were destroyed in the 1530s, many being converted into great houses and others falling rapidly into ruin. Archaeologically, then, we see what in prehistoric jargon might be termed a cultural horizon – the sudden loss and destruction of a whole class of elite monuments. The archaeological biography of any one of these monuments, the way in which their sites and often their fabric were reused in a variety of ways, is a testament again to rupture at an elite level; in many cases, the conversion of these monasteries into elite dwellings has been interpreted as a deliberately meaningful statement of the changing nature of power in a region (Figure 5.4; Everson and Stocker 2003).

Transformation was extended down the social scale, into every community in England, through the reformation of the parish church two decades later. The church, the focus of collective memory, the baptism and burial place of every villager, was utterly transformed. Figures of the Virgin Mary and other saints were smashed or removed; wall-paintings and other depictions were whitewashed over; stained glass

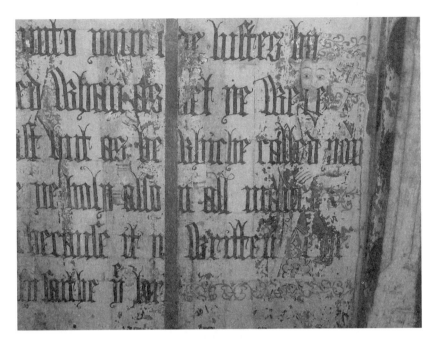

Figure 5.5 Medieval painting from Binham, whitewashed over and covered with lettering as part of the Reformation; the painting has subsequently become less obscured

was smashed to allow clear light into the church, in part for easier popular reading of the Word (Aston 2003). In place of all this, religious texts such as the Ten Commandments were written in black lettering across the whitewash (Figure 5.5). The layout of space inside the church was also transformed, and with it the lived experience of every villager. Internal fixtures and fittings were removed. The rood screen, which stood between the congregation and the altar and thus lent religious ceremony an air of mystery, was cut down or removed entirely. The altar was often moved forward from its formerly distant position, towards the centre of the church. Fragments of the earlier pattern of church space and imagery survive, in part evidence of popular resistance to such changes (Tarlow 2003). At the same time, reformation was extended across the landscape. Holy wells and crosses, the resting places or meeting points for individuals and groups of different kinds, were destroyed or stripped of their religious associations.

Historians have stressed the doctrinal debates and struggles that accompanied these changes, and examined their intersection with high politics. Here I am drawing attention to their archaeology, in the form of the physical, everyday experience of such change. With both depopulation and reformation, I am stressing how these were experienced by the rural population of all social classes, as ruptures in the landscape, and as losses of visible expressions of everyday meaning. They also stand as archaeological testament to the growing power and changing nature of the state. Where peasant culture was strongly regional in nature, as seen for example in variations in house forms and farming practices across the country, changes in the Church had a national pattern, even if from church to church they were applied in a different, contingent way.

Form

The form of late medieval and early modern houses, and the way that form was changing, is well known. I have discussed several times elsewhere how the period from the middle of the 16th century onwards saw a steady abandonment of the open hall, in other words a central room open to the roof that dominated the everyday life and cultural sentiment of the medieval peasant. Houses from the 16th century onwards did not abandon the hall wholesale. A central room in which eating and many other activities of daily life took place was still standard in most houses. However, it was reduced in size, and had its open hearth replaced by a chimney stack; with this, the hearth was moved from the centre to the side of the room. Where the late medieval peasant gazed up into the mysterious recesses of the roof, its apex lost amid the smoke from the hearth, the early modern yeoman sat at the head of the table, with all his family and household gathered around him (Johnson 1993, 1996).

The house was the centre of a working farm and, together with the everyday activities that took place within and around it, was embedded in a landscape context of farming practices. As noted above, these practices were changing rapidly in the 16th century in ways that are seen archaeologically through desertion, inequality between peasant households, and the continued growth of market relationships between towns and rural hinterlands. Its agricultural setting also meant that the house was "charged with production": in other words, the relations within it – between husband and wife, master and servant, parent and child – were also economic relationships.

And these relationships, like those expressed in the church and those in other rural societies, were political relationships too. Any archaeologist working contextually would find it very difficult to ignore a set of parallels between the organization of the parish church and that of the peasant house. Both are rectangular spaces, entered by the long side towards the lower end, and divided into upper and lower ends; in both church and open-hall house the gaze is drawn upwards, to the roof; in both, a table/altar stands at one end; in both, a meal-like ceremony encodes and materializes the social and cultural relations at stake. The common currency here is a *habitus*, a common set of cultural assumptions and practices spanning religion, politics, and economics. Such a linkage using the layout and structure of the house at its centre is, again, a feature of pre-industrial societies which has generated an extensive comparative literature in archaeology and anthropology (Joyce and Gillespie 2000; Beck, in press). In pre-industrial societies ranging from the ancient Maya to medieval Europe, the house is used as a controlling metaphor and symbol of political order and authority: the everyday activities around the house – the relative position of seating, the preparation and serving of food, the differential provision of privacy.

Archaeologically, then, it is not surprising to find a change in the form of the house so closely tied in terms of dates to a change in the form of the church, both unfolding from the middle of the 16th century onwards.

Dating and agency

As was discussed in Chapter 4, the rebuilding of houses is difficult to date as a general process nationally or even regionally. In this respect, the difficulty of dating rebuilding as a general process is similar to the difficulty of dating the creation of villages as a general process. Consequently, we can no longer talk of a Great Rebuilding as such. However, individual houses can be dated very tightly if they are seen a little differently, as actions of individual and household agency. The use of tree-ring dating can isolate a very specific date for the building of a specific house. Each building, each modification of an older house, indeed each action that takes place within and around its walls, is a small or large piece of human agency, whether or not it has specific documents associated with it (Figure 5.6). Human agency is manifested in the "rearing" of the timber frame, the decision to place a date-stone with initials over the threshold, the purchase and installation of window glass to replace wooden shutters, countless everyday actions that amount to a "change in use" of a particular room, the naming of a room as hall, parlour, or chamber in a probate inventory,

Such agency can be quite complex to discern. First, there is the agency of the craftsman, carpenter, and/or mason building or modifying

Figure 5.6 Fairlings, Yetminster, Dorset, built around 1600. As with
other houses in the area, the builder of Fairlings chose to retain a traditional
plan with a cross-passage. The hall, however, had a ceiling and chimney-
stack placed with its back to the cross-passage. In succeeding generations,
a second chimney-stack was added to the service (near) end of the building,
creating separate heating and cooking facilities at the end of the house away
from the hall, and in the process blocking the window in the gable end.
The upper end (on the left) was rebuilt in the form of a gabled wing in the
18th century (Machin 1978:29)

the house, constrained by local materials and working within a craft
tradition. I have argued (Johnson 1993a:38–42) that the archaeology
shows that the craft tradition that framed, literally and metaphorically,
the late medieval house was very strong. Timber frames were prefabri-
cated in the builder's yard, and details such as the position of doors
and windows were predetermined by being carpentered into the main
elements of the timber frame at that early point. Houses before the
Reformation, then, were tightly controlled in their form by a strong
sense of what was culturally appropriate, expressed in what was taken
for granted in the prefabrication of the house.

This tight control was weakened in the later 16th century. Just as the
traditional elements of the wider landscapes and the links between
them were being ruptured, so the craft tradition embedded in the

Figure 5.7 Datestone of 1607, Yetminster. It should probably be read as: "JO(hn) (and) DO(rothy) REDE BE(ne) DO(mum) HA(nc) ED(ificavit)" (Machin 1978:114)

house itself was being pulled apart. A simple and obvious point to make with houses at the time of the Reformation is that, in many areas, their form is very varied. Where the late medieval house always had a hall in a certain spatial relationship to the other rooms, and with a certain door position, this is not so with later houses. Not only is the open hall abandoned; there is, at least initially, no very tight "competence" or system to replace it.

Where houses have date-stones and initials on them, such a placing is not only a useful piece of "evidence" but is itself a social action. Initials are often recorded in pairs, with husband and wife given an apparent equality in the naming of the house – though those of the husband invariably come first (Figure 5.7).

Agency is important in the understanding of not just the construction of the house but also its use. The ceiling-over of the hall had the consequence of making movement along the house possible at the level of the upper floor. The internal dimensions and appearance of these rooms suggest that, in some cases, they were not widely or habitually used for living purposes in the generation immediately after their construction – ceilings were low or non-existent, and the traditional placement of the husband and wife's bed was downstairs in the chamber or parlour. Over the next century, to 1700 and beyond, these upper floors were more and more frequently used for bedrooms in particular. In other words, the move to sleeping upstairs, with its attendant values of greater "privacy" and differentiation of space, was the result of many thousands of individual social actions, new ways of living in old houses, that were not necessarily intended as such by the builders of the house.

The most revealing intersections of archaeology and history lie in the way in which both frame, and are framed through, social action. And such social action is only a very short inferential leap from the archaeological and documentary record. The building of a house is a scene easily envisaged: the distrustful client, insisting on a written contract (Salzman 1952); the comments of neighbours as the foundations of a new stone wing are laid out; the creation of a probate inventory: the group of men of "good credit" moving solemnly through the house, one perhaps impatient to get the job done, another making sure the list is made up meticulously, listing the rooms one by one and taking care to ensure that values of missed items are included in the phrase "in small things forgotten," the third member illiterate and making his mark with a shaky cross; the grieving widow in one corner of the hall. The arrival in the village of outsiders, men with a licence to survey the church and report back to a distant and dimly understood authority; a second visit, an episode of smashing, plunder, and looting, with villagers observing the scene and muttering comments into their beer in the alehouse – *sotto voce*, so they will not be presented in court, and thus of course lost for ever to the documentary record. We can imagine the first church service after the stripping of the altars, villagers now slightly uncertain as to where to sit and how to behave during the service. The priest explains the texts written on the walls to a congregation more than half of whose members are illiterate. The quiet thoughts of the socially middling yeoman, as he tramps home with his family after the service – neither of quiet acceptance nor of radical rejection of this new world, but rather, in more practical terms, to make sure his family has access to this new power: to find the money to send his son to grammar school, to learn how to read and write. The thoughts of his wife: there is a growing demand for cheese and butter from the farm; that is her money, not her husband's; best to keep those activities away from the rest of the house, in a new wing.

And the thoughts of both: if there is a good harvest, and if the income from dairying and brewing continues to flow, the next year will be a good time to add a new wing or a new chimney-stack to the house. After all, the contributions to the Church so generously and piously made by their mothers and fathers have been swept away; by 1580, the Church had undergone four separate settlements according to the religious preferences of changing monarchs, each time involving a new requirement that the parish fund a new set of religious regalia and each involving further destruction and reformation at parish level. It might be best for the family and household, then, to turn away a little from the parish and the village and concentrate on the house.

Hoskins saw the close connections between the rebuilding of rural England and the growing affluence of the middling sort. He also observed that houses "tell us facts about the past life of the parish that no written record ever set out to do, mainly, of course, because the facts were too commonplace at the time to be worthy of record" (1959:108–9). By placing the rebuilding of houses in its archaeological context, by tracing contextual links between different forms of landscape from domestic architecture through to religious and farming systems, and by thinking about houses as products of social action, scholars can take forward those connections. And in the process, a contribution to more general issues of the cultural construction of middle-class culture, and of the role of the house in pre-industrial societies, can be made.

Conclusion

If archaeologists really want to take seriously the injunction to hear the men and women of the past talking and working, there is a need to do more than cite such a sentiment on the first and last pages of books on the historic landscape. I have tried to show how we can do just that, in relatively simple and direct ways that correspond with the strengths of archaeology as a discipline. In the process, I have tried to trace some of the ways forward for a theoretically informed study of landscape that combines the best of the Hoskins tradition with the best of recent insights. In the next chapter, I will argue that such an approach should be argued for in political as well as scholarly terms.

Chapter Six

THE POLITICS OF LANDSCAPE

I want to start this chapter in the present, with two images. They come from the front and back covers of a recent policy document produced by English Heritage, entitled *Power of Place* (Figures 6.1 and 6.2). This document attempted to lay down guidelines and recommendations for what it called the "historic environment" over the next ten years. In so doing, it was informed by a commissioned survey of attitudes of English people towards "heritage," and in its turn has seen its recommendations fed into subsequent government legislation. More broadly, the context of *Power of Place* was the challenge of understanding and enhancing the role of the historic environment with reference to the changing social and political imperatives of modern England.

Archaeology, and intellectual life as a whole, has long moved beyond the point at which academic study of the past can plausibly be held to be independent of and detached from the concerns of the present (Johnson 1999:167–8). It has been accepted that a full account of ideas of landscape must be a reflexive one. That is, landscape is a two-way process: it is about the viewer and his or her social, cultural and political circumstances as well as the viewed (Bender 1993, 1998; Bender and Winer 2001; Stewart and Strathern 2003). An acknowledgement of the context within which we all work, and an open discussion of what could or should be done about it, is thus a necessary counterpart to the discussions of theory, method, and practice that have run through this book.

The 1980s saw a new sharpness in the recognition that the English landscape and the political present were closely related. Robert Hewison's book *The Heritage Industry* (1987) argued that the rise of interest in "heritage" in Britain was closely related to a "climate of decline" in

Figure 6.1 *Power of Place*: front cover. © *English Heritage*

general. Patrick Wright's *On Living in an Old Country* (1985) continued this theme. Both were writing within a specific context – the political victory of a neoliberal economics, whether that of Margaret Thatcher in Britain or Ronald Reagan in the USA, which, it was argued, saw

Figure 6.2 *Power of Place*: back cover. © *English Heritage*

the past as commodified – a packaged product, to be bought, sold, and consumed like any other.

An effective response was mounted by the socialist historian Raphael Samuel (1994). Samuel granted that the construction of "heritage" was ideological and that its packaging as a marketable commodity was part of wider political currents. However, he suggested that rather than being passive consumers of heritage culture, ordinary people drew their own meanings and experiences from their encounter with heritage parks and the English countryside. Samuel saw local history and archaeology groups in the Hoskins tradition as part of this active and bottom-up pattern.

However, to understand the *Power of Place* images we must go to the date of publication of the McPherson report (McPherson 1999). Lord McPherson's brief was to examine the context of the murder of a black British youth, Stephen Lawrence, and the subsequent failure of the police force and judiciary to successfully convict anyone of the crime. McPherson took his brief in the widest possible sense, and what started as a specific inquiry into a judicial and policing failure became a devastating case study in the intersection of race, politics, and cultural institutions in modern Britain. McPherson produced a wide-ranging report whose implications went further and deeper than the expected exposure of "institutional racism" in the police force and judiciary. It was impossible to come away from a reading of the report without the feeling that he had identified just one strand of a wider pattern of institutional racism running across British society as a whole. The implication of McPherson was that the 1950s social consensus, and the social and cultural institutions that embodied that consensus, stood accused of an implicit racism, in part in their acceptance of a single cultural standard to which all should assimilate and in which acceptance of such a single standard was assumed.

The effect of the McPherson report and related developments of the time was to inscribe into the political landscape, and give state sponsorship to, many of the ideas and discourses of multiculturalism and social inclusion that had been a familiar part of academic radical critique for some time. The work of Stuart Hall and other colleagues of Raymond Williams in cultural studies had taken a "multicultural turn," looking beyond a Marxist analysis of class to look at questions of ethnic identity and postcolonialism (Gilroy 1987; Rojek 2003). At the same time, postcolonial and feminist critiques made increasing inroads into academic discourse – though most obviously into prehistoric archaeology, human geography, and the social sciences rather than into landscape history and the archaeology of historic periods.

In the wake of the election of a Labour government in 1997, the whole balance of British institutional politics and culture shifted. "New Labour" instituted a programme of reform based around the language and principles of social inclusion and diversity, terms which were taken to encompass the whole gamut of social, gender, and ethnic identities and extending to related issues such as disability. Government legislation made it incumbent upon institutions to make an active engagement with such issues. Where formerly individuals and institutions were considered beyond reproach unless proven otherwise, it was now incumbent upon institutions to demonstrate that they had reflected on issues of diversity, equality, and social inclusion, were implementing policies to actively tackle the issues raised, and were monitoring the outcomes.

Behind this top-down shift in institutional policy lay an attempt to change what was perceived by many as a national culture of complacency. No longer could universities shrug their shoulders and claim that they would admit more students from underprivileged backgrounds if they made the effort to apply; it was now incumbent upon them to show that they had an active policy of encouraging recruitment and were monitoring its effectiveness. No longer could established heritage bodies like museums, English Heritage, and the National Trust shrug their shoulders and say that they would welcome more ethnic minority visitors if they only came through the doors; relevant policies to attract such visitors and make monuments and displays relevant to them had to be shown to exist, be freely available for inspection, and be subject to a process of regular review.

The most obvious influence of these new imperatives on *Power of Place* was in the choice of pictures. The front and back cover illustrations were clearly chosen to convey the way in which particular landscapes held power and meaning for people, and, to be cynical, to convey a sense of the commitment of English Heritage to this new set of values. What interests us here is the pairing of the two images. The front cover is a street scene from a market in Brixton, south London – explicitly urban and "multicultural." The back cover, on the other hand, is an aerial view of a traditional English village, with church, green, and houses. It is, in one sense, a graphic representation of the Hoskins-derived vision of the English landscape.

Power of Place is revealing in the way it juxtaposes on front and back cover different senses of place. The Chair of the Commission for Racial Equality, Trevor Phillips, has spoken of a "passive apartheid" in the modern English countryside (T. Phillips 2004; see also Solly and Ling Wong 2004); what *Power of Place* hints at is a kind of intellectual apartheid in which other narratives of conflict and diaspora take place elsewhere, somewhere other than the English village. The cosy, insular world of rural landscape history that has evolved from the Hoskins tradition can, it is implied, be left to get on in peace, while more radical and challenging work goes on in the inner cities. My concern in this chapter is to look more closely at this back cover, and ask about its rhetorical pairing with and separation from the front, and then to explore the implications for such an analysis of the role of landscape archaeology in the present.

Post-War Landscapes

As Chapter 3 outlined, the post-war period running into the 1950s was a critical horizon in the formation of the English landscape tradition in intellectual and scholarly terms. It was also a critical horizon in two other senses.

First, the 1950s were a pivotal moment in the mass experience of and encounter with the English landscape. Post-war affluence meant many ordinary people could, for the first time, afford a motor car; weekend drives into the country became ever more popular. The destinations of these drives were closely linked to "England's heritage": country houses (Mandler 1997), ruined castles, villages, and market towns. A walk in the country had been a favourite occupation since the inter-war period and before, first assisted in the 19th century by the spread of the bicycle and Wordsworth's hated railways; the 1950s saw its expansion in popularity. National parks were founded in this period: the first, inevitably, in the Lake District following the injunction of Wordsworth a century and a half earlier. The post-war Labour government passed the National Parks and Access to the Countryside Act in 1949; the Lake District National Park came into being in 1951. The Yorkshire Dales, including Swaledale, became a national park in 1954 (MacEwen and MacEwen 1987); the latest area, the New Forest on the south coast of England, was designated in 2005.

Second, this period saw the formation of a post-war cultural consensus, a critical cultural horizon, stretching beyond the world of academic scholarship into that of the intellectual classes and ordinary people, encompassing aesthetic and moral as well as cultural and political values. *The Making of the English Landscape*, then, was not simply a text that existed in academic isolation. Returning from their countryside expeditions, families turned to the pages of the Book Club magazines and ordered Hoskins's books, or listened to his radio talks, reprinted in *The Listener* (for example Hoskins 1954a, 1964a, 1964b). Hoskins explained to them something about what they saw. He enthused a generation beyond the professional and the academic. We have seen that the post-war formation of landscape history and archaeology tied itself to an explicitly populist ethos, set itself the task of writing accessibly, just as

Wordsworth defined a poet as a man speaking to other men, focused on ordinary people in the past, and was taken up by amateur and continuing education groups.

The post-war period was central to the intellectual formation of the English landscape tradition, as we have seen. It was also central to the formation of intellectual currents in society, culture, and politics. A "post-war consensus" was established during this period that can in many ways be characterized as a hegemonic discourse. It formed a body of shared assumptions about what "culture" was and how to appreciate it, what it was to be literate and educated, in literature, the arts, and in political life – what might be termed, following archaeological methodology, a "cultural horizon." This culture can be characterized as a consciously radical and social democratic one, with left and liberal affiliations (Sinfield 1989, 2000). As a result, the Hoskins view of landscape was inscribed not just into the fabric of the academic practice of landscape archaeology, but also in popular views of landscape as a whole. It was congruent with and reinforced a much wider formation of beliefs and discourses. These discourses, these assumptions about what culture was, how it was disseminated and perpetuated, went hand in hand with the social and economic reforms of the 1945–51 Labour government, which were accepted and indeed reinforced by the Conservative governments of the 1950s. As such, they formed part of a social democratic consensus.

Nevertheless, with the hindsight of fifty years, the 1950s "cultural horizon" now seems to many to be a peculiarly narrow and single-voiced consensus. Its political sensibility was largely one of class. Other dimensions – in particular the politics of gender, race, and disability – were not so explicitly articulated. Lynne Segal notes the blindness, even on the left, towards women's issues in this period (1990:22–5). In this way, the 1950s inscribed the Romantic social exclusivity of class and gender into a culture as a whole in a single orthodoxy into which other genders, cultures, and races could, with hard work and effort on their part, be "assimilated." Debate over what "culture," and the national consciousness that underlay it, was, was quite attenuated. The writer Stefan Collini has pointed out how ideas of Englishness and Britishness are subject to a "muffling inclusiveness" whereby debate about them is implicit and inflected rather than overt and strident (Collini 1991; see also Johnson 2003).

This cultural horizon was not to be questioned until the 1980s. At that point, it came under attack from two sources: the social divisions and break-up of the social democratic consensus under Margaret Thatcher's radical and neoliberal Conservative government, and the increasing prominence and sharpness of a multicultural and postcolonial critique of British society from both within and without.

In spite of these two challenges, I will argue that the culture of the 1950s endures today in the presumed moral underpinnings of study of the English landscape. A fragmentation in ideas of landscape was established at the start of this book, between heavily theorized approaches on the one hand, and common sense and muddy boots on the other. This fragmentation has also been a political one, with the cultural horizon of the 1950s continuing in landscape archaeology not in refutation of more recent critiques, but as if they never happened.

Landscapes of the Past

We have seen how, for Wordsworth, appreciation of landscape tended to push social relations into the background. Every time, then, that a modern writer invites their readers to contemplate the landscape as a symphony, chamber music, or indeed any kind of artistic composition, he or she is implicitly asking them to treat the social relations behind that landscape as somehow secondary or marginal. Comments such as "We tend to sentimentalize old village life but for many it was a lifetime of poverty and extreme hardship and not of roses round the door" (Hoskins 1980:19) do occur in Hoskins's writings, and he wrote extensively as an economic historian on topics such as harvests and hunger (1964b, 1968), but comments on class conflict of whatever form are striking in their rarity, particularly when he is discussing landscape rather than economic and social history as such. "Slave labour" is mentioned in a purely descriptive context, the early medieval construction of an estate boundary (1955:68).

Over and over again in his work, Hoskins explicitly tells us that we should turn away from the present to contemplate the past, perhaps most chillingly when he refers to the need to write one's books before the onset of nuclear war (1954a:xix) or evocatively in his "description" in *Devon* of a country house:

> Here [in a squire's house], where all is quiet, the lunacy of the outside world, the fate that has overtaken it, is an insoluble mystery. One ruminates over it for a few moments after the nine o'clock news, heard religiously each evening in the library on an antique and sizzling battery set. With relief the squire turns to the local newspaper . . . and reads the more intelligible and interesting news of his own countryside.*

*The above description is a composite one. No particular house is intended, but every detail is authentic. (Hoskins 1954b:298)

This nostalgia for a past that is quite obviously sentimentalized even arouses the American critic Meinig's ire in an otherwise celebratory piece on Hoskins's work. Meinig locates what he sees as Hoskins's refusal to discuss the Industrial Revolution in his distaste for modernity in general, and comments:

> to follow him all the way is to abandon landscape analysis and simply indulge one's emotions . . . by militantly, idiosyncratically refusing to describe and analyse one of the greatest eras of change, Hoskins has arbitrarily truncated the story of the making of the English landscape . . . We cannot avoid the conclusion that there is a deep sentimental bias laced through all his landscape writing, and while his incisive impressions of it enliven his books and vivify him in our minds as a strong and engaging personality, they also limit our confidence in his judgment and, at worst, depreciate him as an historian. (Meinig 1979a:207–8)

However, Meinig is only telling part of the story: Hoskins may have decried the present, and before that the Industrial Revolution, but he did not arbitrarily truncate it. *The Making of the English Landscape* does contain a discussion of later historic periods proportionate with earlier themes, even if Hoskins's distaste for what he is discussing is evident: "The Industrial Revolution," "Roads, Canals and Railways," and "The Landscape of Towns" occupy three chapters and sixty-eight pages of *The Making of the English Landscape* (Hoskins 1955:162–230). We saw in Chapter 4 that there is a powerful myth that Hoskins did not understand archaeology, but that such a myth needs at the very least careful critical appraisal if not outright scepticism. The same goes for Hoskins's view of the Industrial Revolution and modernity in general.

In any case, all archaeological and historical writing is by definition a commentary on the present as well as an exploration of the past. We read Hoskins's words, and the words of his contemporaries, in the present, and make sense of them in terms of things we see in the landscape of the present. When it is recalled that the present is unavoidable, Hoskins's flowery prose and other writers' apparent silence on contemporary issues is itself quite eloquent: both reader and writer are taking a position through their very silence.

David Matless has pointed out that the level on which the anti-modernist statements from different writers of the 1930s and 1950s should be taken is quite complex; it is certainly much more, and deserves to be taken more seriously, than a mindless, nostalgic, sentimental, and formless slush. Quoting his sentiments on setting up a "Human Conservancy" area in the tiny and beautiful Midlands county of Rutland, to parallel the burgeoning Nature Conservancy areas across the country in the 1950s, Matless notes that "Hoskins has no real hope that his ironic Conservancy proposal will come to pass." Further, it is a view that "comes not from mindlessness but from expert authority, like Larkin [the English poet] in 'Going, going'" (Matless 1998:274; see also Matless 1993). Hoskins's position of turning away from the present is, then, not really proposed as a practical political strategy, nor is it a position that he maintains at the most serious level. Rather, yet again, it is a blatantly rhetorical device borrowed from the Romantic tradition. It is a sentiment directly prefigured by Wordsworth, in the latter's early radicalism giving way to the sentiment of "this melancholy waste of hope o'erthrown," born in part of the experience of the French Revolution, that action will only lead to something even worse. With both Wordsworth and Hoskins, this retreat is expressed both in temporal and also in geographical terms. Both came to hate London and to seek refuge in the countryside, whether of the Lake District or of "provincial England." In both cases, retreat from the capital was retreat into political quietude and nostalgia and a turn away from the political realities of the present.

This kind of ethic would be a historical footnote if it did not continue in the study of landscapes today. It is repeated, for example, by Muir, who extends the anti-modern trope to the current state of academic study in addition to the countryside in terms which would have appealed to Hoskins (who, after all, cited as one of the reasons for his retirement the growing pressure of university administration):

> The first version of *Reading the Landscape* was written in the hope that, by encouraging the process of landscape discovery, support would be found for more effective conservational measures and improved access to the countryside. Times have changed, conservational and educational budgets have been slashed, while managers, some with fake academic titles, marketing consultants and accountants have replaced the people of real learning and vision . . . With little if any old countryside remaining it is even more important that we should leave records as blueprints for mental or physical reconstructions. (Muir 2000:xv)

Flight into contemplation of the English countryside is, by definition, a flight away from the multicultural urban reality expressed by the front cover of *Power of Place*. Shanks and Tilley wrote that "Archaeology should be conceived as acting as a catalyst in the transformation of the present, for without commitment to one's own historicity, the discipline becomes little more than an escape from our own time and place" (1987:208). Ironically, it was just such an escape that Hoskins appeared to advocate, and which Thirsk (2000:15–16) and others (Muir 2000) appear to endorse. It is symptomatic of the lack of dialogue between different forms of archaeological and historical study that both sides in this debate implicitly treat the other's views as self-evidently absurd and even immoral.

What is wrong with the apparently innocent activity of turning away from the present to contemplate the past? The answer is very simple: it cannot be done. Any piece of writing about the past, or for that matter any fieldwork or other form of landscape scholarship and appreciation, takes place in the present, in the here and now. Therefore, the appeal to study the past for its own sake or as an escape from the present is always and immediately disingenuous. It serves only to conceal the way in which past and present are linked, and to serve as a pretence that a piece of writing about landscape is not always and immediately political in nature.

Landscapes of Beauty

A related problem with the retreat into an unrestrained desire to contemplate the past is that it tends to reinforce the split between the aesthetic and the political that so crippled later Romanticism. If we want to retreat into contemplation of the past, it is in part because, it is implied, the past was so much more beautiful a place.

The split between society and aesthetics has been rejected over and over again, most notably in Raymond Williams's insistence that "we cannot separate literature and art from other kinds of social practice, in such a way as to make them subject to quite special and distinct laws . . . [the arts] may have quite specific features as practices, but they cannot be separated from the general social process" (1980:44). In the early 1960s, the Cultural Studies Department at Birmingham University was initiating a new phase in the study of literature, art, and aesthetics and the connections between them. Drawing on Marxist traditions, Williams and his colleagues were insisting that literature and other forms of cultural production should be seen not as timeless, ahistorical classics suitable for purely aesthetic contemplation, but in their historical context, in particular that of changing class relations: genres such as country house and early landscape poetry, then, were understood in terms of nascent capitalism and class relations in the English countryside (Williams 1959, 1961, 1973, 1976; Hoggart 1957).

In the process, Williams was questioning the "objective" basis of many of the categories that are assumed in Hoskins's work and in that of subsequent scholars, for example landscape, community, aesthetics, Nature and the natural (which he memorably describes as "the most complex word in the English language": Williams 1976:184). In many ways, Williams's analysis of these words and the configuration of ideas they delineated shared similarities with Michel Foucault's exposure of discursive formations as part of his "archaeology of knowledge" (Foucault 1972). It is this view that I have borrowed heavily from in my account of early topographical and landscape writing in the Introduction.

However, despite its obvious relevance to the themes discussed in landscape history and archaeology, mention of such work is entirely absent. Williams's classic book *The Country and the City* (1973), for example, examines the construction of the idea of the English countryside as it changed during and after the Industrial Revolution; yet it makes no appearance in Hoskins's later work, for example the 1977 introduction and selected reading for *The Making of the English Landscape*. I suggest that part of the reason such work was not easily understood from within the English landscape tradition was that it failed to conform to some of its basic assumptions about the aesthetic, just as prehistoric remains in the landscape were underemphasized because they failed to find a place in a lineal story of the ancestors. It was also not easily understood because it questioned the very categories that formed the underlying conceptual geology of the English landscape tradition itself. How could one celebrate the "country" if one recognized that such a category was itself not an immemorial, unchanging entity, but rather was created by the "city"? How could one condemn modernity if the very literary device of such a condemnation was revealed as a characteristically modern way of thinking?

The ideological problem with an elevation of the aesthetic is that it leads into an attempt to demarcate certain kinds of "artistic" practices as beyond critique. Such an attempt to place elements of culture beyond critical comment was, for Roland Barthes, a classic strategy of bourgeois culture: if an art object was somehow ineffable, beautiful in a way that transcended history, the social values and practices that it characterized were similarly elevated beyond critique (Barthes 1989). By creating a separate category of the beautiful, the values and practices that characterize the beautiful are insulated from any kind of politically situated comment, or make such a comment appear vulgar or petty.

One might add to Barthes that it is also a classically English technique of ideology: one appeals to the love of the beautiful as self-evident (Easthope 1999). In short, the back cover of *Power of Place* is insulated from critique. It is unmoving, stable, contented, and sane. What could possibly be problematic about such an image?

Such a split, again, continues in landscape studies today, though the "beautiful" is often replaced by the "muddy." Modern writers may have shied away from Hoskins's purple prose, but the assumption that the chill air on one's face and the mud on one's boots elevates one's observations beyond the disturbing relativism of the "social" remains. In this sense, the idea that muddy boots have an authority that cannot be touched by mere theorizing is not only deeply empiricist; it is also politically reactionary, as it seeks unconsciously to insulate certain observations about the social life of humans from critical analysis. As a result, studies which stress the dominance of an untheorized "environment" tend to underplay class relations, even where in other work their authors have a demonstrated radical commitment.

Landscapes of Nationalism

For Hoskins, the study of landscape, and indeed the study of the past as a whole, is the study of his lineal ancestors. His *Exeter in the 17th Century* was dedicated "to my father 1873–1955, a citizen of Exeter" (Hoskins 1957:v). Elsewhere, the study of "ancestors" is often true in a quite literal sense:

> My ancestors were men and women of no particular eminence even in local history, farmers nearly all of them until the collapse of local communities all over England in the early 19th century drove them off the land and into the towns and across the water to the American continent. But they were the sort of people who form the foundations of any stable society. (Hoskins 1954b:xix–xx; see also Hoskins and Finberg 1952:396–405)

> I was born in Exeter, and my father before me, and his father before that. My great-grandfather came to the city as the son of a failing farmer in the bad years of the 1820s, so we have been here a long time. As a native I have been critical of much that is done now in the name of progress (whatever that vague word may mean) but that is the privilege of belonging to the family. (Hoskins 1960:v)

Hoskins discovers with delight that the parish clerk in the Dartmoor town of Chagford in 1800 was "my great-great-grandfather Richard Thorn," who traced his ancestry in turn to "Robert Atte Thorne in 1332" and back beyond this to

> the first moorland peasant who broke up the ground around the solitary thorn-tree, perhaps in the closing years of the 12th century or the first years of the 13th century. First the ancient tree gave its name to the farm, then the farm gave its name to the owners; and still there are Thorns in Chagford . . . These things delight me when I come across them. This is the immemorial, provincial England, stable, rooted deep in the soil, unmoving, contented, and sane. These are my forebears, who have made me what I am whether I like it or not. (Hoskins 1954b:xx)

Who reads these words, this narration of self, with a corresponding delight and recognition? Who does Hoskins think will share his delight? More broadly, who do contemporary landscape archaeologists and historians write for? Who is it that comprises their imagined audience, and what kind of "imagined community" (Anderson 1989) are they referring to and even creating in their work?

Hoskins's England is in part an England for exiles. Not for those abroad, nor indeed for "locals" living in the countryside, but for those living in English towns and cities. He himself after all first encountered the Devon countryside as a child, on summer holidays as a visitor from Exeter, even if his ancestors came from that countryside; and we have noted (Chapter 3) how his narrative of personal discovery is framed around that encounter. As Raymond Williams would observe, such a Romantic world is not of the country but observes it from the vantage point of the city: it is in part the world of the 1930s "geographer-citizen" (Williams 1973; Matless 1998:77). Its basic tools – the map, the air photograph, the record office where archives are kept – are all produced in the towns or are urban institutions. As Howard Newby has pointed out, it stands at some distance from the problems and issues faced by people actually living in the countryside: "most of us do not know – and do not want to know – about the factors . . . which are shaping modern farming. To do so would merely increase our sense of disillusion. Instead we prefer to allow the countryside to become the repository of nostalgic remembrance" (Newby 1979:19).

The Making of the English Landscape and *Fieldwork in Local History*, in their tone and approach, are written for the intelligent layman (with all the deliberate ambiguity within that term), as are the two popular books emerging from his television series. *Devon* is written for an English visitor to the county, rather than a foreign tourist, on the one hand, or a "local," on the other. For example:

> [Totnes] has excellent shops and markets . . . the excellent cider, like a golden *vin du pays*, solaces the historical traveller all over this part of Devon . . . Among the many minor pleasures of Totnes, one can still embark on the steam-packet for Dartmouth, an 8-m. journey down what is unquestionably the loveliest river in England. There is, alas, no second-hand and antiquarian bookshop in the town, a notable lack of enterprise on someone's part. (Hoskins 1954b:506)

We saw in Chapter 3 that Hoskins, sharing in the hegemonic culture of the 1950s, was opposed to what he saw as class distinctions. Like the contemporary archaeologist Mortimer Wheeler, Hoskins believed passionately in communicating to the masses, and, like Wheeler, some academic contemporaries thought the less of him for it (Hawkes 1982).

In his choice of audience, Hoskins was referring to a world in which "England appeared to be feminized, stable and coherent" (Taylor 1994:4). It was moulded in a country where after the First World War there was "a move away from formerly heroic and officially masculine public rhetoric of national destiny to an Englishness at once less imperial and more inward-looking, more domestic and more private – and, in terms of pre-war standards, more 'feminine'" (Light 1991:8). This England became, in the view of many, safe and smug; they moved abroad, to what in their perception were the raw edges and the hard bright sunlight of the colonial periphery. The less imperial, more inward-looking domestic and private England is, of course, the England that Hoskins and his contemporaries described and inhabited.

The English tradition of landscape history and archaeology could not have succeeded in its post-war project without a growing middle-class belief that they had a stake in the landscape without actually owning it, a belief most obviously evident in the rise among ordinary people of the practice of country-house visiting (Mandler 1997; land-ownership in Britain continues to be highly restricted, both in absolute terms and relative to other countries in Europe, with around 6,000 families owning over half the country according to Cahill 2001). Then, as now, this paradox was resolved, as it continues to be resolved, by the turn to emotion: "History in the form of feeling – ancestral, aesthetic and moral – was a conventional form. It resolved the puzzle of instability by turning it into the bedrock of certainty" (Taylor 1994:200).

There is nothing intrinsically wrong with such an emotional turn; indeed, a writer who claimed to be immune to the idea of history in the form of feeling would either be intellectually dishonest or an automaton. However, when it is not accompanied by serious critical analysis, an emotional link between landscape and nation can be politically suspect. The search for rootedness in place, in other times and places, has led to politically unpleasant consequences: the German conception of *Heimat* is an obvious case in point (Morley 2000:32–3). Where there is an idea of rootedness, of place and locality, with all the warmth, cosiness, and sense of belonging that such an idea implies, there is also its dark side, its obverse – an implicit concept of strangers, of foreigners, of the excluded, those who because of a different ancestry and background have in this view no claim to rootedness.

Other nations have constructed their national pasts around conflicting sets of ideas: that of citizenship on the one hand, or blood and soil on the other (Diaz-Andreu and Champion 1996). An exception proves the rule: the Professor of Geography at Queen's University Belfast, Emyr Estyn Evans, an opponent of Irish nationalism, stressed the differences in physical geography between Ulster and the rest of Ireland as determinants of deep-seated differences in culture between the two regions; it has been argued that this stress served to legitimate the 1921 partition between North and South (Stout 1996; see also Graham 1994 for a more sympathetic view). Hoskins's writing, as one might expect of someone writing from the 1930s onwards, skirts around these issues. While Hoskins refers over and over again to his own blood ancestors, identity is for him nevertheless not quite blood. However, it is not quite citizenship either. And while a sense of place and of locality is a central element of identity, it is clearly not the only element. Occasionally, it can even be climatic: he writes that the urban grid plan is "basically unhuman . . . the British climate calls for the warm pub rather than the open spaces of the piazza" (1970:246–7). It certainly stands at some distance from Benedict Anderson's view of nation as defined by print language (Gilroy 1987:44). The celebratory use of the term *genius loci* sits, in my view, ambiguously and fuzzily somewhere between all these ideas. Like the use in English of many Latin tags, it can be used to disguise lack of conceptual clarity under the cloak of a foreign language. Such usage is closely linked with geographers' and historians' deployment of the French term *pays*, drawn from the work of Vidal de la Blache and others, where again the meaning is not directly reducible to this or that factor (economics, society, culture, environment), but is, rather, holistic and even sensual and emotive (see for example Everitt 1970; Phythian-Adams 1993:24). *Genius loci* also turns up in similarly vague and ineffable contexts in the architectural historian Nikolaus Pevsner's radio talks, where it is explicitly linked with a distinctive sense of Englishness that, according to Pevsner, is connected with England's identity as a middle-class nation (Pevsner 2002:232–4). It has also been used by later writers on landscape to capture the essence of Hoskins's own "genius" (Phythian-Adams 1992).

One of the advantages of using words like *pays* or *genius loci* is that their meaning does not have to be fully explicated; it becomes in part ineffable, beyond rational analysis, and thus insulated from critical comment, like the Romantic aesthetic sensibility discussed above. There is a close connection here with claims that the sum total of all these regions, "England" itself, is somehow ineffable, and therefore beyond critique, and also a close connection with essentialism, or the belief in a defining essence to nation, a belief undercut by postmodern geography (Curry 1992). It is certainly a place that cannot be left, whatever its faults: towards the end of his career, in a private letter, Hoskins wrote that "I often feel this country is dead – perhaps it is just twelve unbroken years of the stinking Tories and their Affluent Society, which seems to breed whores chiefly – but then I think of all my interests here and I know I should feel rootless and lost in any other country" (private letter, 1963, cited in Millward 1992:68).

Many people do *not* belong to a particular place; they are, nevertheless, just as much part of the national community as the most rotund, bewhiskered "English" gentleman. These placeless, diasporic people tend in the course of history to be those against whom those that do "belong" have committed terrible crimes. What is the imagined community behind the tiny, commonsensical, but utterly pernicious word "we"? There is no discussion of who this sense of locatedness and place is meant for – its relevance is habitually deemed to be self-evident, "what everyone knows." This lack of discussion, and the assumption of shared knowledge, is revealing. The question, "How might a British person of colour whose parents were immigrants find rootedness in this landscape?" is not simply denied – it is never even considered. Muir writes "Globalisation, the tyranny of economics over higher values and the phenomenon described by one geographer as 'time-space com-pression' magnify a longing for identity and roots . . . the inner craving for stability, predictability and belonging may guide us into explorations of the bonds between past communities and their settings" (Muir 2000:xiii). But what Muir sees as an inner craving common to all humanity is actually a very specific feeling, the offspring of Wordsworthian Romanticism, close to the heart of a particularly conservative (with a small *c*) version of Englishness. Joan Thirsk is even more explicit when she sums up the present state of landscape studies: "such an enquiry," she writes, "could be an unexpectedly satisfying experience in a world that is being made more and more impersonal by technology." According to Thirsk, such an experience is all the more satisfying in its resonance with English literature: H. E. Bates, Wordsworth, and J. E. Cary all wrote about a mix of social classes, "harmonious because all classes accepted their place, whether low or high, in a hierarchy that allowed and acknowledged both duties and rights" (Thirsk 2000:16).

When many scholars write about a sense of place, they implicitly have in their mind's eye the back rather than the front cover of *Power of Place*. The "imagined community" of landscape history and archaeology is, then, a geographically, socially and culturally stable and homogeneous group. Populations of diaspora – of movement and exile (Bender and Winer 2001, prefatory dedication) – have a very different relationship to the landscape. For such peoples, "landscapes are never taken for granted and are often a source of pain." This would not matter were it not that it is a truism that those of Jewish or Muslim religion, or West Indian, African, or Asian parentage, are no more or less British or English than anyone else.

Diaspora is not a new or late-arriving feature in the landscape. In prehistory, the old view of successive waves of migration has long been unfashionable, but diaspora of various kinds is well recorded in the historic landscape. Gypsies, drovers, and squatters were all cohesive groups with a close sense of cohesion and community, not to mention a strong sense of pride in their past, even if by definition they lay outside an uncritical celebration of rootedness in the landscape. The patron saint of England, St George, is habitually rendered pictorially as a typical medieval knight; however, he was allegedly born in Turkey of Palestinian parentage, and as such was hailed as one of the hundred greatest Black Britons in a poll for the British Broadcasting Corporation (Young 2004) and never actually set eyes on the country that took him to its heart. Diasporic groups such as the Jews have a long history and archaeology (Hinton 2003). In the early modern period, local communities' paranoia about "masterless men," that is, those who moved from parish to parish with no fixed master or authority, was not only a desire to move them on before they became a burden on the parish; it was also in part fear of rising numbers of Gypsies and Irish people. The latter were ordered back to Ireland in 1572, with obvious lack of success, and over succeeding centuries individuals and communities of Irish descent became a routine focus of cultural and religious prejudice in both countryside and town (Beier 1985). There has been a Black community in England since the end of the 16th century, alongside better-known groups such as the Flemings and Huguenots (Gerzina 1995). Diasporic groups do have landscapes which are meaningful to them. They often link their identity to a sense of place, but in a complex and heterogeneous way not easily approximated to the place-dependent models discussed above. Tolia-Kelly (2004) has shown, for example, how British Asian women relate their experiences of diaspora and migration to movement within their present, British landscape; a sense of place for them, then, is not at all what traditional writers on landscape history have in mind.

My point is not that historians and archaeologists write in a way that deliberately excludes marginalized groups; most of them, like Hoskins before them, are conscious liberals. Rather, it is that, in its discursive assumptions and implied audience, *the discourse of historic landscapes continues as if the issues of multiculturalism do not exist*. This is not meant as a criticism of Hoskins's writings, which are after all over fifty years old and come from a very different social and cultural context, but it is meant as a comment on a continuing uncritical celebration of that tradition.

Even over fifty years ago, however, such sentiments could be – and were – questioned. It is very easy for the modern reader to forget precisely what social changes writers on landscape in the 1950s were turning their back on. It was not just the obscene shape of the atom-bomber; it was also "the immigration of black people from the West Indies and West Africa, and the formation of modern multiracial Britain." In this respect, there is a profound and revealing silence in landscape history and archaeology, just as there is a silence in 1950s art and culture generally (Philips 2004:6; see also Sinfield 1989:125–50).

Patriotism, and the potential in an unthinking love of country for an implied politics of exclusion, has always been a difficult issue for the Romantic left. The most distinctive and paradigmatic case is that of the writer and social critic George Orwell, who moved from a rejection of patriotism on anti-imperialist grounds to a fervent belief in "my country right or left" within the space of the admittedly eventful eighteen months of 1939–40 (Crick 1980:376).

Landscapes of Recreation

In Chapter 4 I looked at a standard set of techniques – the map, the air photograph, the hachured plan – used by academics to understand the landscape. I made the point that the map in particular was deeply embedded in popular consciousness. I now want to repeat and expand that point with reference to its political dimensions. The map formed, and forms, part of a set of basic tools which are used by the recreational visitor to the English countryside. These tools are apparently objective records, impartial guides, but in other ways they act as filters. They tell the visitor what he or she should be looking at, where to direct his or her gaze, and even what he or she should be thinking about the view around them. Such a direction and control, extending to valuation of the landscape, is most evident in Pevsner's county guides, but also includes the different editions of the Shell guides and the older Batsford guides to the countryside (Matless 1998; Figures 6.3 and 6.4).

All these volumes, in complementary ways, tell their readers how they should look at the landscape. The map tells them where they can and cannot walk. Pevsner tells them not just the date and type of the buildings they look at, but in some cases whether they should "approve" or "disapprove" of the building in question. Like many students of landscape, I always prefer to take a first-edition Pevsner with me, as it is not only smaller and more easily portable but the force and asperity of his value judgements shine through more clearly; many passages in the guides are clearly meant to be read out in ceremonial style in front of the building in question – thus descriptions of churches routinely start by describing the exterior, façade by façade as one walks round the building, before moving to the interior. A typical description, for the church at Down St Mary in Devon, reads:

> ST MARY. The most interesting feature of the church is the Norman tympanum of the S door. It illustrates Daniel in the Lion's Den. The date must be C12. Otherwise the exterior has little of interest: W tower with buttresses of type B and no pinnacles, NE stair-turret. The body of the church thoroughly renewed 1878–80. Inside, the N aisle separated from the nave by three low granite arcades; the piers of A-type with capitals only to the main shafts. – FONT. Perp, moulded. – SCREEN of standard type-A tracery with ribbed coving and cornice with cresting, mostly the work of Mr Bushell, the village carpenter. – BENCH-ENDS. Unusually many, of the current Devon and Cornwall type. Amongst the representations monograms, profiles, a siren with comb, a cherub with scourge (cf. Lapford). – PLATE. Dwarf Cup by Jons of Exeter, 1577. (Pevsner 1952:81)

Pevsner guides the visitor round the building from exterior to interior; he directs the visitor's attention to key features of interest; he assumes a degree of background knowledge of history and the Judaeo-Christian tradition ("Norman," "Daniel in the Lion's Den"); his abbreviations

Figure 6.3 1930s Batsford guide: front cover

Figure 6.4 Pevsner's first edition to the *Yorkshire The North Riding*: front cover. © 1966 by Nikolaus Pevsner. *Reprinted with permission of the Penguin Books Ltd*

refer to a wider narrative (thus "Perp" is an abbreviation for Perpendicular, a form of Late Gothic art and architecture distinctive to England); he refers the readers to other buildings that are implicitly also on their itinerary of countryside visiting ("Lapford").

The guidebook and map thus turn that most superficially innocent and pleasurable of activities – a visit to the countryside – into a pedagogical and ideological exercise. Wandering around the humps and bumps that mark a deserted medieval village or tracing the history of a parish church with the aid of a Pevsner becomes an exercise in reminding oneself of what it means to be English, just as a visit to Yosemite or the Grand Canyon, far from being an unmediated encounter with the natural world, is a reminder of what it means to be an American (Schama 1995).

The view of the landscape delineated by any guidebook, of course, can never be an objective one, but is always historically and culturally situated. The French structuralist and cultural commentator Roland Barthes made this point with reference to the Blue Guides, a book series with which tourists are still armed as they visit the great cultural capitals of Europe. Barthes examined the selection of sites and the commentary upon them, and saw both as reflecting what he terms a "Helvetico-Protestant" view of the world in which morality is equated with "effort and solitude." His comments, in my view, only touch on a fraction of the meanings and ideologies that can be found in the Blue Guides, but it is certainly the case that they prioritize Christian monuments over those of other religions and classify in terms of cultural and ethnic essences (Barthes 1989).

The natural next step from the Sunday visit was to the extramural class, where the Hoskins/Crawford tradition held and continues to hold sway. Hoskins's own classes in Leicester before the war were followed by a huge post-1945 expansion in adult and continuing education. Such classes were filled with people with a variety of occupations and interests, but all animated by a love of the countryside, frequently that of their own locality, and a passionate desire to learn more about it.

Landscape history and archaeology has immense pedagogical power in such contexts. It is not a set of techniques dependent on excavation; useful work can be done over the course of a weekend or even an afternoon; students get involved in their own locality, about which they often care passionately; they can make real "discoveries" (O'Brien and Wheeler 1978). It is an outdoor activity: Leslie Grinsell noted how "barrow-hunting is strongly recommended as an outdoor hobby for hikers" (cited in Matless 2000:79). And it is an activity which combines affection, pedagogy, and the enthusiasm of any Sunday outing: thus Maurice Beresford dedicated the second edition of *History on the Ground* (1957) to "my mother, who packed the sandwiches." But these same kinds of students, and indeed their teachers, are often hostile to what they see as more abstract theorizing. The world of the extramural class is at some distance from that of academia, especially its upper reaches in the senior common rooms of the colleges of Oxford and Cambridge. We have seen how both Hoskins and Crawford shared negative feelings about Oxford. Though Oxford has Ruskin College and both Oxford and Cambridge have thriving continuing education departments, both stand at some intellectual and cultural distance from the older and more prestigious elements of their respective universities.

At the same time as the Hoskins tradition was placed centre stage in extramural classes, so it was marginalized and excluded from the higher reaches of academic history. In Boyd's *Encyclopaedia of Histories and Historical Writing*, there is only a single passing reference to Hoskins in the context of early modern history, though there is space for entries on "Historical Geography" and "Local History" (Boyd 1999). In Bentley's *Companion to Historiography* (1997), there is also no mention of Hoskins. Perhaps the most surprising omission is from Peter Mandler's short book *History and National Life* (2002), which tells the story of the relationship between popular consciousness of "heritage" and the writing of English national history. In other words, the more Hoskins is embedded as a father-figure for certain kinds of landscape history and for the amateur practice of landscape history and archaeology, the less he impinges on the consciousness of the higher academic echelons of metropolitan history. This is a common pattern: it is related to the writing of academic historiography, in which, for example, antiquarians of the 18th century and their researches in the English countryside were "written out" of the story of the development of history as a discipline in favour of the "great national historians" writing in a metropolitan register such as Macaulay and Trevelyan (Sweet 2004).

Colonial Landscapes

I have argued in earlier chapters that a denial of otherness is questionable in scholarly terms, but it is more than this. It was this confidence in there being one right way of relating to the landscape or to "nature" that led to the extermination of other ways of life in the name of the British empire in the 19th century, and to the intellectual perception of cultures that failed to approximate to such models as primitive, backward, esoteric, or otherwise eminently qualified to receive the benefits of Western cultural domination (Said 1978; Orser 1996). It is a fact that the model of landscape that occupies such a central position in English landscape appreciation – rolling hills, fertile green fields neatly divided with hedges – was the landscape form that the British attempted to impose, with varying degrees of success, on colonized landscapes around the world, from Ireland (Aalen et al. 1997) to Puritan New England (Bowden 1992) to South Africa (Winer 2001) to New Zealand and Australia (Burke 1999).

No modern writer would seek to justify such an imposition and appropriation. However, there is a general lack of discussion in English landscape writing about the relationships between the English landscape on the one hand and that of "the colonies" on the other. The relationship between English and colonial landscapes is not a new or fashionable topic. Eric Williams argued, in his doctoral thesis published in 1944, that the development of capitalism in 18th-century England was directly dependent on the proceeds of the sugar plantations of the Caribbean. Williams's thesis provoked a major and continuing debate in academic circles. And yet, while the clear implication of Williams was that the Georgian parks and gardens of the English countryside were funded by wealth produced through the misery of enslaved men and women, references to such a relationship are extremely rare. This omission is found, for example, in my own work (Johnson 1996). Where references do occur, they do so within the genre of comparative historical and urban archaeology rather than the English landscape tradition (Hicks 2003).

One consequence of this lack of discussion is a perpetuation of the classic elision between "England" and "Britain." Any casual visitor to the United Kingdom knows how difficult it is to get a "native" to give a coherent historical explanation of the relationship between England, Wales, Scotland, and Northern Ireland, and why in much national discourse "England" and "Britain" become mysteriously coterminous (most infamously in the characterization of "Britain" using southern English stereotypes: Johnson 1999:113). An ethnic component to this confusion is given particular sharpness when many second-generation British citizens feel happy to identify themselves as "British" but not "English." The English landscape tradition tends to view "England" as a unit whose nature is essential and unquestioned; where debate occurs, it is over the nature or regions or *pays* within this unit. However, by

1600 (and indeed well before) no discussion of English society and politics can be disentangled from that of the other three nations – Wales, Scotland and Ireland – which in different ways were politically connected to England. Revisionist scholarship of the civil wars of the 1640s focused in part on the way political events in one nation triggered off crisis in another, most obviously when the revolt of the Scottish Kirk against King Charles's policies meant that he had to call on an English Parliament to raise funds in England for an army, a Parliament that he found unable to control (Morrill 1993).

References to Wales are infrequent in, and to Scotland and Ireland close to absent from, Hoskins's work; there is almost no reference to "Britain" at all. Hoskins is drawing here on a well of English political and cultural sentiment that links a rejection of modernity with a rejection of what are perceived as the "Celtic fringes" and even implicitly of the political creation of British union in the early modern period. As a result, analysis of the historical processes through which English, Welsh, Scottish, and in part Irish identities were to become articulated within a common conception of Britishness (as discussed most recently by Colley 1992; see also Johnson 2003) was entirely bypassed in the work of both Hoskins and his contemporaries in historic landscape archaeology, despite the centrality of the idea of "England" to its intellectual formation. It is expressed in the directly empirical terms of the map. In Figure 5.1, Wales becomes a *tabula rasa* and Scotland disappears entirely; in this case the structure of the map is a consequence of the "English Heritage" funding of the project it derives from, but the composition is typical of the genre (see for example the map in Johnson 1996:22, where England seems to have become an island).

As a result, one critical route within which a more generalizing and comparative view of landscape archaeology, not to mention a view in which questions of conflict, power, and inequality would be more effectively foregrounded, was lost. At different historic periods, English forms of landscape have been imposed on other parts of the British Isles, and in their turn they have been resisted in different ways. A landscape history and archaeology of the four nations of England, Wales, Scotland, and Ireland would include, among other episodes: the 13th-century imposition of royal castles and new towns in North Wales; the subsequent Tudor division of Wales into English shires and its absorption within the English political structure until recent times; plantations and attempted reorganizations of different regions of Ireland such as Munster and Ulster from the later 16th century onwards; the reorganization of Scottish agriculture culminating in the Highland clearances; local and "native" rebellion and resistance to all these episodes; Irish nationalism and partition of that island after the First World War. These episodes are not merely the subject of fashionable postcolonial discourse; they were part of the traditional history of the "British Isles" taught to most British schoolchildren before the fragmentation of history teaching in the 1980s.

In this respect, a celebration of the particular and an aversion to the generalizing and comparative has the unintended consequence of leading towards a politics that draws a veil over the conflicted colonial history of Britain, as opposed to the stable, unmoving, contented and sane history of little England. It is also a turning away from contexts where national identity is obviously and immediately created rather than essential, and an object of contestation rather than apparent consensus. For a large part of the second millennium A.D., Ireland was under the dominion of the English Crown, and, from the 18th to the early 20th centuries, Ireland was officially part of Great Britain. The violent struggles attendant upon that relationship, and the con-demnation of British policy as complicit with the events and under-lying causes of for example the Great Famine, and the way in which these processes are inscribed on the Irish landscape, are a matter of record, yet much writing on the English landscape is completely silent on such issues – for the excellent and undeniable reason that England is not Britain. In this respect, the stable, contented, and sane English landscape and the archaeology of British imperialism (Diaz–Andreu 2004) contain little cross-reference to each other for a very good reason – they are precisely complementary; they fit like lock and key.

The Romantic turning away from the metropolis of London, with its origins in classical discourse, is a turning away from one of the key sites where Englishness and colonial heritage intersect. Richard Muir is a notable exception when he writes of the depopulation of villages:

> Similar roads of bitter despair would be walked by countless innocents – Russian Jews, the Gaels of Ulster, the Sioux, the Highland peasants and the modern Afghans – but the villagers that we have met were English. Their tragedy was not proclaimed, then or now, and nobody bothered to write about it. It was not unique; it was not even unusual, and with only the smallest changes of detail this reconstructed scene was enacted at over a thousand medieval villages. (Muir 1982:20)

Whether Muir's picture is an accurate one or not is beside the point in this context. What is omitted or at best implicit in other narratives is here given prominence.

Indigenous Landscapes

The tensions and violence associated with landscape can be seen most clearly in contexts around the world where the perspectives of indigenous peoples have clashed with those of the West in different circumstances. An extensive literature has built up in these contexts, most obviously in the work of the World Archaeological Congress, prompted in part by the recognition that archaeology needs to engage with the world-views of indigenous peoples rather than treating their pasts as an intellectual playground (Ucko and Layton 1999; Smith and Wobst 2005). For example, archaeologists, anthropologists, and indigenous peoples in Australia have stressed that landscapes once regarded as "natural," "wilderness," or "*tabula rasa*" by colonial settlers were not only extensively modified by indigenous groups: they were full of meaning, with complex narratives linking the natural world to the world of humans, or, to put it another way, writing human concerns into the landscape itself.

For the indigenous peoples of Australia, the landscape is part and parcel of the "dreaming," a complex term which refers to the origins and identities of all living things, and which embraces both past and present. Within this view, there is no opposition between human and natural – places like Uluru, called Ayers Rock by the colonists, are both at the same time. Features that might be classified as "natural" by Western observers are part of a network of symbolic relationships that relate back to the spirit world of the ancestors. Particular physical features are the bodies of animals and/or the ancestors (David 2002; David and Wilson 2002).

We might fruitfully ask: what is the indigenous culture at stake in the study of the English landscape? The moral and political differences between the landscapes of England and of other areas of the world are such that there might be argued to be no "indigenous culture" to deal with in the English case. Welsh and Cornish popular writers have claimed to be the lineal descendants of the British dispossessed by the Anglo-Saxon invaders of the fifth and sixth centuries A.D., but while this is an assertion that cannot be evaluated independently of claims of cultural and economic marginalization in the present, the evidence for such a claim is tenuous at best (James 1999).

But the assertion of the lack of an indigenous community, again, is not quite the whole truth. There is an indigenous culture of the English; the Hoskins tradition, and behind it the discursive formations of Romanticism and empiricism, form important components of that indigenous culture. When the Sex Pistols snarled that there was "no future, no future" in England's dreaming, they were referring to a powerful well of ideas and experiences. However, it needs critical examination to go alongside nostalgic celebration if it is not to become a culture that excludes rather than embraces.

Conclusion

Where does this leave the study of landscape? I propose that it leaves us with a series of imperatives. The move away from a view of landscape dominated by Wordsworth is not simply a scholarly advance: it has a social, cultural, and political imperative as well as an academic one.

Is there a future in England's dreaming? Only if we embrace the insight that what is being celebrated in such a view of landscape is not an objective method, independent of space and time, but rather a particular discourse, a particular cultural formation. The people who put such a cultural formation together were and generally are from a particular social class and ethnic identity. This is not to invalidate such a view or to suggest that it has no further use, nor is it to suggest that it is morally and politically good or bad. However, it does relativize it radically, undercutting any protestations of innocence, and it does suggest that other views of the English landscape are possible and indeed should be encouraged. Richard Benjamin's recent discussion of Hadrian's Wall, where units of North African soldiers were stationed at the time of the Roman empire, as a possible marker and locus of Black British identity is a case in point. Benjamin writes that "archaeology and heritage in Britain propagate the image of Black people as newcomers, not active citizens in British history" (2004:11). In other words, the English landscape tradition remains important, but its importance derives from its place as one of a series of different discourses about landscape, or if you like one indigenous view – that of "the English" – among several, or indeed among many of the "tribes of Britain" (Miles 2003).

I propose, then, four very simple steps for the academic practice of the English tradition of landscape archaeology in its political context.

First, the acknowledgement of anthropological otherness in the past. These people may have been "our ancestors," but this does not mean that they were "like us" – the past is a foreign country (Lowenthal 1985). If we acknowledge that life in the past, even for "our ancestors," was different, the implication is that life can be different in the future. In other words, celebration of the landscape and the human history it expresses ceases to be an inherently conservative enterprise, and can instead be an exploration of human possibility.

Second, open discussion of Englishness in the landscape as a construct, and an acknowledgement that the making of the English landscape cannot simply be told in celebratory terms as an unfolding of essentials, but rather is a constructed story with spiritual dimensions. In a Seattle hotel room a few years ago at an archaeology conference I was asked by a Native American: "Do the English have a spiritual view of landscape?" In subsequent years I have returned to this question over and over again. I think the summation of this book must be rather banal: the answer must be both Yes and No. Values of Englishness are embedded in views of landscape, but the English habitually insist that their understanding of landscape is somehow ineffable, beyond politics. As a result, many social groups in modern England, from the Sex Pistols onwards, both White and Black, feel that they are not part of that culture (Jeater 1992). Discussion of Englishness as a culture dominates contemporary discourse (Porter 1992; Colley 1992; Bassnett 1997; Easthope 1999; Paxman 1999; Strong 2000); but, perhaps fortunately, it lies beyond the scope of this book.

Third, the writing of mobility, conflict, and change back into the past. People moved around, had conflicts with each other, and often saw very sudden change in their lifetime, for example at the moment of parliamentary enclosure. The stable, contented, and sane England was only part of the story; other stories need to be told. One of those stories is that of migration and diaspora – not just that of the *Windrush* in 1948 and the ensuing immigration, but a much longer story going back to the Renaissance and beyond (Gerzina 1995; Benjamin 2004). And part of that story is the creation of place out of space by immigrant and other groups in ways that are ambivalent, tentative, and shifting rather than stable, unmoving, contented, and sane, but just as important and valid nevertheless (see for example Western's (1993) discussion of the post-1948 history of Brixton and Notting Hill).

Fourth, and perhaps most vitally, a questioning of the assumption that there is one single way of understanding the landscape. When Alan Sinfield writes of literary appreciation that "the crucial property that cannot be restored is that of universality," he might be talking about our understanding of the English landscape: "If a lower-class person, woman, student, person of colour, lesbian or gay man does not 'respond' in an 'appropriate' way to 'the text', it is because they are reading wrongly – i.e. not from the position that has traditionally been privileged in the literary-critical apparatus (white, adult, male, middle-class, heterosexual). To be sure, almost anyone may be coached to internalize and produce an 'appropriate' response, but that will be at the expense of the person they thought they were" (Sinfield 1989:290).

If these four elements are taken together, then the front and back covers of *Power of Place* become not two different stories, but, to use an analogy that should by now be familiar to readers of this book, different harmonies on the same theme.

Chapter Seven

CONCLUSION

In writing this book I have drawn a distinction between two ways of thinking about landscape: the one comparative, theoretical, interested in process, with close links to anthropology; the other humanistic, particularistic, interested in *genius loci*, and closely implicated in the concerns of history. I have argued that this difference in approach is much deeper than much of the surface froth of theoretical debate: thus much of postprocessual archaeology is actually seated in the former, generalizing and processual, tradition while the latter owes its roots to 18th-century Romanticism and even deeper national traditions of empiricism.

One might see the origins of archaeology as a whole in terms of two conflicting impulses. The first is to make generalizing statements about humankind; from this impulse springs evolutionary archaeology in all its forms, and, I would argue, an emphasis on theory of all stripes and also an emphasis on prehistory. The second is curiosity about what is in one's own backyard – not to explain the general sweep of history, but to answer questions about the fields around one's home, one's local community. From this impulse stems a strong topographical and empirical tradition, and an interest in historic periods, accompanied by a particularism and an unreflective empiricism – that specifically all one really needs to understand what one is looking at when one ventures in to the countryside is a countryman's eye and a good pair of boots. I have stated that these impulses are equal yet conflicting: what we have seen in this book is that one or the other predominates in different circumstances.

It could be argued that this divergence happened before the 18th century, and is inscribed into the very conception of archaeology in the development of anthropological and antiquarian enquiry. The origins of archaeology are habitually traced to the intellectual developments of the Renaissance. Renaissance Europe produced, on the one hand, an exploration and contact with other parts of the globe, an encounter with "native peoples." This encounter led to a nascent anthropology: why did these groups have customs so very different from "us"? It produced, on the other hand, an emergent tradition of local topography and an exploration by the gentry classes of the local landscape. Both traditions, then, were there at the genesis of archaeology, and the creative tension between them continues to structure much archaeological debate.

North American Romanticism

Inevitably, however, this distinction has been over-drawn, in particular in its national parameters. There is, for example, a vibrant North American tradition of Romantic writing about landscape that must be acknowledged, stemming in part from the writings of Thoreau, Emerson, Muir, and the Sierra Club (Leighly 1963:7). Again, in these writings we see a tension between a landscape for "the people" and that of elitism. Thoreau's *Walden* was a retreat into solitary contemplation, not a place for the urban masses; the environmentalist Sierra Club in its earlier history was seen as a rather elitist organization, and there was a tension between its appreciation of landscape and the more populist sentiments expressed, for example, by Woody Guthrie (Partridge 2002).

There is a clear parallel to the work of the English landscape tradition in the writings of two North American scholars in particular: Carl Sauer and J. B. Jackson. Writing from within a humanist perspective on academic geography, Sauer's work identified itself as part of long humanist/conservationist tradition that set itself the aim of retreating from the "obtrusive ugliness of our culture." Sauer wrote with passion: "Whatever the problems of the day that claim the specialist . . . there remains a form of geographic curiosity that is never contained by systems. It is the art of seeing how land and life have come to differ from one part of the earth to the other." Calling this approach to landscape "regional interpretation" Sauer, like Hoskins, borrowed from what he called "Sir Cyril Fox's admirable study of the cultural backgrounds of the British Isles" (Leighly 1963:105, citing Fox 1938).

Much of Sauer's thinking stemmed from a very strong tradition of Romantic writing about the landscape in literary studies. This was particularly so of the conception of the wilderness, so central to North American historical thinking in its conception of the "frontier," and in part framed by 17th-century Puritan writing about New England discussed in Chapter 1 (Jackson 1979), but then extended to the perceived wilderness of the American West. Just as Wordsworth called for a national park, so the nascent United States National Park ethos was expressed in Romantic and nationalist terms (Schama 1995). In the 19th-century United States, the Romantic impulse to include humans as ant-like figures to be objectively observed as part of the landscape gained an even more explicit form. George Catlin, famous for his records and observations on Native Americans, called for a "magnificent park" in the American West where landscape, animals, and humans would be on display: "where the world could see, for ages to come, the native Indian in his classic attire . . . amid the fleeting herds of elks and buffaloes . . . a nation's Park, containing man and beast, in all the wild and freshness of their nature's beauty!" (Harmon 1989:106–11). Such a Romantic tradition continued into the 20th century with the landscape gardens and writing of Frederick Law Olmsted and the photographs of Ansel Adams.

At the same time as Hoskins was forging his vision of the English landscape, J. B. Jackson was founding his landmark journal *Landscapes*. Like Hoskins, Jackson was not easily confined within disciplinary boundaries. He also freely used the analogy of text; he chose to open *Landscapes* with a quotation from the poet Robert Frost, and with the words: "A rich and beautiful book is always open before us. We have but to learn to read it" (cited in Meinig 1979b:196).

The ethos of *Landscapes* was pedagogical, conservationist, and humanist. It took a stand against grand urban designs and sought to develop a love of the unplanned roadside strip. Where others, influenced by western European thinking, saw tat and sleaze in the roadside strip, Jackson sought to celebrate it in nationalist terms as quintessentially American. In early editions *Landscapes* concentrated on the American Southwest, but later broadened its scope to a "magazine of human geography." "There was an urgent need for the public to have a better understanding of how their local communities and countrysides were being changed, and that understanding must be grounded upon some knowledge of how these settlements were created and how they have endured" (Meinig 1979b:315). In this project, a central tool was to be the air photograph. *Landscapes* concentrated on "the dwelling," with an early essay on the American front yard.

Meinig summarizes the principles of J.B. Jackson as follows:

1 Landscape is anchored upon human life
2 Landscape is a unity: "man" is part of nature
3 Therefore, landscape must be assessed in living terms
4 The elementary unit is the individual dwelling
5 Primary attention should be given to the vernacular
6 All landscapes are symbolic
7 All landscapes are changing.

Jackson saw that landscape problems were political, but he was basically uninterested in politics. Like Hoskins, he turned away from the
present, though in his case the present was the social tension and
radicalism of the 1960s: "he turned away from *Landscapes* just as the
political and social critique of American society, including what it was
doing to its landscapes, was becoming very shrill and intense. That
critique made good use of a basic Jacksonian premise: that landscape
mirrors society" (Meinig 1979a:230). Like Hoskins also, Jackson did
not write in an overly theoretical style, though it has been argued that
he was deeply aware of theoretical currents; he simply did not see the
need to cite the relevant texts in order to gain intellectual legitimacy
(Wright 1998:474–5).

In summary, then, much of North American humanistic study has
been tied to a love of place and a close association with history that
would have been recognized by Hoskins, and which continues to play
a central role in much contemporary academic and popular thought
(for example Leuchtenburg 2000). However, it has to be said that
neither Sauer nor Jackson, nor North American humanistic geography
in general, had much explicit impact on Americanist archaeology and
its understanding of landscape in the second half of the 20th century.
Where Hoskins directly prefigures the present state of English landscape archaeology, there is almost no mention of Sauer or Jackson in
North American archaeological literature.

The only exception proves the rule: some North American historical
archaeology draws on a Romantic tradition via citation of "folklife"
and related traditions. In particular, the development by James Deetz of
the "Georgian Order" thesis (Deetz 1977) drew heavily on one particular book: *Folk Housing in Middle Virginia*, written by the folklorist
Henry Glassie (1975; see also Glassie 2000). There is no coincidence in
having a Romantic intellectual ancestry here: the historical archaeology
of the east coast of North America, of course, in other words the world
(in part) of the Puritans of New England and the settlers of Virginia, is

arguably the only context in which North American archaeologists are in the Romantic situation of dealing with a group seen explicitly as "ancestors." Further, the story of those ancestors, from the *Mayflower* to the Declaration of Independence and beyond, is part of a strongly teleological view of American history.

This divergence is best explained by the different disciplinary configuration in the two contexts. To state the obvious, Americanist archaeology was and continues to be part of anthropology, characteristically described as one of a "four-field approach" (archaeology, cultural anthropology, physical anthropology, linguistic anthropology). Such an approach has tremendous strengths; we have seen that a critical weakness in much in the landscape tradition is its inability to take seriously an anthropological approach. However, it did distance archaeology and its study of landscape from relevant traditions in history and geography. This distance was reinforced by Walter Taylor's sharp division between anthropology and history, and his preference for the former, in his *A Study of Archeology* (1948). The New Archaeology of the 1960s reinforced the divergence between a scientific anthropology on the one hand and humanistic traditions on the other. Consequently, early New Archaeology looked for "objective" ways of defining and researching landscape, as discussed in earlier chapters.

As a result, the overwhelming majority of archaeological studies of North American landscape have been in the broadly processual and comparative tradition. Again, however, this is an oversimplification. The last twenty years have seen a much greater diversity in the literature. James Snead has traced how the archaeology of the American Southwest has, like its English counterpart, always been embedded in questions of society and culture (Snead 2001). Snead has also described the making of Ancestral Pueblo trails in terms that reference phenomenological and interpretative traditions (2002). More broadly, discussions of Ancestral Pueblo art and landscape have shown an interpretative turn that means that a simple binary contrast is at the very least too simplistic. Christine Ward has talked of Chacoan ritual landscapes, referring to memory and social tradition, for example (2003).

In the case of the American Southwest, this turn towards more empathetic and interpretative approaches can be explained in part by the increasing recognition of and respect for cultural continuity between "indigenous peoples," such as the Hopi and Zuni, and the archaeological remains that they claim as those of their ancestors. There are political as well as intellectual reasons for this shift and recognition. Such a shift is seen most obviously in the changing preference for the name of the most famous of the archaeological cultures of the Southwest; formerly the "Anasazi" or "vanished ones"; now for many the preferred terms is "Ancestral Pueblo," stressing direct historical links to the pueblo-dwelling Hopi. In many areas, the active involvement of Native Americans in research programmes has again resulted in such a turn (Varien and Wilhusen 2002).

Prehistory

The distinction has also been over-drawn between the landscape archaeology of prehistoric and historic periods. It is an overstatement to suggest that Romanticism is entirely absent from the intellectual formation of British prehistoric archaeology, or that the divergence I traced back to the 1950s between the methods of prehistorians and historical archaeologists left prehistory entirely free from Romantic underpinnings. As discussed in earlier chapters, Romanticism and empiricism have been so successful as discursive formations that their habits of thought have become implicit and unspoken; Foucault might say that they are deeply embedded in the underlying geology of the study of the past (Foucault 1972). As such, empiricist ways of thinking periodically resurface. John Barrett has argued that much of British prehistory, whatever its overt theoretical orientation, continues to exhibit a form of empiricism where features in the archaeological record are seen as more or less straightforward reflections of cultural realities in the past (Barrett 2005, 2006). I would also argue that the recent turn to phenomenological approaches, although legitimated by reference to Heidegger and other Continental theorists, owes more to Romanticism than it cares to admit.

When postprocessual writing on the British prehistoric landscape stresses memory, place, locale, the everyday, texture, and feeling, the references given are routinely to French and German writers in structural and phenomenological traditions: the names that recur include Bourdieu (1979), Heidegger (1953), Gadamer (1975, 1976) and Benjamin (1999). However, the ideas expressed in such postprocessual writing have been formed in part not simply by a reading of certain theoretical texts, but also by an encounter with the landscape, an encounter that was mediated through many of the intellectual and bodily processes described in previous chapters, most obviously the activity of walking, the inductive pattern of field research, the social context of academic research. Further, the ideas put forward in such postprocessual writing are evaluated and gain intellectual currency, are deemed "successful" or "fashionable," within a wider academic and cultural context. This wider context of British academic and popular culture continues to refer, as we have seen, to a Romantic view of the world as a critical cultural horizon.

I suggest that one of the reasons for the greater *intellectual* success of prehistory lies in a paradox. For better or worse, the historic English landscape is heavily freighted with meaning. It remains a powerful marker of identity for many people. Prehistoric monuments and landscapes, and the writings of prehistorians, have had a more marginal impact on and resonance with popular habits of thinking. When English Heritage searched for two images to place on the cover of *Power of Place*, images that they intended to convey power and meaning, the picture editors chose a modern urban street scene with 19th-century buildings in the background and a village of medieval origin. When the residents of Yorkshire refer to their identity, they refer to Richard III and the Yorkists, not to the Mesolithic inhabitants of Starr Carr. Hoskins did not come to his story of lineal ancestors by accident or in a vacuum. The generic images of the parish church, the cottage, the 18th-century parkland, then, occupy a place in the English imagination, however defined, that prehistory does not. When prehistory does carry an emotional charge, it is through the work of "alternative" writers rather than of established prehistorians; Julian Cope's *The Modern Antiquarian* continues to outsell the books on British prehistory by academics (Cope 1998).

One can argue, then, that the relative success of processual and postprocessual archaeology in rewriting prehistory has not simply been a result of the epistemological issues involved. It has also succeeded because the rewriting of prehistory was dealing with a "soft target." By contrast, scholars of historic landscapes deal in symbols and narratives that are much more dense and resonant in their meaning for people today. As such, the political and cultural stakes are higher, and the cultural material that the historic landscape archaeologist seeks to remould is much more dense and intractable. One might suggest that the difficulty of remoulding the study of historic landscapes, relative to the success of prehistory, is testament to its greater cultural importance.

Two Cultures

However, large and disabling gaps remain between different academic schools, different habits of thought. In a sense, they might be characterized as two academic tribes, each with its own discursive rules and patterns of thought and behaviour (Becher and Trowler 2001). In itself, diversity is not necessarily a bad thing in epistemological terms: the philosopher of science Alison Wylie writes of different contexts in archaeological thought that "the question of what epistemic stance is appropriate . . . should be settled locally, in the light of what we come to know about specific subject matters and about the resources we have for their investigation. We should resist the pressure to adopt a general epistemic stance appropriate to all knowledge claims" (Wylie 1992:35). I agree, with the proviso that the reverse is also true: we should resist the pressure to adopt an uncritical position where each tradition is regarded as no more or less valid than the next one, and in which critique, comparison, and relative evaluation are not attempted.

One of the key problems in traditional landscape archaeology and history is a culture of academic deference to "established authorities" and "senior figures." This is not so marked in Britain as it is in some Continental European countries, but it is more marked in Britain than in America, more in landscape history than in prehistoric archaeology, and more in medieval than in early modern studies. Archaeological and social theorists of whatever intellectual stripe are used to the sound and fury of a new generation of scholars heralding their arrival by the ritual denunciation of the previous generation. Both processual and post-processual changes in thinking were accompanied by polemics, clear position statements, an uncompromising tone, and a rhetoric that was often bruising (see for example Binford 1972; Shanks and Tilley 1987). In traditional landscape studies, and in studies of local history and related topics, things are often taken to the other extreme. Often, critiques of an established position are simply ignored, not in refutation, but as if they had never happened. Gelling notes how place-name studies continued in stagnation and confusion, in part because of a reluctance to challenge the academic and social standing of leading authorities (1988: 10). Collision between these two views and the communities they come from can lead to misunderstanding and unintended offence: when Philip Rahtz presented an anthropological view of Wharram his comments were seen as disrespectful (Rahtz 2001).

Such deference, however, does not mean that views that seriously challenge the existing discursive hegemony are not treated with hostility. Much of the project outlined in this book shares intellectual territory with Kathleen Biddick's reassessment of the future of British medieval peasant studies (1993). Biddick's suggestions, however, stand at some distance from what is considered established practice, to the extent that her 1993 paper was excluded from a student "reader" at the insistence of an anonymous British historian. Biddick's account of this exclusion, and of the way that she felt she had been "frozen out" as an archaeologist, a woman, and an American, is a model account of the processes of academic discourse in traditional circles, in which dissenting voices are muffled or excluded rather than confronted or engaged with (Biddick 1998). Her account resonates with the reception of the American journalist Paula Weideger's critique of that most British and Romantic of institutions, the National Trust (Weideger 1994).

There also exists a disabling gap between different elements of the academic community. As we have seen, landscape archaeology occupies a marginal place at Oxford and Cambridge; it is there, but within the interstices of the structures, for example in the Continuing Education Departments at both institutions or with individuals holding college fellowships rather than established positions. This marginal position can be traced back to Hoskins's own discomfort within the academic structures of Oxford, and also the metropolitan stress of much of the practice of history. I would argue that there has been a resulting intellectual loss on both sides. Oxford and Cambridge archaeology and history continue, in some parts, to have a rather rarefied existence. Grahame Clark's "world prehistory" spread Cambridge graduates across the globe (Clark 1989), while a generation of Oxford and Cambridge historians "discovered" the local as part of a shift in cultural attention to the small-scale and the everyday in the 1980s, rather than as a direct influence of the Hoskins tradition (for example Wrightson 1982). But as a result, much of landscape archaeology and history has been set at a certain remove from two of the sharpest critical environments in the country and indeed the world.

This marginal position can also be seen in the way in which the story of landscape history and archaeology has been marginalized from the established narrative of the history of archaeology as a whole. Histories of archaeology have, until recently, tended to stress prehistory over historic periods and excavation over other forms of fieldwork. Historians of archaeology do not mention Hoskins, and their discussion of O. G. S. Crawford often limits examples of his work to prehistoric sites (Daniel 1975:297–9). This pattern is continued by Trigger (1989) and other writers who concentrate on prehistory; Lucas (2001) treats "fieldwork" and "excavation" as largely coterminous.

In writing this book, I feel as if I am bringing two very old and much-loved friends together. As a Cambridge graduate, and as one of the generation who followed the lead of Ian Hodder and Shanks and Tilley in forging what came to be known as postprocessual archaeology, I find that the insistence on theory, on the intellectual integrity of archaeology, and on a wide-ranging approach in which one's work contributes to critical debates in the human sciences in general is second nature. But as someone brought up in the English county of Norfolk, about which Hoskins wrote, in classic style, that it was "a part of England that draws me like a woman" (Chalkin and Havinden 1974:xxv), who read *The Making of the English Landscape* and *Fieldwork in Local History* at an early age, and who was fascinated by the particularities of Norfolk's gently undulating landscape and lonely churches, and who went on to dig at Wharram, pore over hachured plans with Chris Taylor, and tramp across countless fields of humps and bumps in all weathers, my second friend is no less important.

Can the two traditions get on, will the one tradition find intellectual interest and stimulation from the other? Can we be more positive than lapsing into a disabling relativism in which "both views have their merits," where both schools refuse to engage with the other's concerns, but simply carry on talking past each other? I believe passionately that we can; in this sense, I hope this book marks a beginning in the study of landscape rather than an end.

GLOSSARY

assarting   the clearing of trees and bushes from land, in order to cultivate it

coppice   a tree is coppiced when its trunk is cut off near the base, so that young shoots grow quickly from the stump that remains

croft   a bounded area to the rear of the peasant toft, often used as a garden or paddock, and occasionally ploughed

demesne   manorial land retained for the private use of the lord

depopulation   the removal of the population of a settlement, for example the removal of tenants from a manor by the lord

diocese   the district under the jurisdiction of a bishop

diplomatic   the study of the form of old official documents and their age and authenticity

Domesday Book   a large-scale administrative survey of most of England, compiled by order of William the Conqueror in the 1080s, now important as a historical source

ecclesiastical   pertaining to the Church

empiricism   the belief that data speak for themselves, without the need for intervening theory

enclosure   The act of surrounding land with a fence or hedge/ditch, and/or the private appropriation of formerly common land

English Heritage   the organization responsible for the conservation and understanding of the "historic environment" in England (it has counterparts in Historic Scotland and, for Wales, Cadw). It is sponsored by and advises the government; its duties are defined by government legislation

forest   an area subject to forest law (often but not always or completely wooded)

genius loci   a Latin term from classical thought, referring to the presiding spirit of a locality or specific place; later used by both Wordsworth and Hoskins

gentry   a social class, of substantial landowners and agents of government, below that of the aristocracy

hachuring   hachures are the lines used as a convention in field survey and mapping to indicate the line, steepness, etc. of a slope; resembling and referred to colloquially as "tadpoles"

hermeneutics   the study of meanings

hundred   an administrative subdivision of a county, perhaps originally not a region

husbandman   the social class below that of the yeoman

ineffable   said of something that (according to the writer) through its very nature is somehow beyond critique, for example a work of art, or a view of landscape

liturgy   a prescribed set of forms for religious worship

lynchet   a ridge formed along the downside of a terraced plot, along the slope, presumed by ploughing

manor   the district over which a lord had domain (the manor house being his residence, from which domain was exercised; see also **demesne**)

messuage   a house and adjacent lands and buildings; see also **tenement**

mimesis   in art or literature, imitative representation of the real world

mnemonic   a device which aids memory

Ordnance Survey   the government agency responsible for drawing up and producing maps of Britain, at various scales

osteology   the study of bones

palaeography   the study of ancient writing systems and manuscripts

phenomenology   the study of lived bodily experience

pollard   as with coppicing, the cutting off of a tree trunk to encourage the growth of shoots from the stump, but done at a sufficient height to stop animals grazing on the shoots

postprocessualism   a loose set of ideas in archaeological theory that opposes many of the tenets of processualism and positivism; closely related to postmodernism; see also **processualism**

probate inventory   a list of movable goods and their value drawn up on a person's death, often compiled room by room

processualism   a movement in archaeological theory that stresses the idea of process, tends to generalize, and adopts a broadly positivist approach. It can be seen as a developed, more mature form of the New Archaeology; see also **postprocessualism**

reave   a form of prehistoric field boundary

ridge and furrow earthwork traces of medieval or later agriculture, generally assumed to be created by a heavy plough being driven up and down a narrow holding of land. The mouldboard of the plough turns the soil inwards, so creating a ridge through time. The pattern is then "fossilized" if and when ploughing ceases and the field is turned over to pasture

Royal Commission on Historical Monuments bodies set up in England, Scotland, and Wales for the purpose of researching the architecture and archaeology of each country county by county; the English body is now merged with English Heritage

stratigraphy in geology, the understanding of the order and relative sequence of geological layers; developed in archaeology as the understanding of sequences of features from their relative position

taphonomy the study of processes of burial, decay, and preservation of objects

tenement property, especially human habitation, held by one person from another

toft the farmyard around the medieval peasant house, often defined by a bank and ditch

trope a term from the study of text, referring to a common pattern or rhetorical turn

vill a term used in medieval law to refer to various entities, not necessarily a village in form

yeoman a socially middling farmer

REFERENCES

Aalen, F. H., Whelan, K., and Stout, M., eds. 1997   Atlas of the Irish Rural Landscape. Toronto: University of Toronto Press.

Aberg, F. A. 1978   Medieval Moated Sites. CBA Research Report 17. York: Council for British Archaeology.

Addy, S. O. 1898   The Evolution of the English House. London: Allen & Unwin.

Aers, D., and L. Staley 1996   The Powers of the Holy: Religion, Politics and Gender in Late Medieval Culture. Philadelphia: Pennsylvania University Press.

Ainsworth, S., D. Field, and P. Pattison, eds. 1999   Patterns of the Past: Essays in Landscape Archaeology for Christopher Taylor. Oxford: Oxbow Books.

Aitchison, C., N. E. MacLeod, and S. J. Shaw 2000   Leisure and Tourism Landscapes: Social and Cultural Geographies. London: Routledge.

Albarella, U. 1999   "The Mystery of Husbandry": Medieval Animals and the Problem of Integrating Historical and Archaeological Evidence. Antiquity 73:867–875.

Alcock, N. W. 1993   People at Home: Living in a Warwickshire Village 1500–1800. London: Phillimore.

Anderson, B. 1989   Imagined Communities: Reflections on the Origin and Spread of Nationalism. London: Verso.

Anonymous 1992   Professor W. G. Hoskins. Local Historian 22(3):144–146.

Appleton, J. 1975   The Experience of Landscape. London: John Wiley.

Ashmore, W., and B. Knapp, eds. 1999   Archaeologies of Landscape: Contemporary Perspectives. Oxford: Blackwell.

Astill, G. 1988   Rural Settlement: The Toft and the Croft. In The Countryside of Medieval England. G. Astill and A. Grant, eds. Pp. 36–61. Oxford: Blackwell.

Astill, G., and A. Grant, eds. 1988   The Countryside of Medieval England. Oxford: Blackwell.

Astill, G., and J. Langdon, eds. 1997 Medieval Farming and Technology: The Impact of Agricultural Change in Northwest Europe. Leiden: Brill.

Aston, M. 1983 The Making of the English Landscape: The Next 25 Years. Local Historian 15(6):323–332.

Aston, M. 1985 Interpreting the Landscape: Landscape Archaeology in Local Studies. London: Batsford.

Aston, M. 2002 Interpreting the Landscape from the Air. Stroud: Tempus.

Aston, M. 2003 Public Worship and Iconoclasm. In The Archaeology of Reformation 1480–1580. D. Gaimster and R. Gilchrist, eds. Pp. 9–28. Leeds, Maney.

Aston, M., D. Austin, and C. Dyer, eds. 1989 The Rural Settlements of Medieval England: Studies Dedicated to Maurice Beresford and John Hurst. Oxford: Blackwell.

Aston, T. H., ed. 1987 Landlords, Peasants and Politics in Medieval England. Cambridge: Cambridge University Press.

Atkinson J. A., Iain Banks, and Jerry O'Sullivan, eds. 1996 Nationalism and Archaeology. Glasgow: Cruithne Press.

Augé, M. 1995 Non-Places: Introduction to an Anthropology of Supermodernity. London: Verso.

Austin, D. 1990 The "Proper Study" of Medieval Archaeology. In From the Baltic to the Black Sea: Studies in Medieval Archaeology. D. Austin and L. Alcock, eds. Pp. 9–42. London: Unwin Hyman.

Austin, D. 1996 Review of Bodmin Moor: An Archaeological Survey, vol. 1: The Human Landscape to c.1800, by Nicholas Johnson and Peter Rose. Medieval Archaeology 40:340–343.

Austin, D., and L. Alcock, eds. 1990 From the Baltic to the Black Sea: Studies in Medieval Archaeology. London: Unwin Hyman.

Bakhtin, M. 1986 The Dialogic Imagination. Austin: University of Texas Press.

Barker, K., and T. Darvill, eds. 1997 Making English Landscapes: Changing Perspectives. Oxford: Oxbow Books.

Barley, M. W. 1961 The English Farmhouse and Cottage. London: Routledge.

Barnes, T. J., and J. S. Duncan, eds. 1992 Writing Worlds: Discourse, Text and Metaphor in the Representation of Landscape. London: Routledge.

Barrett, J. 1993 Fragments from Antiquity: Archaeology of Social Life in Britain 2900–1200 BC. Oxford: Blackwell.

Barrett, J. 2005 Material Culture, Humanity and the Beginnings of the Neolithic. In Die Dinge als Zeichen. Kulturelles Wissen und materielle Kultur. T. L. Kienlin, ed. Pp. 111–124. Bonn: Habelt.

Barrett, J. 2006 Archaeology as the Investigation of the Contexts of Humanity. In Deconstructing Context: A Critical Approach to Archaeological Practice. D. Papaconstantinou, ed. Pp. 194–211. Oxford: Oxbow Books.

Barthes, R. 1989 Mythologies. London: Paladin.

Bassnett, S., ed. 1997 Studying British Cultures. London: Routledge.

Bate, J. 1991   Romantic Ecology: Wordsworth and the Environmental Tradition. London: Routledge.

Becher, T., and P. R. Trowler 2001   Academic Tribes and Territories: Intellectual Enquiry and the Culture of Disciplines. Buckingham: Open University Press.

Beck, R., ed. In press   The Durable House: Material, Metaphor and Structure. Carbondale: Southern Illinois University Centre for Archaeological Investigations.

Beier, A. L. 1985   Masterless Men: The Vagrancy Problem in England 1560–1640. London: Methuen.

Bender, B., ed. 1993   Landscape: Politics and Perspectives. Oxford: Berg.

Bender, B. 1998   Stonehenge: Making Space. Oxford: Berg.

Bender, B. 1999   The Case for a Living Giant. In The Cerne Giant: Antiquity on Trial. T. Darvill, K. Barker, B. Bender, and R. Hutton, eds. Pp. 126–161. Oxford: Oxbow Books.

Bender, B., and M. Winer, eds. 2001   Contested Landscapes: Movement, Exile and Place. Oxford: Berg.

Benjamin, R. 2004   Roman Wall: Barrier or Bond? British Archaeology 77:10–15.

Benjamin, W. 1999   The Arcades Project. London: Belknap Press.

Bennett, Judith M. 1996   Ale, Beer and Brewsters in England: Women's Work in a Changing World, 1300–1600. Oxford: Oxford University Press.

Bentley, M., ed. 1997   Companion to Historiography. London: Routledge.

Beresford, G. 1987   Goltho: The Development of an Early Medieval Manor. London: English Heritage.

Beresford, M. W. 1948   Ridge and Furrow and the Open Field. Economic History Review 2nd series, 1:34–45.

Beresford, M. W. 1956   The Lost Villages of England. London: Lutterworth.

Beresford, M. W. 1957   History on the Ground, 2nd edition. London: Methuen.

Beresford, M. W., and J. G. Hurst, eds. 1971   Deserted Medieval Villages: Studies. London: Lutterworth Press.

Beresford, M. W., and J. G. Hurst, eds. 1990   Wharram Percy: Deserted Medieval Village. London: Batsford.

Beresford, M. W., and J. K. St Joseph 1978   Medieval England: An Aerial Survey, 2nd edition. Cambridge: Cambridge University Press.

Bermingham, A. 2000   Learning to Draw: Studies in the Cultural History of a Polite and Useful Art. New Haven: Yale University Press.

Biddick, K. 1990   People and Things: Power in Early English Development. Comparative Studies in Society and History 32(1):3–23.

Biddick, K. 1993   Decolonising the English Past: Readings in Medieval Archaeology and History. Journal of British Studies 32(1):1–24.

Biddick, K. 1998   The Shock of Medievalism. Durham: Duke University Press.

Binford, L. R. 1962   Archaeology as Anthropology. American Antiquity 11:198–200.

Binford, L. R. 1964 A Consideration of Archaeological Research Design. American Antiquity 29:425–441.

Binford, L. R. 1972 An Archaeological Perspective. New York: Seminar Press.

Binford, L. R. 1983 In Pursuit of the Past. London: Thames & Hudson.

Binford, L. R. 1987 Data, Relativism and Archaeological Science. Man 22:391–404.

Block, H. 1962 The Visionary Company: A Reading of English Romantic Poetry. London: Faber.

Bloom, H., ed. 1961 English Romantic Poetry: An Anthology. New York: Doubleday.

Boivin, N., and M. A. Owoc, eds. 2004 Soils, Stones and Symbols: Cultural Perceptions of the Mineral World. London: UCL Press.

Bond, J. 2000 Landscapes of Monasticism. In Landscape: The Richest Historical Record. SLS Supplementary Series 1. D. Hooke, ed. Pp. 63–72. Amesbury: Society for Landscape Studies.

Boots, B. 1986 Voronoi (Thiessen) Polygons. Norwich: Geo Books.

Bourdieu, P. 1979 Outline of a Theory of Practice. Cambridge: Cambridge University Press.

Bowden, M. 1992 The Invention of American Tradition. Journal of Historical Geography 18:3–26.

Bowden, M. 2001 Mapping the Past: OGS Crawford and the Development of Landscape Studies. Landscapes 2:29–45.

Boyd, K., ed. 1999 Encyclopaedia of Histories and Historical Writing. London: Fitzroy Dearborn.

Bradbury, M., ed. 1996 The Atlas of Literature. London: De Agostini.

Bradley, R. 1993 Altering the Earth: The Origins of Monuments in Britain and Continental Europe. Edinburgh: Society of Antiquaries of Scotland.

Bradley, R. 1998 The Significance of Monuments: On the Shaping of Human Experience in Neolithic and Bronze Age Europe. London: Routledge.

Bradley, R. 2000 Mental and Material Landscapes in Prehistoric Britain. In Landscape: The Richest Historical Record. SLS Supplementary Series 1. D. Hooke, ed. Pp. 1–11. Amesbury: Society for Landscape Studies.

Bradley, S., and B. Cherry, eds. 2001 The Buildings of England: A Celebration. Harmondsworth: Penguin.

Bragg, M. 1996 The Lake District of the Romantics. In The Atlas of Literature. M. Bradbury, ed. Pp. 58–61. London: De Agostini.

Brewer, William D. 1998 Unnationalized Englishmen in Mary Shelley's Fiction. Romanticism on the Net 11. Electronic document, <http://users.ox.ac.uk/scat0385/mwsfiction.html>.

Britnell, R. H. 1996 The Commercialisation of English Society, 1000–1500, 2nd edition. Manchester: Manchester University Press.

Brocklehurst, H., and R. Philips, eds. 2004 History, Nationhood and the Question of Britain. Basingstoke: Macmillan.

Brookner, A. 2000 Romanticism and its Discontents. London: Viking.

Brumfiel, E., and J. W. Fox, eds. 1994   Factional Competition and Political Development in the New World. Cambridge: Cambridge University Press.

Burke, H. 1999   Meaning and Ideology in Historical Archaeology: Style, Social Identity and Capitalism in an Australian Town. New York: Kluwer.

Cahill, K. 2001   Who Owns Britain: The Hidden Facts Behind Ownership in the UK and Ireland. Edinburgh: Canongate.

Camille, M. 1998   Mirror in Parchment: The Luttrell Psalter and the Making of Medieval England. London: Reaktion.

Canuto, M. A., and J. Yaeger, eds. 2000   An Archaeology of Communities: A New World Perspective. London: Routledge.

Carter, P. 1987   The Road to Botany Bay. London: Faber.

Chalkin, C. W., and M. A. Havinden, eds. 1974   Rural Change and Urban Growth 1500–1800: Essays in English Regional History in Honour of W. G. Hoskins. London: Longman.

Chandler, J. 2000   The Discovery of Landscape. *In* Landscape: The Richest Historical Record. SLS Supplementary Series 1. D. Hooke, ed. Pp. 133–142. Amesbury: Society for Landscape Studies.

Chapelot, J., and R. Fossier 1980   The Village and House in the Middle Ages. London: Batsford.

Cherry, B. 1998   The Buildings of England, Ireland, Scotland and Wales: A Short Bibliography. Harmondsworth: Penguin.

Cherry, J. F., J. L. Davis, and E. Mantzourani, eds. 1991   Landscape Archaeology as Long-Term History: Northern Keos in the Cycladic Islands from Earliest Settlement Until Modern Times. UCLA Institute of Archaeology monograph. Los Angeles: University of California Press.

Clark, G. 1989   Prehistory at Cambridge and Beyond. Cambridge: Cambridge University Press.

Clark, M., and M. Sleeman 1991   Writing the Earth, Righting the Earth: Committed Presuppositions and the Geographical Imagination. *In* New Words, New Worlds: Reconceptualising Social and Cultural Geography. C. Philo, ed. Pp. 49–60. Lampeter: St David's University College.

Clarke, D. L. 1968   Analytical Archaeology. London: Methuen.

Clarke, D. L., ed. 1972   Models in Archaeology. London: Duckworth.

Claval, P. 1993   Autour de Vidal de la Blache: La Formation de l'école française de géographie. Paris: Centre National des Recherches Scientifiques.

Cloke, P., I. Cook, P. Crang, M. Goodwin, J. Painter, and C. Philo 2003   Practicing Human Geography. London: Sage.

Coleman, S., and J. Elsner 1999   Pilgrimage to Walsingham and the Re-Invention of the Middle Ages. *In* Pilgrimage Explored. J. Stopford, ed. Pp. 189–214. Woodbridge: Boydell.

Colley, L. 1992   Britons: Forging the Nation 1707–1837. New Haven: Yale University Press.

Collingwood, R. G. 1946   The Idea of History. Oxford: Oxford University Press.

Collini, S. 1991   Genealogies of Englishness: Literary History and Cultural Criticism in Modern Britain. *In* Ideology and the Historians. C. Brady, ed. Pp. 128–145. Dublin: Lilliput Press.

Combe, W. 1812   The Tour of Dr Syntax, in Search of the Picturesque: A Poem. London: Ackermann.

Conkey, M., and J. Spector 1984   Archaeology and the Study of Gender. Advances in Archaeological Method and Theory 7:1–38.

Cope, J. 1998   The Modern Antiquarian: A Pre-Millennial Odyssey through Megalithic Britain: Including a Gazetteer To Over 300 Prehistoric Sites. London: Thorsons.

Corcos, N. 2001   Churches as Prehistoric Ritual Monuments: A Phenomenological Perspective from Somerset. Artefact 6. Electronic document, <http://www.shef.ac.uk/assem/issue6/Corcos_web.html>.

Cosgrove, D. 1984   Social Formation and Symbolic Landscape. London: Croom Helm.

Cosgrove, D. 2000   Apollo's Eye: A Cartographic Genealogy of the Earth in the Western Imagination. Baltimore: Johns Hopkins.

Cosgrove, D., and S. Daniels, eds. 1988   The Iconography of Landscape. Cambridge: Cambridge University Press.

Crawford, O. G. S. 1928   Wessex from the Air. Oxford: Clarendon Press.

Crawford, O. G. S. 1953   Archaeology in the Field. London: Phoenix House.

Crawford, O. G. S. 1955   Said and Done: Autobiography of an Archaeologist. London: Weidenfeld & Nicolson.

Crick, B. 1980   George Orwell: A Life. London: Secker & Warburg.

Cronon, W. 1983   Changes in the Land: Indians, Colonists and the Ecology of New England. New York: Hill & Wang.

Crown, P. L., and W. J. Judge 1991   Chaco and Hohokam: Prehistoric Regional Systems in the American Southwest. Santa Fe: School of American Research Press.

Crumley, C. L., ed. 1994   Historical Ecology: Cultural Knowledge and Changing Landscapes. Santa Fe: School of American Research Press.

Currie, C. 1988   Time and Chance: Modeling the Attrition of Old Houses. Vernacular Architecture 19:1–9.

Currie, C. 2004   The Unfulfilled Potential of the Documentary Sources. Vernacular Architecture 35:1–11.

Curry, M. R. 1992   The Architectonic Impulse and the Reconceptualisation of the Concrete in Contemporary Geography. *In* Writing Worlds: Discourse, Text and Metaphor in the Representation of Landscape. T. J. Barnes and J. S. Duncan, eds. Pp. 91–117. London: Routledge.

Curry, P. 1998   Defending Middle-Earth: Token, Myth and Modernity. London: HarperCollins.

Daniel, G. 1975   150 Years of Archaeology, 2nd edition. London: Duckworth.

Daniel, G., and A. C. Renfrew 1988   The Idea of Prehistory. Edinburgh: Edinburgh University Press.

Daniels, S. 1992   Fields of Vision: Landscape Imagery and National Identity in England and the United States. Cambridge: Polity.

Darby, H. C., ed. 1936   An Historical Geography of England Before AD1800. Cambridge: Cambridge University Press.

Darvill, T., K. Barker, B. Bender, and R. Hutton, eds. 1999   The Cerne Giant: Antiquity on Trial. Oxford: Oxbow Books.

David, B. 2002   Landscapes, Rock Art and the Dreaming: An Archaeology of Pre-Understanding. Leicester: Leicester University Press.

David, B., and M. Wilson, eds. 2002   Inscribed Landscapes: Marking and Making Place. Honolulu: University of Hawaii Press.

De Man, P. 1984   The Rhetoric of Romanticism. New York: Columbia University Press.

de Selincourt, E., ed. 1906   Wordsworth's Guide to the Lakes: The Fifth Edition (1835). Oxford: Oxford University Press.

de Selincourt, E., ed. 1967   The Letters of William and Dorothy Wordsworth, vol. 1. Oxford: Clarendon Press.

Deetz, J. F. 1977   In Small Things Forgotten: The Archaeology of Early American Life. New York: Anchor.

Devereux, P. 2001   Shamanism and the Mystery Lines: Ley Lines, Spirit Paths, Out-of-Body Travel and Shape-Shifting. London: Quantum.

Diamond, J. 1997   Guns, Germs and Steel. London: Jonathan Cape.

Diaz-Andreu, M. 2004   Britain and the Other: The Archaeology of Imperialism. *In* History, Nationhood and the Question of Britain. H. Brocklehurst and R. Philips, eds. Pp. 227–241. Basingstoke: Macmillan.

Diaz-Andreu, M., and T. Champion, eds. 1996   Nationalism and Archaeology in Europe. London: University College London Press.

Dimbleby, D., ed. 2005   A Picture of Britain. London: Tate.

Dobres, M.-A., and J. Robb, eds. 2000   Agency in Archaeology. London: Routledge.

Docker, J. 2001   1492: The Politics of Diaspora. London: Continuum.

Douglas, M. 1978   Purity and Danger: An Analysis of Concepts of Pollution and Taboo. London: Routledge.

Drescher, S. 1987   Eric Williams: British Capitalism and British Slavery. History and Theory 26:180–196.

Driver, F. 2000   Editorial: Fieldwork in Geography. Transactions of the Institute of British Geographers 25:267–268.

Driver, F. 2001   Geography Militant: Culture of Exploration and Empire. Oxford: Blackwell.

Duffy, E. 1992   The Stripping of the Altars: Traditional Religion in England 1400–1580. New Haven, Yale University Press.

Duffy, E. 2001   The Voices of Morebath: Reformation and Rebellion in an English Village. New Haven: Yale University Press.

Duncan, J., and D. Ley 1993   Place/Culture/Representation. London: Routledge.

Dunant, S., ed. 1993   The War of the Words: The Political Correctness Debate. London: Virago.

Dussart, F., ed. 1971   L'Habitat et les paysages ruraux d'Europe. Liège: no publisher given.

Dyer, C. C. 1980   Lords and Peasants in a Changing Society: The Estates of the Bishopric of Worcester, 680–1540. Cambridge: Cambridge University Press.

Dyer, C. C. 1994   Everyday Life in Medieval England. London: Hambledon.

Dyer, C. C. 1997   Medieval Farming and Technology: Conclusion. *In* Medieval Farming and Technology: The Impact of Agricultural Change in Northwest Europe. G. Astill and J. Langdon, eds. Pp. 293–312. Leiden: Brill.

Dyer, C. C. 2002   Making a Living in the Middle Ages: The People of Britain, 850–1520. New Haven: Yale University Press.

Dymond, D., and E. Martin, eds. 1998   An Historical Atlas of Suffolk. Ipswich: Suffolk County Council.

Eagleton, T. 1990   The Ideology of the Aesthetic. Oxford: Blackwell.

Earle, T. 2002   Bronze Age Economics: The Beginnings of Political Economies. Oxford: Westview Press.

Easthope, A. 1999   Englishness and National Culture. London: Routledge.

Ebbatson, L. 1994   Context and Discourse: Royal Archaeological Institute Membership 1845–1942. *In* Building on the Past: Papers Celebrating 150 Years of the Royal Archaeological Institute. B. Vyner, ed. Pp. 22–74. London: Royal Archaeological Institute.

Edgeworth, M. 2003   Acts of Discovery: An Ethnography of Archaeological Practice. BAR International Series 1131. Oxford: Archaeopress.

Edmonds, M. 1999   Ancestral Geographies of the Neolithic. London: Routledge.

Elliott, J. 1999   Laurence Stone. Past and Present 164:3–5.

Erickson, A. 1993   Women and Property in Early Modern England. London: Routledge.

Erickson, C. 1993   The Social Organisation of Prehispanic Raised Field Agriculture in the Lake Titicaca Basin. Research in Economic Anthropology Supplementary Series 7:369–426.

Erickson, C. L. 1999   Neo-Environmental Determinism and Agrarian "Collapse" in Andean Prehistory. Antiquity 73:634–642.

Evans, J. G. 2003   Environmental Archaeology and the Social Order. London: Routledge.

Everitt, A. 1970   New Avenues in English Local History: An Inaugural Lecture. Leicester, Leicester University Press.

Everson, P., and D. Stocker 2003   The Archaeology of Vice-Regality: Charles Brandon's Brief Rule in Lincolnshire. *In* The Archaeology of Reformation 1480–1580. D. Gaimster and R. Gilchrist, eds. Pp. 145–158. Leeds: Maney.

Ewart Evans, G. 1960   The Horse in the Furrow. London: Faber.

Ewart Evans, G. 1966   The Pattern Under the Plough: Aspects of the Folk-Life of East Anglia. London: Faber.

Faith, R. 1997   The English Peasantry and the Growth of Lordship. Leicester University Press.

Faroghi, S. 1999   Approaching Ottoman History: An Introduction to the Sources. Cambridge: Cambridge University Press.

Feinman, G., and D. Price, eds. 2001   Archaeology at the Millennium: A Sourcebook. New York: Kluwer.

Field, J. 1989   English Field Names: A Dictionary, 2nd edition. Gloucester: Alan Sutton.

Fieldhouse, R., and B. Jennings 1978   A History of Richmond and Swaledale. Chichester: Phillimore.

Finberg, H. P. R. 1964   Local History in the University: An Inaugural Lecture Delivered in the University of Leicester 26 May 1964. Leicester: Leicester University Press.

Fisher, H. A. L., ed. 1911   The Collected Papers of F. W. Maitland. 3 vols. Cambridge: Cambridge University Press.

Flannery, K. V., ed. 1976   The Early Mesoamerican Village. New York: Academic Press.

Fleming, A. 1988   The Dartmoor Reaves: Investigating Prehistoric Land Divisions. London: Batsford.

Fleming, A. 1998   Swaledale: Valley of the Wild River. Edinburgh: Edinburgh University Press.

Foucault, M. 1972   The Archaeology of Knowledge. London: Tavistock.

Fowler, D. D. 2000   A Laboratory for Anthropology: Science and Romanticism in the American Southwest. Albuquerque: Museum of New Mexico Press.

Fox, C. 1923   The Archaeology of the Cambridge Region: A Topographical Study of the Bronze, Early Iron, Roman and Anglo-Saxon Ages, with an Introductory Note on the Neolithic Age. Cambridge: Cambridge University Press.

Fox, C. 1938   The Personality of Britain: Its Influence on Inhabitant and Invader in Prehistoric and Historic Times. Cardiff: National Museum of Wales.

Fox, Sir Cyril, and Lord Raglan 1951   Monmouthshire Houses: A Study of Building Techniques and Smaller House-Plans in the 15th to 17th Centuries. 3 vols. Cardiff: National Museum of Wales.

Frantzen, A. J. 1994   The Work of Work: Servitude, Slavery and Labour in Medieval England. In Frantzen and Moffat, eds., pp. 1–15.

Frantzen, A. J., and D. Moffat, eds. 1994   The Work of Work: Servitude, Slavery and Labour in Medieval England. Glasgow: Cruithne.

Frodeman, R. 2004   Reading the Earth: Philosophy in/of the Field. In Soils, Stones and Symbols: Cultural Perceptions of the Mineral World. N. Boivin and M. A. Owoc, eds. Pp. 203–216. London: UCL Press.

Gadamer, H.-G. 1975   Truth and Method. London: Continuum.

Gadamer, H.-G. 1976   Philosophical Hermeneutics. Berkeley: University of California Press.

Gaimster, D., and R. Gilchrist eds. 2003   The Archaeology of Reformation 1480–1580. Leeds, Maney.

Gardiner, M. F. 2000   Vernacular Buildings and the Development of the Later Medieval Domestic Plan in England. Medieval Archaeology 44:159–179.

Gardner, A., ed. 2004   Agency Uncovered: Archaeological Perspectives on Social Agency, Power and Being Human. London: University College London Press.

Garmonsway, G. N. 1978   Ælfric's "Colloquy". Exeter: University of Exeter.

Gelling, M. 1988   Signposts to the Past: Place-Names and the History of England, 3rd edition 1997. London: Phillimore.

Gelling, M., and A. Cole 2000   The Landscape of Place-Names. Stamford: Shaun Tyas.

Gerrard, C. M. 2003   Medieval Archaeology: Understanding Traditions and Contemporary Approaches. London: Routledge.

Gerzina, G. 1995   Black England: Life Before Emancipation. London: John Murray.

Gilroy, P. 1987   "There Ain't No Black in the Union Jack": The Cultural Politics of Race and Nation. London: Hutchinson.

Glassie, H. 1975   Folk Housing in Middle Virginia: A Structural Analysis of Historic Artifacts. Knoxville: University of Tennessee Press.

Glassie, H. 1982   Passing the Time: Folklore and History of an Ulster Community. Philadelphia: University of Pennsylvania Press.

Glassie, H. 2000   Vernacular Architecture. Bloomington: University of Indiana Press.

Goldberg, P. J. P., ed. 1997   Women in Medieval English Society, 2nd edition. Stroud: Sutton.

Gorringe, T. 2002   A Theology of the Built Environment: Justice, Empowerment, Redemption. Cambridge: Cambridge University Press.

Gower, B. 1997   Scientific Method: An Historical and Philosophical Investigation. London: Routledge.

Graham, B. J. 1994   The Search for the Common Ground: Estyn Evans' Ireland. Transactions of the Institute of British Geographers 19(2):183–201.

Graham, H. 1997   "A Woman's Work . . .": Labour and Gender in the Late Medieval Countryside. In Women in Medieval English Society, 2nd edition. P. J. P. Goldberg, ed. Pp. 126–148. Stroud: Sutton.

Graves, C. P. 2000   The Form and Fabric of Belief: An Archaeology of the Lay Experience of Religion in Medieval Norfolk and Devon. BAR British Series 311. Oxford: British Archaeological Reports.

Greenblatt, S. 1991   Marvelous Possessions: The Wonder of the New World. Oxford: Clarendon Press.

Greenblatt, S. 1994   The Eating of the Soul. Representations 48:97–116.

Greene, J. P. 1992   Medieval Monasteries. Leicester: Leicester University Press.

Gregory, D. 1994   Geographical Imaginations. Oxford: Blackwell.

Griffiths, D., ed. 2003   Boundaries in Early Medieval Britain. Oxford: Oxford University School of Archaeology.

Grove, A. T., and O. Rackham 2001   The Nature of Mediterranean Europe: An Ecological History. New Haven: Yale University Press.

Guelke, L. 1982   Historical Understanding in Geography: An Idealist Approach. Cambridge: Cambridge University Press.

Hadfield, J., ed. 1973   The Shell Guide to England. London: Joseph.

Hadfield, J., ed. 1980   The Shell Book of English Villages. London: Joseph.

Hanawalt, B. 1986   The Ties That Bound: Peasant Families in Medieval England. Oxford: Oxford University Press.

Harley, J. B. 1992   Deconstructing the Map. In Writing Worlds: Discourse, Text and Metaphor in the Representation of Landscape. T. J. Barnes and J. S. Duncan, eds. Pp. 231–247. London: Routledge.

Harley, J. B. 2000   The New Nature of Maps: Essays in the History of Cartography. Johns Hopkins.

Harmon, D., ed. 1989   Mirror of America: Literary Encounters with National Parks. Boulder: Roberts Rinehart.

Harrison, B., and B. Hutton 1984   Vernacular Houses in North Yorkshire and Cleveland. Edinburgh: Donald.

Harvey, D. 1990   The Condition of Postmodernity: An Enquiry into the Conditions of Cultural Change. Oxford: Blackwell.

Harvey, P. D. A. 1996   Mappa Mundi: The Hereford World Map. Hereford: Hereford Cathedral.

Hatcher, J., and M. Bailey 2001   Modelling the Middle Ages: The History and Theory of England's Economic Development. Oxford: Oxford University Press.

Hawkes, J. 1982   Mortimer Wheeler: Adventurer in Archaeology. London: Weidenfeld & Nicolson.

Heidegger, M. 1953   Sein und Zeit. Tübingen: Niemeyer.

Helgerson, R. 1992   Forms of Nationhood: The Elizabethan Writing of England. Chicago: University of Chicago Press.

Hettinger, M. J. 1994   Defining the Servant: Legal and Extra-Legal Terms of Employment in 15th-Century England. In The Work of Work: Servitude, Slavery and Labour in Medieval England. A. J. Frantzen and D. Moffat, eds. Pp. 206–228. Glasgow: Cruithne.

Hewison, R. 1987   The Heritage Industry: Britain in a Climate of Decline. London: Methuen.

Hicks, D. 2003   Archaeology Unfolding. Oxford Journal of Archaeology 22(3):315–329.

Hill, C. 1964   Society and Puritanism in Pre-Revolutionary England. London: Secker & Warburg.

Hill, C. 1993   The English Bible and the 17th Century Revolution. London: Allen Lane.

Hills, C. M. 1979   The Archaeology of Anglo-Saxon England in the Pagan Period: A Review. Anglo-Saxon England 8:297–330.

Hills, C. M. 2003   Origins of the English. London: Duckworth.

Hilton, R. H. 1977   Bond Men Made Free: Medieval Peasant Movements and the English Rising of 1381. London: Methuen.

Hines, J. 2004   Voices in the Past: English Literature and Archaeology. Cambridge: Brewer.

Hinton, D. 1967   A Cruck House at Lower Radley, Berkshire. Oxoniensa 32:13–33.

Hinton, D. 2003   Medieval Anglo-Jewry: The Archaeological Evidence. *In* The Jews in Medieval Britain: Historical, Literary and Archaeological Perspectives. P. Skinner, ed. Pp. 97–112. Woodbridge: Boydell.

Hobsbawm, E., ed. 1984   The Invention of Tradition. Oxford: Past and Present.

Hobsbawm, E. 1990   Myths and Nationalism Since 1780: Programme, Myth, Reality. Cambridge: Cambridge University Press.

Hodder, I. 1990   The Domestication of Europe. Oxford: Blackwell.

Hodder, I. 1999   The Archaeological Process. Oxford: Blackwell.

Hodder, I., and S. Hutson 2003   Reading the Past: Current Approaches to Interpretation in Archaeology. Cambridge: Cambridge University Press.

Hoggart, R. 1957   The Uses of Literacy: Aspects of Working-Class Life with Special Reference to Publications and Entertainments. London: Chatto & Windus.

Hooke, D., ed. 1985   Medieval Villages. OUCA Monograph 5. Oxford: Oxford University Committee for Archaeology.

Hooke, D. 1997   Lamberde leie, dillameres dic: A Lost or a Living Landscape? *In* Making English Landscapes: Changing Perspectives. K. Barker and T. Darvill, eds. Pp. 26–45. Oxford: Oxbow Books.

Hooke, D., ed. 2000   Landscape: The Richest Historical Record. SLS Supplementary Series 1. Amesbury: Society for Landscape Studies.

Hoskins, W. G. 1949   Midland England. London: Batsford.

Hoskins, W. G. 1953   The Rebuilding of Rural England, 1570–1640. Past and Present 4:44–59.

Hoskins, W. G. 1954a   The Anatomy of the English Countryside: 1. The Anatomy of the English Countryside; 2. A Hand-Made World; 3. The Road Between; 4. The "Rash Assault"; 5. The House through the Trees. The Listener, 732–734, 772–774, 819–820, 864–866, 917–918.

Hoskins, W. G. 1954b   Devon. London: Collins.

Hoskins, W. G. 1955   The Making of the English Landscape. London: Hodder & Stoughton.

Hoskins, W. G. 1957   Exeter in the 17th Century: Tax and Rate Assessments 1602–1699. Devon and Cornwall Record Society new series 2. Torquay: Devonshire Press.

Hoskins, W. G. 1959   Local History in England. London: Longman.

Hoskins, W. G. 1960   Two Thousand Years in Exeter: An Illustrated Social History of the Mother-City of South-Western England. Exeter: Townsend.

Hoskins, W. G. 1964a   Harvest and Hunger. The Listener 72:931–932.

Hoskins, W. G. 1964b   Harvest Fluctuations and English Economic History, 1480–1619. Agricultural History Review 12:28–47.

Hoskins, W. G. 1965   Provincial England. London: Macmillan.

Hoskins, W. G. 1966a   Old Devon. London: David and Charles.

Hoskins, W. G. 1966b   English Local History: The Past and the Future. Leicester: Leicester University Press.

Hoskins, W. G. 1967   Fieldwork in Local History. London: Faber.

Hoskins, W. G. 1968   Harvest Fluctuations and English Economic History, 1620–1759. Agricultural History Review 16:15–31.

Hoskins, W. G. 1970   Review of Bell and Bell, City Fathers: The Early History of Town Planning in Britain. Antiquity 44:246–247.

Hoskins, W. G. 1973   English Landscapes: How to Read the Man-Made Scenery of England. London: British Broadcasting Corporation.

Hoskins, W. G. 1976   The Age of Plunder: King Henry's England 1500–1547. London: Longman.

Hoskins, W. G. 1977   The Making of the English Landscape. Reprinted with new introduction. London: Hodder & Stoughton.

Hoskins, W. G. 1978   One Man's England. London: British Broadcasting Corporation.

Hoskins, W. G. 1979   Review of T. Rowley, Villages in the Landscape. Antiquity 53:157.

Hoskins, W. G. 1980   The Fabric of the Village. *In* The Shell Book of English Villages. J. Hadfield, ed. Pp. 11–19. London: Joseph.

Hoskins, W. G. 1983   Local History in England, 3rd edition. London: Longman.

Hoskins, W. G., and H. P. R. Finberg 1952   Devonshire Studies. London: Jonathan Cape.

Hoskins, W. G., and L. D. Stamp 1963   Common Lands of England and Wales. London: Collins.

Huntley, J., and S. Stallibrass, eds. 2000   Taphonomy and Interpretation. Oxford: Oxbow Books.

Hurst, J. G. 1984   The Wharram Research Project: Results to 1983. Medieval Archaeology 28:77–111.

Husbands, C. R. 1985   The Hearth Tax and the Structure of the English Economy. Cambridge: Cambridge University Press.

Hutton, R. 1994   The Rise and Fall of Merry England: The Ritual Year 1400–1700. Oxford: Oxford University Press.

Hutton, R. 1999   The Case for a Post-Medieval Giant. *In* The Cerne Giant: Antiquity on Trial. T. Darvill, K. Barker, B. Bender, and R. Hutton, eds. Pp. 69–124. Oxford: Oxbow Books.

Innocent, C. 1916   The Development of English Building Construction. Cambridge: Cambridge University Press.

Jackson, B., and D. Marsden 1962   Education and the Working Class. London Routledge.

Jackson, J. B. 1979 The Order of a Landscape: Reason and Religion in Newtonian America. *In* The Interpretation of Ordinary Landscapes: Geographical Essays. D. W. Meinig, ed. Pp. 153–163. Oxford: Oxford University Press.

James, S. 1999 The Atlantic Celts: Ancient People or Modern Invention? London: British Museum.

Jardine, L. 1994 Canon to Left of Them, Canon to Right of Them. *In* The War of the Words: The Political Correctness Debate. S. Dunant, ed. Pp. 97–115. London: Virago.

Jardine, L. 1996 Reading Shakespeare Historically. London: Routledge.

Jeater, D. 1992 Roast Beef and Reggae Music: The Passing of Whiteness. New Formations 16:107–121.

Jenkins, S. 2001 "Si monumentum Pevsnerianum." *In* The Buildings of England: A Celebration. S. Bradley and B. Cherry, eds. Pp. 54–58. Harmondsworth: Penguin.

Johnson, M. H. 1993a Housing Culture: Traditional Architecture in an English Landscape. London: University College London Press.

Johnson, M. H. 1993b Rethinking the Great Rebuilding. Oxford Journal of Archaeology 12:117–125.

Johnson, M. H. 1994 Ordering Houses, Creating Narratives. *In* Architecture and Order: Approaches to Social Space. M. Parker-Pearson and C. Richards, eds. Pp. 170–177. London: Routledge.

Johnson, M. H. 1996 An Archaeology of Capitalism. Oxford: Blackwell.

Johnson, M. H. 1999 Archaeological Theory: An Introduction. Oxford: Blackwell.

Johnson, M. H. 2002 Behind the Castle Gate: From Medieval to Renaissance. London: Routledge.

Johnson, M. H. 2003 Muffling Inclusiveness: Some Notes Towards an Archaeology of the British. *In* Archaeologies of the British: Explorations of Identity in Great Britain and its Colonies 1600–1945. S. Lawrence, ed. Pp. 17–30. London: Routledge.

Johnston, K. R. 1999 Romantic Anti-Jacobins or Anti-Jacobin Romantics? Romanticism on the Net 15. Electronic document, <http://users.ox.ac.uk/scat0385/antijacobin.html>.

Jones, B. 1984 Past Imperfect: The Story of Rescue Archaeology. London: Heinemann.

Jones, G. R. J. 1971 The Multiple Estate as a Model Framework for Tracing Early Stages in the Evolution of Rural Settlement. *In* L'Habitat et les paysages ruraux d'Europe. F. Dussart, ed. Pp. 251–267. Liège: no publisher given.

Jones, R., and M. Page 2003 Characterising Rural Settlement and Landscape: Whittlewood Forest in the Middle Ages. Medieval Archaeology 47:53–84.

Jope, E. M. 1972 Models in Medieval Studies. *In* Models in Archaeology. D. L. Clarke, ed. Pp. 963–990. London: Duckworth.

Joyce, R., and S. Gillespie, eds. 2000   Beyond Kinship: Social and Material Re-production in House Societies. Philadelphia: University of Pennsylvania Press.

Kaplan, C. 1986   Sea Changes: Essays on Culture and Feminism. London: Verso.

Kiernan, V. G. 1989   Poets, Politics and People. London: Verso.

Kitson, P. J. 1991   Coleridge and the Armory of the Human Mind: Essays on his Prose Writings. London: Cass.

Leech, R. 1977   The Upper Thames Valley in Gloucestershire and Wiltshire: An Archaeological Survey of the River Gravels. Bristol: Committee for Rescue Archaeology in Avon, Gloucestershire and Somerset.

Leighly, J., ed. 1963   Land and Life: A Selection from the Writings of Carl Ortwin Sauer. Berkeley: University of California Press.

Lekson, S. H. 1999   The Chaco Meridian. Walnut Creek: Altamira.

Leone, M., ed. 1972   Contemporary Archaeology: A Guide to Theory and Contributions. Carbondale: Southern Illinois University Press.

Leone, M., and C. Crosby, with Constance A. Crosby 1987   Middle-Range Theory in Historical Archaeology. In Consumer Choice in Historical Archaeology. Suzanne Spencer-Wood, ed. Pp. 397–410. New York: Plenum Press.

Leuchtenburg, W. E., ed. 2000   American Places: Encounters with History. Oxford: Oxford University Press.

Lewis, C., P. Mitchell-Fox, and C. C. Dyer 1997   Village, Hamlet and Field: Changing Medieval Settlements in Central England. Manchester, Manchester University Press.

Light, A. 1991   Forever England: Femininity, Conservatism and Literature between the Wars. London: Routledge.

Linklater, A. 2002   Measuring America. London: HarperCollins.

Liu, A. 1989   Wordsworth: The Sense of History. Stanford: Stanford University Press.

Lowe, P. 1989   The Rural Idyll Defended: From Preservation to Conservation. In The Rural Idyll. G. E. Mingay, ed. Pp. 113–131. London: Routledge.

Lowenthal, D. 1985   The Past Is a Foreign Country. Cambridge: Cambridge University Press.

Lowenthal, D. W., and H. C. Prince 1965   English Landscape Tastes. Geographical Review 55:192.

Lucas, G. 2001   Critical Approaches to Fieldwork: Contemporary and Historical Archaeological Practice. London: Routledge.

Luce, J. ed. 1998   Livy, The Rise of Rome: Books 1–5. Oxford: Oxford University Press.

Lyman, R. L. 1994   Vertebrate Taphonomy. Cambridge: Cambridge University Press.

Macculloch, D. 1999   Tudor Church Militant. Harmondsworth: Penguin.

MacEwen, A., and M. MacEwen 1987   Greenprints for the Countryside? The Story of Britain's National Parks. London: Allen & Unwin.

Machin, R. 1977   The Great Rebuilding: A Reassessment. Past and Present 77:33–56.

Machin, R. 1978 The Houses of Yetminster. Bristol: University of Bristol Department of Extra-Mural Studies.

Maitland, F. W. 1897 Domesday Book and Beyond: Three Essays in the Early History of England. Cambridge: Cambridge University Press.

Malachuk, D. S. 2002 Labour, Leisure and the Yeoman in Coleridge's and Wordsworth's 1790s Writings. Romanticism on the Net 27. Electronic document, <http://www.erudit.org/revue/ron/2002/v/n27/006564ar.html>.

Mandler, P. 1997 The Fall and Rise of the Stately Home. London: Yale University Press.

Mandler, P. 2002 History and National Life. London: Profile.

Marshall, J. D. 1996 Communities, Societies, Regions and Local History. Perceptions of Locality in High and Low Furness. Local Historian 26: 36–47.

Marshall, J. D. 1997 The Tyranny of the Discrete: A Discussion of the Problems of Local History in England. Aldershot: Scolar Press.

Martinez, K., and K. L. Ames, eds. 1997 The Material Culture of Gender: The Gender of Material Culture. Delaware: Wintherthur.

Massingham, H. J. 1936 The English Downland. London: Batsford.

Massingham, H. J. 1939 The English Countryside. London: Batsford.

Massingham, H. J. 1943 Men of Earth. London: Chapman & Hall.

Matless, D. 1993 One Man's England: W. G. Hoskins and the English Culture of Landscape. Rural History 4:187–207.

Matless, D. 1998 Landscape and Englishness. London: Reaktion.

Mawer, A., and F. M. Stenton 1929 Introduction to the Survey of English Place-Names. Cambridge: Cambridge University Press.

McDowell, L., ed. 1997 Undoing Place? A Geographical Reader. London: Arnold.

McGann, J. 1984 The Romantic Ideology: A Critical Investigation. Chicago: University of Chicago Press.

McGuire, R., and M. Shanks 1996 The Craft of Archaeology. American Antiquity 61:75–88.

McKeon, M. 1992 Historicising Patriarchy: The Emergence of Gender Difference in England, 1660–1760. 18th Century Studies 28:295–322.

McPherson, W. 1999 The Stephen Lawrence Enquiry. London: Her Majesty's Stationery Office.

Meinig, D. W. 1979a Reading the Landscape: An Appreciation of W. G. Hoskins and J. B. Jackson. In D. W. Meinig, ed., pp. 195–243.

Meinig, D. W., ed. 1979b The Interpretation of Ordinary Landscapes: Geographical Essays. Oxford: Oxford University Press.

Merrifield, R. 1978 The Archaeology of Ritual and Magic. London: Batsford.

Miles, D. 2003 The Tribes of Britain. London: English Heritage.

Miller, A. L. 1997 Space, Cultural Authority, and the Imagery of Feminine Influence. In The Material Culture of Gender: The Gender of Material Culture. K. Martinez and K. L. Ames, eds. Pp. 311–336. Delaware: Wintherthur.

Millward, R. 1992 William George Hoskins, Landscape Historian (1908–1992). Landscape History 14:65–70.

Mingay, G. E., ed. 1989 The Rural Idyll. London: Routledge.

Montefiore, J. 1994 Feminism and Poetry: Language, Experience, Identity in Women's Writing. London: Pandora.

Moore, H. 1988 Feminism and Anthropology. Oxford: Polity Press.

Moreland, J. 2001 Archaeology and Text. London: Duckworth.

Morley, D. 2000 Home Territories: Media, Mobility and Identity. London: Routledge.

Morrill, J. 1993 The Nature of the English Revolution: Essays. London: Longman.

Morris, R. 1989 Churches in the Landscape. London: Dent.

Morton, H. V. 1927 In Search of England. London: Methuen.

Muir, R. 1982 The Lost Villages of Britain. London: Joseph.

Muir, R. 1998 Approaches to Landscape. London: Macmillan.

Muir, R. 2002 Editorial. Landscapes 3(1):1–3.

Muir, R. 2000 The New Reading the Landscape: Fieldwork in Landscape History. Exeter: University of Exeter Press.

Myrdal, A., and V. Klein 1956 Women's Two Roles. London: Routledge.

Myres, J. N. L. 1986 The English Settlements. Oxford: Oxford University Press.

Newby, H. 1979 Green and Pleasant Land? Social Change in Rural England. London: Hutchinson.

O'Brien, C., and H. Wheeler 1978 Discovery Learning in Landscape Archaeology. Adult Education 51:352–357.

Obeyeskere, G. 1992 The Apotheosis of Captain Cook: European Mythmaking in the Pacific. Princeton: Princeton University Press.

Olson, M. C. 2003 Fair and Varied Forms: Visual Textuality in Medieval Illuminated Manuscripts. London: Routledge.

Orser, C. 1996 An Historical Archaeology of the Modern World. New York: Plenum.

Owen, T., and E. Pilbeam 1992 Ordnance Survey: Map Makers to Britain Since 1791. London: Her Majesty's Stationery Office.

Owoc, M. A. 2004 Epilogue: Humans in a Mineral World. In Soils, Stones and Symbols: Cultural Perceptions of the Mineral World. N. Boivin and M. A. Owoc, eds. Pp. 217–225. London: UCL Press.

Parker-Pearson, M., and C. Richards, eds. 1994 Architecture and Order: Approaches to Social Space. London: Routledge.

Partridge, E. 2002 This Land Was Made for You and Me: The Life and Songs of Woody Guthrie. New York: Viking.

Patterson, A. 1989 Shakespeare and the Popular Voice. Oxford: Oxford University Press.

Paxman, J. 1999 The English: Portrait of a People. London: Penguin.

Pearson, S. 1985 House of the Lancashire Pennines. London: Her Majesty's Stationery Office.

Pease, B., and A. Pease 2001   Why Men Don't Listen and Women Can't Read Maps: How We're Different and What To Do About It. London: Orion.

Persyn, M. 2002   The Sublime Turn Away from Empire: Wordsworth's Encounter with Colonial Slavery, 1802. Romanticism on the Net 26. Electronic document, <http://www.erudit.org/revue/ron/2002/v/n26/005700ar.html>.

Pevsner, N. 1952   The Buildings of England: North Devon. Harmondsworth: Penguin.

Pevsner, N. 1956   The Englishness of English Art: An Expanded and Annotated Version of the Reith Lectures Broadcast in October and November 1955. London: Architectural Press.

Pevsner, N. 2002   Pevsner on Art and Architecture: The Radio Talks. London: Methuen.

Phatz, R. 1985   Wharram Percy Memorial Stones: An Anthropological View from Mars. In Medieval Villages. OUCA Monograph 5. D. Hooke, ed. Pp. 215–223. Oxford: Oxford University Committee for Archaeology.

Philips, C. 2004   Kingdom of the Blind. Guardian, Review Section, 17 July, 4–6.

Phillips, T. 2004   Ethnic Minorities in Rural Areas. Unpublished press release, Commission for Racial Equality, 8 October.

Philo, C., ed. 1991   New Words, New Worlds: Reconceptualising Social and Cultural Geography. Lampeter: St. David's University College.

Phythian-Adams, C. 1987   Re-Thinking English Local History. Department of English Local History Occasional Papers, 4th series, 1. Leicester: Leicester University Press.

Phythian-Adams, C. 1992   Hoskins' England: A Local Historian of Genius and the Realisation of his Theme. Local Historian 22:170–183.

Phythian-Adams, C., ed. 1993   Societies, Cultures and Kinship, 1580–1850: Cultural Provinces and English Local History. Leicester: Leicester University Press.

Pite, R. 2002   Hardy's Geography: Wessex and the Regional Novel. Basingstoke: Macmillan.

Pitts, M. 2005   Alan Sorrell: Hysteria, Gloom and Foreboding. British Archaeology 83:16–19.

Platt, C. 1981   The Parish Churches of Medieval England. London: Secker & Warburg.

Plumwood, V. 1993   Feminism and the Mastery of Nature. London: Routledge.

Pollard, J., and A. Reynolds 2002   Avebury: The Biography of a Landscape. Stroud: Tempus.

Poos, L. R. 1991   A Rural Society after the Black Death: Essex 1350–1525. Cambridge: Cambridge University Press.

Porteous, J. D. 1990   Landscapes of the Mind: Worlds of Sense and Metaphor. Toronto: University of Toronto Press.

Porter, R., ed. 1992 Myths of the English. Cambridge: Polity.

Power, E. 1924 Medieval People. London: Methuen.

Privateer, P. 1991 Romantic Voices: Identity and Ideology in British Poetry, 1789–1850. Athens: University of Georgia Press.

Rackham, O. 1990 Trees and Woodland in the British Landscape, 2nd edition. London: Dent.

Rackham, O. 1994 The Illustrated History of the Countryside. London: Weidenfeld & Nicolson.

Rackham, O., and A. T. Grove 2001 The Nature of Mediterranean Europe: An Ecological History. New Haven: Yale University Press.

Rackham, O., and J. A. Moody 1994 The Making of the Cretan Landscape. Manchester: Manchester University Press.

Raczowski, W. 2002 Archaeologia Lotznica: Metoda Wobec Teori. Poznan: Adam Mickiewicz University Press.

Radford, R., and J. Hylton 1995 Australian Colonial Art 1800–1900. Adelaide: Art Gallery of South Australia.

Rahtz, P. 2001 Living Archaeology. Stroud: Tempus.

Rawling, E. 2002 Changing the Subject: The Impact of National Policy on School Geography 1980–2000. London: Geographical Association.

Razi, Z. 1987 Family, Land and the Village Community in Later Medieval England. In Landlords, Peasants and Politics in Medieval England. T. H. Aston, ed. Pp. 377–393. Cambridge: Cambridge University Press.

Relph, E. 1976 Place and Placelessness. London: Pion.

Renfrew, A. C. 1973a Monuments, Mobilisation and Social Organisation in Neolithic Wessex. In Renfrew, ed., pp. 539–558.

Renfrew, A. C., ed. 1973b The Explanation of Culture Change. London: Duckworth.

Reynolds, A. 1999 Anglo-Saxon Law in the Landscape: An Archaeological Study of the Old English Judicial System. London: University of London.

Reynolds, F. 2002 Interview for Desert Island Discs. BBC Radio Four. <http://www.bbc.co.uk/radio4/factual/desertislanddiscs_20020407.shtml>.

Richardson, J. 1986 The Local Historian's Encyclopaedia. New Barnet: Historical Publications.

Richeson, W. 1966 English Land Measuring to 1800: Instruments and Practices. Cambridge: MIT Press.

Riding, C. 2005 War and Peace. In A Picture of Britain. D. Dimbleby, ed. Pp. 61–83. London: Tate.

Riley, H., and R. Wilson-North 1999 From Pillow Mounds to Parterres: A Revelation at Cerne Abbas. In Patterns of the Past: Essays in Landscape Archaeology for Christopher Taylor. S. Ainsworth, D. Field, and P. Pattison, eds. Pp. 71–76. Oxford: Oxbow Books.

Roberts, B. K. 1990 The Field Study of Village Plans. Department of Geography Occasional Publication 24. Durham: University of Durham Press.

Roberts, B. K., and S. Wrathmell 2000 An Atlas of Rural Settlement in England. London: English Heritage.

Roberts, B. K., and S. Wrathmell 2002 Region and Place: A Study of English Rural Settlement. London: English Heritage.

Robin, C. 2003 New Directions in Classic Maya Household Archaeology. Journal of Archaeological Research 11(4):307–356.

Rockland, M. A. 1997 The Masculine Bias of the Vernacular. In The Material Culture of Gender: The Gender of Material Culture. K. Martinez and K. L. Ames, eds. Pp. 299–310. Delaware: Wintherthur.

Rodaway, P. 1994 Sensuous Geographies: Body, Sense and Place. London: Routledge.

Rogers, P. 1980 Hacks and Dunces: Pope, Swift and Grub Street. London: Methuen.

Rogers, P., ed. 1989 Daniel Defoe: A Tour through the Whole Island of Great Britain. London: Webb & Bower.

Rojek, C. 2003 Stuart Hall. Cambridge: Polity.

Rose, G. 1993 Feminism and Geography: The Limits of Geographical Knowledge. Cambridge: Cambridge University Press.

Rothman, B. 1982 The 1932 Kinder Trespass: A Personal View of the Kinder Scout Mass Trespass. Altrincham: Willow.

Rothnie, N. 1992 The Baedeker Blitz: Hitler's Attack on Britain's Historic Cities. Shepperton: Ian Allan.

Rudwick, M. J. S. 2005 Lyell and Darwin, Geologists: Studies in the Earth Sciences in the Age of Reform. Aldershot: Ashgate.

Ruffing, J. 1994 The Labour Structure of Ælfric's Colloquy. In The Work of Work: Servitude, Slavery and Labour in Medieval England. A. J. Frantzen and D. Moffat, eds. Pp. 55–70. Glasgow: Cruithne.

Sabloff, J. A., and W. Ashmore 2001 An Aspect of Archaeology's Recent Past and its Relevance in the New Millennium. In Archaeology at the Millennium: A Sourcebook. G. Feinman and D. Price, eds. Pp. 11–37. New York: Kluwer.

Sahlins, M. 1972 Stone Age Economics. New York: Aldine.

Sahlins, M. 1977 Culture and Practical Reason. Chicago: University of Chicago Press.

Sahlins, M. 1995 How "Natives" Think: About Captain Cook, For Example. Chicago: University of Chicago Press.

Sahlins, M. 1996 The Sadness of Sweetness: The Native Anthropology of Western Cosmology. Current Anthropology 37(3):395–428.

Said, E. W. 1978 Orientalism: Western Conceptions of the Orient. London: Routledge.

Salzman, F. 1952 Building in England Down to 1540: A Documentary History. Oxford: Oxford University Press.

Samuel, R. 1994 Theatres of Memory. London: Verso.

Sauer, C. O. 1963 Land and Life: A Selection from the Writings of Carl Ortwin Sauer. Berkeley: University of California Press.

Scarfe, N. 1992 W. G. Hoskins: Giving Life to History. Guardian, 14 January.

Schama, S. 1995 Landscape and Memory. New York: Knopf.

Schiffer, M. B. 1976 Behavioral Archaeology. New York: Academic Press.

Schiffer, M. B. 1987 Formation Processes of the Archaeological Record. Albuquerque: University of New Mexico Press.

Schiffer, M. B., A. P. Sullivan, and T. C. Klinger 1978 The Design of Archaeological Surveys. World Archaeology 10(1):1–28.

Schnapp, A. 1993 The Discovery of the Past. London: British Museum.

Schubert, C. 1996 Land und Raum in der Romischen Republik. Die Kunst des Teilens. Darmstadt: Wissenschaftliche Buchgesellschaft.

Sebastian, L. 1992 The Chaco Anasazi: Sociopolitical Evolution in the Prehistoric Southwest. Cambridge: Cambridge University Press.

Seebohm, F. 1884 The English Village Community Examined in its Relations to the Manorial and to the Common or Open Field System of Husbandry: An Essay in Economic History. London: Longman.

Segal, L. 1990 Slow Motion: Changing Masculinities, Changing Men. London: Virago.

Serematakis, N. 1991 The Last Word: Women, Death and Divination in Inner Mani. Chicago: University of Chicago Press.

Shanks, M. 1992 Experiencing the Past: On the Character of Archaeology. London: Routledge.

Shanks, M., and R. McGuire 1996 The Craft of Archaeology. American Antiquity 61:75–88.

Shanks, M., and C. Tilley 1987 Re-Constructing Archaeology: Theory and Practice. Cambridge: Cambridge University Press.

Sheeran, G., and Y. Sheeran 1999 Reconstructing Local History. Local Historian 29:256–262.

Shoard, M. 1999 A Right to Roam. Oxford: Oxford University Press.

Sinfield, A. 1989 Literature, Politics and Culture in Post-War Britain. Oxford: Blackwell.

Sinfield, A. 2000 British Culture of the Postwar: An Introduction to Literature and Society. London: Routledge.

Smith, Adam T. 2003 The Political Landscape: Constellations of Authority in Early Complex Societies. Berkeley: University of California Press.

Smith, Angela 2003 Landscape Representation: Place and Identity in 19th-Century Ordnance Survey Maps of Ireland. In Landscape, Memory and History: Anthropological Perspectives. P. J. Stewart and A. Strathern, eds. Pp. 71–88. London: Pluto.

Smith, C., and M. Wobst, eds. 2005 Indigenous Archaeologies: Decolonising Theory and Practice. London: Routledge.

Smith, E. A. 1983 Archaeological Applications of Optimal Foraging Theory: A Review. Current Anthropology 24:625–651.

Smith, J. 1992 The Slightly Different Thing That Is Said: Writing the Aesthetic Experience. In Writing Worlds: Discourse, Text and Metaphor in the Representation of Landscape. T. J. Barnes and J. S. Duncan, eds. Pp. 73–85. London: Routledge.

Smith, J. T. 1993   Hertfordshire Houses: Selective Inventory. London, Royal Commission on the Historical Monuments of England.

Snead, J. E. 2001   Ruins and Rivals: The Making of Southwestern Archaeology. Tucson: University of Arizona Press.

Snead, J. E. 2002   Ancestral Pueblo Trails and the Cultural Landscape of the Pajarito Plateau, New Mexico. Antiquity 76:756–765.

Sofaer, J. 2006   The Body as Material Culture: A Theoretical Osteoarchaeology. Cambridge: Cambridge University Press.

Sofaer, J., and J. Sofaer Derevenski 2002   Disinter/est: Digging Up our Childhood. Performance Research 7:45–56.

Sofaer Derevenski, J. 2000   Sex Differences in Activity-Related Change in the Spine and the Gendered Division of Labour at Ensay and Wharram Percy, UK. American Journal of Physical Anthropology 111:333–354.

Solly, R., and J. Ling Wong 2004   Green and Pleasant Land for All. Church and Race 19:1.

Spender, D. 1980   Man Made Language. London: Routledge.

Spufford, M. 1974   Contrasting Communities: English Villagers in the 16th and 17th Centuries. Cambridge: Cambridge University Press.

Spufford, M. 1981   Small Books and Pleasant Histories: Popular Fiction and its Readership in 17th Century England. London: Methuen.

Spufford, M. 2000   Contrasting Communities: English Villagers in the 16th and 17th Centuries. Stroud: Sutton.

Steane, J. M. 2001   The Archaeology of Power: England and Northern Europe AD600–1800. Stroud: Tempus.

Stenton, D. M. 1957   The English Woman in History. London: Allen & Unwin.

Steward, J. H., ed. 1955   Irrigation Civilisations: A Comparative Study. A Symposium on Method and Result in Cross-Cultural Regularities. Washington: Department of Cultural Affairs.

Stewart, P. J., and A. Strathern, eds. 2003   Landscape, Memory and History: Anthropological Perspectives. London: Pluto.

Stoddart, S., ed. 2000   Landscapes from Antiquity. Cambridge: Antiquity Publications.

Stopford, J., ed. 1999   Pilgrimage Explored. Woodbridge: Boydell.

Stout, M. 1996   Emyr Estyn Evans and Northern Ireland: The Archaeology and Geography of a New State. In Nationalism and Archaeology. J. A. Atkinson, Iain Banks, and Jerry O'Sullivan, eds. Pp. 111–127. Glasgow: Cruithne Press.

Strong, R. 2000   The Spirit of Britain: A Narrative History of the Arts. London: Pimlico.

Sweet, R. 2004   Antiquaries: The Study of the Past in 18th Century England. London: Hambledon.

Tarlow, S. 1999   Bereavement and Commemoration: An Archaeology of Mortality. Oxford: Blackwell.

Tarlow, S. 2003   Reformation and Transformation: What Happened to Catholic Things in a Protestant World? *In* The Archaeology of Reformation 1480–1580. D. Gaimster and R. Gilchrist, eds. Pp. 108–121. Leeds: Maney.

Tarlow, S. In press   The Archaeology of Improvement. Cambridge: Cambridge University Press.

Tarlow, S., and S. West, eds. 1999   The Familiar Past? Archaeologies of Later Historic Britain. London: Routledge.

Tate, W. E. 1969   The Parish Chest, 3rd edition. Cambridge: Cambridge University Press.

Tawney, R. 1912   The Agrarian Problem in the 16th Century. London: Longman.

Tawney, R. 1941   The Rise of the Gentry, 1558–1640. Economic History Review 11:1–38.

Taylor, C. C. 1974   Fieldwork in Medieval Archaeology. London: Batsford.

Taylor, C. C. 1989   Whittlesford: The Study of a River-Edge Village. *In* The Rural Settlements of Medieval England: Studies Dedicated to Maurice Beresford and John Hurst. M. Aston, D. Austin, and C. Dyer, eds. Pp. 207–227. Oxford: Blackwell.

Taylor, C. C. 1992   Medieval Rural Settlement: Changing Perceptions. Landscape History 14:5–15.

Taylor, C. C. 2000   The Plus Fours in the Wardrobe: A Personal View of Landscape History. *In* Landscape: The Richest Historical Record. SLS Supplementary Series 1. D. Hooke, ed. Pp. 157–163. Amesbury: Society for Landscape Studies.

Taylor, J. 1994   A Dream of England: Landscape, Photography and the Tourist's Imagination. Manchester: Manchester University Press.

Taylor, W. 1948   A Study of Archeology. Menasha: American Anthropological Association.

Thirsk, J. 1992   Obituary: Professor W. G. Hoskins. Independent, 14 January.

Thirsk, J., ed. 1992   Making a Fresh Start: 16th Century Agriculture and the Classical Inspiration. *In* Culture and Cultivation in Early Modern England: Writing and the Land. M. Leslie and T. Raylor, eds. Pp. 15–34. Leicester: Leicester University Press.

Thirsk, J., ed. 2000   The English Rural Landscape. Oxford: Oxford University Press.

Thomas, J. 1991   Rethinking the Neolithic. Cambridge: Cambridge University Press.

Thomas, J. 1996   Time, Culture and Identity: An Interpretative Archaeology. London: Routledge.

Thomas, J. 2004   Archaeology and Modernity. London: Routledge.

Thomas, K. 1971   Religion and the Decline of Magic: Studies in Popular Beliefs in Sixteenth and Seventeenth Century England. London: Weidenfeld & Nicolson.

Thomas, K. 1983   Man and the Natural World: Changing Attitudes in England 1500–1800. London: Allen Lane.

Thompson, E. P. 1963 The Making of the English Working Class. London: Gollancz.

Thompson, E. P. 1978 The Poverty of Theory and Other Essays. London: Merlin.

Thompson, E. P. 1991 Customs in Common. London: Merlin Press.

Thorpe, H. 1975 Air, ground, document. *In* Aerial Reconnaissance for Archaeology. D. R. Wilson, ed. CBA Research Report 12. London: Council for British Archaeology.

Tiller, K. 1992 English Local History. London: Sutton.

Tilley, C. 1994 A Phenomenology of Landscape: Places, Paths and Monuments. Oxford: Berg.

Todd, J. 1988 Feminist Literary History: A Defence. Oxford: Polity.

Tolia-Kelly, D. P. 2004 Landscape, Race and Memory: Biographical Mapping of the Routes of British Asian Landscape Values. Landscape Research 29:277–292.

Trigger, B. G. 1980 Archaeology and the Image of the American Indian. American Antiquity 45:662–676.

Trigger, B. G. 1989 A History of Archaeological Thought. Cambridge: Cambridge University Press.

Tuan, Y.-F. 1974 Topophilia. Englewood Cliffs: Prentice-Hall.

Tuan, Y.-F. 1979 Landscapes of Fear. Minneapolis: University of Minneapolis Press.

Turner, J. 1979 The Politics of Landscape: Rural Scenery and Society in English Poetry 1630–1660. Oxford: Blackwell.

Ucko, P., and R. H. Layton, eds. 1999 The Archaeology and Anthropology of Landscape: Shaping Your Landscape. London: Routledge.

Varien, M. D., and R. H. Wilshusen 2002 A Partnership for Understanding the Past: Crow Canyon Research in the Central Mesa Verde Region. *In* Seeking the Center Place: Archaeology and Ancient Communities in the Mesa Verde Region. M. D. Varien and R. H. Wilshusen, eds. Pp. 3–23. Salt Lake City: University of Utah Press.

Vaughan, A. T. 1979 New England Frontier: Puritans and Indians, 1620–1675. London: University of Oklahoma Press.

Vigarello, G. 1988 Concepts of Cleanliness: Changing Attitudes in France since the Middle Ages. Cambridge: Cambridge University Press.

Wallace, G. 2004 Digging the Dirt: The Archaeological Imagination. London: Duckworth.

Wallis, R. J. 2003 Shamans/Neo-Shamans: Ecstasy, Alternative Archaeologies and Contemporary Pagans. London: Routledge.

Ward, C. 2003 The Great Bluff House: Research on the Periphery of the Chacoan World. Expedition 45(3):9–14.

Warner, M. 1976 Alone of All Her Sex: The Myth and the Cult of the Virgin Mary. London: Weidenfeld & Nicolson.

Warnke, M. 1994 Political Landscape: The Art History of Nature. London: Reaktion.

Watkins, A. 1925 The Old Straight Track: Its Mounds, Beacons, Moats, Sites and Mark Stones. London: Methuen.

Weideger, P. 1994 Gilding the Acorn: Behind the Façade of the National Trust. London: Simon & Schuster.

Western, J. 1993 Ambivalent Attachments to Place in London: Twelve Barbadian Families. Environment and Planning D: Society and Space 11: 147–170. Reprinted in L. McDowell, ed. (1997), Undoing Place? A Geographical Reader. Pp. 82–93. London: Arnold.

White, L. 1959 The Evolution of Culture. New York: McGraw-Hill.

White, M. 2001 Tolkien: A Biography. London: Little, Brown.

White, R. 1997 The Yorkshire Dales: Landscapes through Time. London: Batsford.

Whyte, N. 2003a The Deviant Dead in the Norfolk Landscape. Landscape History 4(1):24–39.

Whyte, N. 2003b The After-Life of Barrows: Prehistoric Monuments in the Norfolk Landscape. Landscapes 25:5–15.

Williams, E. 1944 Capitalism and Slavery. Chapel Hill: University of North Carolina Press.

Williams, R. 1959 Culture and Society 1780–1950. London: Chatto & Windus.

Williams, R. 1961 The Long Revolution. London: Chatto & Windus.

Williams, R. 1973 The Country and the City. London: Chatto & Windus.

Williams, R. 1976 Keywords: A Vocabulary of Culture and Society. London: Fontana.

Williams, R. 1980 Problems in Materialism and Culture. London: Verso.

Williamson, T. 1983 Ley Lines in Question. Kingswood: World's Work.

Williamson, T. 1988 Ancient Landscapes. In An Historical Atlas of Suffolk. D. Dymond and E. Martin, eds. Pp. 40–41. Ipswich: Suffolk County Council.

Williamson, T. 1998 The "Schole–Dickleburgh Field System" Revisited. Landscape History 20:19–28.

Williamson, T. 2000 Understanding Enclosure. Landscapes 1:56–79.

Williamson, T. 2002 The Transformation of Rural England: Farming and the Landscape, 1700–1870. Exeter: Exeter University Press.

Williamson, T. 2003 Shaping Medieval Landscapes: Settlement, Society, Environment. London: Windgather Press.

Williamson, T., and E. Bellamy 1983 Ley Lines in Question. Kingswood: World's Work.

Williamson, T., and E. Bellamy 1987 Property and Landscape: A Social History of the English Countryside. London: Allen.

Winchester, A. J. L. 2000 Hill Farming Landscapes of Medieval Northern England. In Landscape: The Richest Historical Record. SLS Supplementary Series 1. D. Hooke, ed. Pp. 75–84. Amesbury: Society for Landscape Studies.

Winchester, S. 2001 The Map that Changed the Word: The Tale of William Smith and the Birth of a Science. London: Viking.

Winer, M. 2001   Landscapes, Fear and Land Loss on the 19th-Century South African Colonial Frontier. *In* Contested Landscapes: Movement, Exile and Place. B. Bender and M. Winer, eds. Pp. 257–272. Oxford: Berg.

Wittfogel, K. 1957   Oriental Despotism: A Comparative Study of Social Power. New Haven: Yale University Press.

Woodcock, P. 2000   This Enchanted Isle: The Neo-Romantic Vision from William Blake to the New Visionaries. Glastonbury: Gothic Image.

Wordsworth, J., ed. 1987   Dorothy Wordsworth: The Grasmere Journal. New York: Holt.

Wordsworth, W. 1951   A Guide through the District of the Lakes, with Illustrations by John Piper. London: Hart-Davis.

Wright, D., ed. 1970   Thomas de Quincey: Recollections of the Lakes and the Lake Poets. Harmondsworth: Penguin.

Wright, G. 1998   On Modern Vernaculars and J. B. Jackson. Geographical Review 88(4):474–482.

Wright, P. 1985   On Living in an Old Country: The National Past in Contemporary Britain. London: Verso.

Wright, P. 2005   Last Orders. Review, Guardian, 9 April, 2–4.

Wrightson, K. 1982   English Society 1580–1680. London: Hutchison.

Wylie, A. 1992   The Interplay of Evidential Constraints and Political Interests: Recent Archaeological Research on Gender. American Antiquity 57:15–35.

Yaeger, P. 1989   Towards a Feminist Sublime. *In* Gender and Theory: Dialogues on Feminist Criticism. L. Kaufman, ed. Oxford: Blackwell.

Young, R. 2004   Crimea Nurse Voted Greatest Black Briton. The Times, 10 February.

INDEX

"Back to the Earth" movement 67
Bacon, F. 82
Bagenal, H. 52
Barley, M. W. 74–5, 142–3
Barrett, J. 136, 142, 147, 151, 198
Barthes, R. 173
  and the Blue Guides 184
Bate, J. 23, 30
Batsford guides 181–2
Bender, B. 1, 139, 147, 151–2, 162
  and M. Winer 179
Benjamin, R. 190
Benjamin, W. 2, 198
Beresford, M. xx, 34, 68, 75, 89,
    92–3, 105, 106–7, 185
Bermingham, A. 22, 28, 72, 85
Betjeman, J. 76
Biddick, K. 6, 200–1
Binford, L. 72, 73, 82, 106, 111,
    121, 126, 136, 200
  see also region
Black Death 151
Blackmore, R., *Lorna Doone* 79
Blake, W. 25, 29, 32, 45
Bloom, H. 29
Bond, J. 137
boundaries 98–9, 105
  linear xxi
  see also field(s); hedge(s)
Bourdieu, P. 142, 198
Bowden, M. 55, 58
Bradley, R. 1, 137
British Broadcasting Corporation
    67, 179
Brookner, A. 22, 25
Burke, E. 28

Cambridge University 201
Cambridgeshire 133
Camden, W. 14
Camille, M. 146
Catlin, G. 195
chalk-cut figures 137–9
  Cerne Abbas Giant 136–9
  Long Man of Wilmington 136–9

Charles II 11, 187
chorography 16–17
church 7–9, 98, 106, 108, 110,
    130, 132–3, 147, 151, 154–6,
    160–1, 181–4, 199
Clarke, D. 61, 75, 121–2, 127, 136,
    201
Coleridge, S. T. 27
Collingwood, R. G. 83
Collini, S. 168
Commission for Racial Equality 166
common law 104
common sense 83, 96, 102, 105
Conservative government 168
Cook, Captain 128–9
Coombe, W., *The Tour of Dr*
    Syntax, in Search of the
    Picturesque 70–2
  see also Grizzle; picturesque
Cope, J. 199
Corcos, N. 133, 136–7
Cosgrove, D. 1, 8, 65, 85
  and S. Daniels 57
Cowper Powys, J. 51
Crawford, O. G. S. xx, 43, 50, 66,
    89, 97–8, 201
  use of ethnographic material 56
  Archaeology in the Field 39, 55–6
  Wessex from the Air 89
croft(s) 59, 95, 106, 150–1, 203
Currie, C. 101, 117

Daniel, G., and A. C. Renfrew xx,
    16, 201
Daniels, S. 1
Darby, H. C. 54
de Man, P. 41
De Quincey, T. 20, 28–9
Deetz, J. 196
Defoe, D. 23
Denham, J. "Coopers Hill" 14
depopulation 11, 91, 148, 153, 156,
    188, 203
Derbyshire 13
  Brassington 13

of liberal individualism 30
of topography 14–15
of work 143
indigenous people(s) 100
    Ancestral Pueblo (Anasazi) 97–8,
      100, 197, 198
    Australia 4, 22, 189
    English 190
    Hopi 197–8
    Irish 15
    Native American(s) 97, 191,
      195
    Zuni 197–8
Industrial Revolution 60, 170, 173
ineffable 28, 48, 83, 178, 191, 204
innocence, loss of xxi, 70–118
Ireland 15–16, 32, 87, 177, 179,
    186–8
    see also indigenous people(s)
irrigation hypothesis 5, 140
Irwin, M. 47

Jackson, J. B. 194–6
Jardine, L. 66, 102
Johnson, M. H. 1, 9, 14–15, 57,
    62, 66, 73, 87, 92, 103, 116,
    121, 127, 130, 147, 153, 156,
    162
Jones, R., and M. Page 122, 141
Jope, E. M. 61

Kant, I. 27
Keats, J. 30
Kinder mass trespass 49
Kingsley, C., *Westward Ho!* 79
kinship 80, 97, 104–5
Knapp, B. xix, 1

Labour government 165–8
Labour Party 25
Lake District 19
    Cumbrian Lakes 23–4
    Helvellyn 19, 21
    as national park 167
    see also national parks

landscape(s)
    agrarian 153, 156
    American 184
    archaeology of historic landscapes
      149–51
    of beauty 172–4
    birth of landscape archaeology
      16–17
    of colonialism 15–16, 87–8,
      185–9
    definitions of 2–4
    East Midlands 111–13
    English landscape tradition xx,
      xxii, 1
    gendered 31, 44, 50–1, 89, 150,
      176
    history 1
    indigenous 189–90; *see also*
      indigenous people(s)
    medieval 11
    Mediterranean 144
    of nationalism 174–80
    of patriarchy 101–5
    phenomenology of 136–7
    politics of 152, 162–92
    post-war 167–9
    power and conflict in 103
    prehistoric 58–61
    of recreation 180–5
    of religion 130–4, 153–6
    Renaissance 8–11
    of satire 32
    studies 1; origins of 5–8
    as symphony and chamber music
      43, 49, 169
    as text 44–5, 57
Larkin, P. 65–6, 171
Latin xix, 6, 9, 101, 131
Lawrence, S. 165
Layton, R. 1, 4, 18
Leicestershire 11
    archaeology and history society
      37
    Hamilton 12, 63
    Hoskins's visits to 37

Rebuilding, the Great 113–18,
    152–61
record office(s) 55, 99–100, 115,
    128, 175
record(s)
    bureaucratic 16
    court 6, 147
    environmental 72
    estate 6
    geological 73
    historical 152
    juridical 103
    manorial 147
    parish 101
    of public rights of way 88
    tax 101
    wills and inventories 99, 101
Reformation, English 154–6,
    158–9
region (or *pays*) 53, 141, 150, 186
regional identity 69
    studies 114–15
    survey 123
relativism xxii, 174, 202
Renaissance 8–11, 16, 114, 194
    see also under landscape(s)
Renfrew, A. C. 136
revolution
    English 13–14, 57, 101, 116
    French 23, 28, 116, 171
    see also Industrial Revolution
Reynolds, A. 149
Richeson, W. 12, 14
ridge and furrow xvii, 106, 118,
    205
Roberts, B. K., and S. Wrathmell
    87, 110, 124–6, 141, 143
Romanticism 18–33
    art 22
    discontents 26–30, 70–4
    formative influence on landscape
        archaeology 33
    German Romantic philosophy 25
    and left-wing thought 68
    legacy 119–20

methodology, and Hoskins 49
nationalistic agenda 32; *see also*
    nation
neo-Romantic art 51
North American 194–8
politics of 25, 28
Rothman, B. 49
Royal Commissions
    on Common Land 49–50
    on Dartmoor 90
    on Historical Monuments 63, 89,
        114, 205

Sabloff, J. A. 123
Sahlins, M. 128–9
Said, E. 185
St George 179
Samuel, R. 164–5
Sauer, C. 54, 194, 196
Saxon, *see* Anglo-Saxon
Schiffer, M. xviii, 123
Schubert, C. 5
science 121–7
Scotland 46, 187
    Scottish Highlands 86
    Scottish landscapes 23
Seebohm, F. 6
Semeratakis, N. 103
settlement(s) 15, 122, 124, 126,
    153, 195
    see also New England
Sex Pistols 190–1
sexist language 103–4
    see also landscape(s), gendered
Shakespeare, W. 18
Shanks, M. xix, 27, 120, 171–2,
    200–1
    and C. Tilley xix, 136
Sheeran, G., and Y. Sheeran 135
Shell guides 50, 53, 181
Shelley, M. 32
Shoard, M. 7, 20
Sierra Club 194
Sinfield, A. 52, 168, 180, 191–2
slave labour 169